172

A STUDY OF
GAWAIN AND THE GREEN KNIGHT

BY

GEORGE LYMAN KITTREDGE

Gloucester, Mass.
PETER SMITH
1960

TO
JOHN MATTHEWS MANLY
MY FRIEND FOR ALMOST
THIRTY YEARS

PREFACE

THIRTEEN years ago this volume was announced, in a foot-note to *Arthur and Gorlagon*, as something that the writer hoped to publish in a few months. It was then practically finished, but procrastination has deferred its appearance beyond all accounting. However, the world has somehow got along without it, and meantime the manuscript has undergone revision from year to year, and has submitted to a final overhauling at the last moment, with the printer at the door.

Such as it is, the book has two objects — to trace the history of a great romance, and to illustrate certain topics in folk-lore and mediæval literature. Accordingly it is divided into two parts. The first eschews footnotes; the second accumulates them without scruple. Those friendly readers, therefore, who find such things distasteful may profitably leave the volume unopened, or close it at the hundred and forty-third page.

The author does not play bridge, — and it is impossible to swim or to sail a boat in a New England winter. Let this suffice as an answer to anybody who thinks that he has wasted his time. At all events, it is his own time that he has spent — and *suum cuique* is a venerable precept.

Acknowledgment is due to a number of friends and colleagues for out-of-the-way facts or useful criticism. Several precious references to oracular heads come from the learning of Professor George F. Moore, and in Celtic matters Professor Robinson has given invaluable help at every turn.

CAMBRIDGE, February 11, 1916.

CONTENTS

PART I

GAWAIN AND THE GREEN KNIGHT

PART II

ILLUSTRATIVE MATERIAL

PART I

GAWAIN AND THE GREEN KNIGHT

GAWAIN AND THE GREEN KNIGHT

I. THE ENGLISH ROMANCE

THE English romance of *Gawain and the Green Knight* is a very distinguished piece of work. The plot is one of the best that an age of good stories has transmitted to us, and the unknown author handles his material with a combination of power and delicacy rare in even the best periods of literature. His sense of fitness and proportion entitles him to high rank as an artistic writer. His descriptive ability is extraordinary; yet he does not allow description to clog the narrative. His ideal of life is noble, and his knowledge of human nature is at once minute and sympathetic. Finally, his command of a difficult metre, and the ease and felicity with which he handles an amazingly elaborate diction, bending its conventions to his will and never impeded or dominated by its inherited mannerisms, mark him as a master of expression. Some of the best of the Middle English romances are rough and artless compositions: they live by their freshness and naïve energy, or by the bare fact that they embody a good tale, whose merits are independent of phraseology. But for *Gawain and the Green Knight* no allowances need be made. Both in plan and in execution, in gross and in detail, it would be a credit to any literature. The author was a poet and an artist as well as a lively *raconteur*.

That the immediate source of *Gawain and the Green Knight* was a French poem is altogether probable. Nor can there be much question in what the obligations of the English writer consist. He is certainly indebted to his unknown predecessor for the plot as a whole. Yet the English romance is by no means a mere translation. The French original is lost, but if it resembled those episodical romances of its class that have come down to us, it was simply a good story fluently told in a clear and engaging style. The qualities which distinguish *Gawain and the Green Knight* from other English romances distinguish it no less from that class of French romances to which its lost original presumably belonged. For example, if the French poem is ever recovered, we shall doubtless find that it lacks the fine transitional passage on the changing seasons, by means of which the English poet spans the interval of a year between the two acts of his drama. In like manner, we shall look in vain for the elaborate account of the arming of Gawain, for the spirited details of the three hunting scenes, and for the " breaking of the deer "; nor will the conversations between Gawain and his hostess appear at such length as in the English, or show such delicacy of characterization. In short, the French original was, in all probability, a straightforward narrative, written in a lively but not an elevated style, with no more description and reflection than are necessary to clearness, and with little poetical embellishment of any kind. Even in the plot, it is likely that the English poet has introduced some modifications, though these, we may safely assume, were not such as to affect the essential integrity of the story.

The plot of *Gawain and the Green Knight* is familiar to all students of mediæval literature and has been made generally accessible in more than one translation; but a brief summary is necessary at this point to make clear the comparisons that are to follow.

King Arthur is holding court at Camelot in the Christmas season. New Year's Day has come and the feast is ready. But Arthur himself will not touch food until all the company is served; for it is his custom never to eat on such a high day until he has heard some strange tidings or some adventure has happened.[1] Everybody else is seated, but the king remains standing before the high table. Suddenly there enters the hall on horseback a huge knight, splendidly attired, and armed only with a battle-axe. His face, hair, and beard, his coat and mantle, his horse and its accoutrements, are all green, and in one hand he bears a holly bough, " that is greatest in green when groves are bare." Riding up to the dais, he challenges the court to contend with him in a Christmas game: — he will take a blow with the axe without resistance, provided that, a twelvemonth and a day hence, his opponent will receive from him a stroke in return. Everybody hesitates, and the stranger taunts the knights with cowardice: " What, is this Arthur's house, that is so renowned in many realms ? Where is your pride now? Where are your conquests, your valor, and your great words ? Now are the splendor and the renown of the Round Table overcome by the words of one man's speech! " Arthur springs forward and grasps the axe; but Gawain interposes and begs the contest for himself. The king gives way, by the advice of his council. The Green Knight then subjoins the condition that Gawain, after dealing the blow, shall visit him at his home to receive the return stroke: — "If I speak after the blow, and tell thee my name, and where I live, then art thou bound to visit me; otherwise thou art free of the covenant." Gawain then smites off the challenger's head with one sweep of the weapon. The Green Knight picks up the head and mounts his horse. The head, thus held up by the hair, calls upon Gawain to fulfil the compact by presenting himself at the Green Chapel on next New Year's morn, — the challenger, says the head, is called the Knight of the Green Chapel. Then the Green Knight, his head in his hand, rides out of the hall at full speed.

When the year's term has nearly expired, Gawain sets out in quest of the Green Chapel. After long and toilsome wanderings, he comes, on Christmas night, to a fine castle, where he is hospitably entertained. The lord of the castle is a tall and stalwart knight, " of high age," with a broad beaver-hued beard and a " face fell as the fire." He receives Gawain with much courtesy, and, learning his name, expresses his satisfaction at the honor of a visit from so distinguished a personage. The lady of the castle is of great beauty, fairer than Guine-

[1] See Child, *Ballads*, I, 257, note ‡; III, 51, note §; cf. *[Harvard] Studies and Notes in Philology and Literature*, VIII, 210, note 4.

vere herself. There is another lady in the household, old and very ugly, but held in high honor by all, and there are many guests. On the morrow of St. John's day, the guests take their departure. The lord of the castle urges Gawain to stay longer, but he declines, alleging his errand. When, however, the lord learns that Gawain is bound for the Green Chapel, he tells him that this is not two miles distant, and Gawain accordingly consents to remain until New Year's morn.

For the last three days of Gawain's stay, his host proposes a merry bargain: Gawain, wearied by his hard journey, is to lie abed till mass-time and spend the day indoors, in the lady's company, while the host goes a-hunting. In the evening they are to exchange what they have won during the day. Gawain accepts the proposition with no thought of guile. He will be ruled in all things, he says, by his friendly entertainer.

On the morning of each of the three days that follow, Gawain is visited, before he rises, by the lady of the castle, who offers him her love. He withstands temptation, though he is in great peril. The first morning, the lady gives him a kiss; the second morning, two; and these he faithfully bestows on her husband at nightfall, when, in accordance with the compact, the avails of the hunt are turned over to *him*. On the third morning, the lady bestows on Gawain three kisses, and also a green lace which she avers will protect him from death in fight. That night he renders up the kisses to his host, but he says nothing about the lace.

On the next morning, which is New Year's day, a retainer is detailed to conduct Gawain to the Green Chapel. Before they reach it, Gawain's guide warns him that the Chapel is guarded by a huge and merciless man, who kills everybody that passes: — " Therefore, good Sir Gawain, let the man alone. Go away in some other direction, and I swear to keep your secret." Gawain thanks his friendly guide, but insists on fulfilling his covenant. The servant then gives him further directions, and rides off, protesting that he would not visit the Green Chapel for all the gold in the world.

Gawain rides down into a valley, but at first can see nothing of the Chapel. At last, by the side of a roaring stream, he perceives a mound overgrown with turf, and having a hole at the end and on either side. It seems to him " an old cave, or the crevice of an old crag." " Perhaps this is the Green Chapel," says Gawain to himself. " It is a place where the devil might well say his matins at midnight! It is a chapel of mischance! It is the cursedest kirk that e'er I came in!" Then he hears, on the other side of the stream, a noise as of one grinding a scythe upon a grindstone. "Who is here," he calls out, " to keep appointment with me ? Gawain is now at hand, if anybody wishes to meet him. It is now or never!" "Abide!" answers a voice, and immediately a huge man comes out of a hole, axe in hand, vaults over the stream, and approaches Gawain. It is the Green Knight. "Thou art trusty in keeping thine appointments," is his greeting.

Then Gawain bends his neck, and the axe is raised. As it descends, however, he "shrinks a little with his shoulders," whereupon the Green Knight pauses, and upbraids him with cowardice. The second time the Green Knight makes a feint with the axe, and Gawain stands firm. "Now thy heart is whole," says the Green Knight, "and it behoves me to strike." Gawain grows angry at the delay. "Why, thresh on, thou fierce man!" he cries, "thou threatest too long. I think thou art terrified at thine own self." The axe comes down a third time, but, instead of striking off Gawain's head, it merely makes a little gash in his neck. Then Gawain springs away more than a spear's length, and puts on his helm. "No more!" he cries, "I have endured one stroke, as I agreed. If thou strikest another, I shall repay thee!"

But the Green Knight has no wish to pursue the matter. He reveals himself as identical with Gawain's host of the castle. He knew all about the actions of his lady; — in fact, he says, it was at his instance that she had wooed Gawain, merely as a test of the visitor's fidelity. The first two blows had been harmless, he adds, because Gawain had faithfully rendered up all that he had received on the first two days, — the kisses that the lady had given him. The third blow had taken effect because Gawain had concealed the lace. In spite of this peccadillo, the Green Knight, who now discloses his name as Bernlak de Hautdesert, commends Gawain for the truest of knights, and invites him to go back with him to the castle. But Gawain is abashed and takes his leave. The Green Knight tells him that the "ancient lady" whom Gawain has seen at the castle is "Morgne la Faye," and that it was by her instructions that he had paid a visit to Arthur's court. Morgan's purpose was, he says, to drive all the knights mad with terror and cause the death of Guinevere from fright. Gawain and his host part with expressions of mutual esteem. Gawain returns to Arthur's court and gives a truthful account of his adventure, though he is sore ashamed. King Arthur and his household laugh, and agree that all the knights "that belong to the Table" shall henceforth wear a green lace or baldric like Gawain's.

As the plot of *Gawain and the Green Knight* lies before us, it is immediately and obviously divisible into two distinct adventures: — (1) the exchange of blows with the axe, which for brevity's sake we may entitle " The Challenge," and (2) the experiences of Gawain at the castle of Bernlak, which we may conveniently designate as " The Temptation." In the structure of the romance, the second of these adventures is inserted in the first, and the combination is very skilfully worked, so that the hero is made to emerge unharmed from the dangers of the Challenge because he has stood the test imposed by the Temptation. Nor is this all, — Gawain is tested without knowing it. His fortitude in withstanding the lady's blandishments is made to result purely and simply from his character. He rejects her advances, not because he is aware of the vital necessity of rejecting them, — for he has no suspicion of the identity of the lady's husband, and no thought of any connection between his own conduct at the castle and the upshot of the beheading game, — but because he would remain faithful to his knightly ideal of " truth," that is, in this instance, of fidelity to the general obligation of guest to host and to the special obligation involved in his compact as to each day's winnings.

Structurally considered, then, the adventure of the Temptation becomes an incident of the adventure of the Challenge; the Challenge brings about the Temptation, and the Temptation, in its turn, determines the issue of the Challenge. Nevertheless, our division of the plot into these two adventures is neither arbitrary nor mechanical. It accords with known facts. Both the Challenge and the Temptation exist elsewhere in literature, and each is quite independent of the other in origin and history. Indeed, it is only in this particular romance of *Gawain and the Green Knight* that the two are woven together in a single plot.[1] We must therefore

---

[1] The romance of *Humbaut* contains both the Challenge and a form of the Temptation, but the two episodes are not combined.

study them separately, in the first instance, before we can understand the changes to which they have been subjected in this special combination. The study is not uninteresting for its own sake, and it may throw some light on the narrative technique of the middle ages.

The Challenge has already been examined with more or less care by several scholars, but the importance of the Temptation seems not to have been sufficiently recognized.

II. THE CHALLENGE; OR, THE BEHEADING GAME

The Irish Versions

Our study of the extraordinary tale known as The Beheading Game — or, as we have agreed to call it, for brevity, The Challenge — is much facilitated by a fortunate chance which enables us, in a manner, to begin at the beginning instead of working back to a purely hypothetical source. The Challenge is not only extant in several Old French documents; it is also preserved in Middle Irish in a highly developed literary form, essentially identical, even in details, with the shape which it takes in *Gawain and the Green Knight*. We may be certain, therefore, that the incident is Celtic, and that it somehow passed from Irish literature into French. The details of this process are not altogether clear, but the main fact admits of no dispute, and affords a firm basis for our investigation. In calling the Challenge story " Celtic," I do not mean to assert that the mere incident, in its elements or its simplest form, actually originated on Celtic soil. Such a proposition would be equally gratuitous and venturesome. What is certain is that, long before the earliest date which can be assigned to any conceivable French work embodying this incident in its developed form,

this developed form existed, *in literary shape,* in Ireland.   In
other words, the Challenge in the form in which it appears in
Old French and Middle English literature, is unquestionably of Celtic origin.   More than this the conditions of the
investigation do not require one to postulate.

The Irish story bears the separate and distinct title of
The Champion's Bargain,[1] and occurs as the concluding
adventure in the great epic saga of *Fled Bricrend,* or *Bricriu's
Feast.*   The subject of this saga is the contention of the three
most distinguished champions of Ulster for the *curathmír* or
" hero's portion " — a special ration or allowance assigned
to the preëminent warrior at feasts.   The manuscript that
contains *Bricriu's Feast,* the famous *Lebor na hUidre* (or
Book of the Dun Cow), was written at the end of the eleventh
or the beginning of the twelfth century (the scribe of this
portion of the *Fled Bricrend* was killed in 1106), and the saga
itself is much older than the manuscript.   *The Champion's
Bargain* is incomplete in the *Lebor na hUidre,* on account of
the mutilation of the manuscript, but enough of it is there
preserved to warrant our accepting the complete text contained in a later manuscript as an accurate reproduction of
the story in every particular.[2]   The adventure must be
translated in full, for it is too important to be abridged.

The Champion's Bargain

Once upon a time, when the Ulstermen were in Emain Macha,[3]
after the fatigue of the gathering and games, Conchobar and Fergus
mac Roig and likewise the nobles of Ulster came from the playing
field outside and took their seats in the Red Branch [4] of Conchobar.
Neither Cuchulinn nor Conall the Victorious nor Loegaire the Triumphant was there that night; but all the rest of the host of valiant
warriors of Ulster were present.   While they were there at the hour
of evening at the close of day, they saw a carl, great and very hideous,

---

[1] *Cennach ind Ruanada.*   [3] The Ulster capital.
[2] See p. 291.   [4] Conchobar's royal residence or hall.

coming toward them into the house. It seemed to them that there was not among the Ulstermen a hero who would reach half his size. Terrible and hideous was the appearance of the carl. An old hide next his skin, and a black tawny cloak about him, and upon him the bushiness of a great tree the size of a winter-fold in which thirty yearlings could find shelter.[1] Fierce yellow eyes in his head, each of those two eyes standing out of his head as big as a cauldron that would hold a large ox. As thick as the wrist of any other man each one of his fingers. In his left hand, a block in which was a load for twenty yoke of oxen. In his right hand, an axe into which had gone thrice fifty measures of glowing metal; the handle was so heavy that it would take the strength of six oxen to move it; it would cut hairs against the wind for sharpness.

In that guise he went and took his stand at the base of the forked beam which was by the fire. " Is the house too small for you," said Dubthach Chafer-tongue [2] to the carl, "that you find no other place there except at the base of the forked beam, — unless it pleases you to claim the position of light-bearer for the house ? Only you are more likely to burn the house down than to give light to the household."

"Whatever my art may be," [said the carl,] "surely it will be judged, however tall I may be, that the whole household shall have light and yet the house shall not be burned.

" Still," said he, " that is not my only art; I have other arts besides. However, the thing which I have come in quest of," said he, " I have found neither in Ireland nor in Scotland nor in Europe nor in Africa nor in Asia as far as Greece and Scythia and the Orkney Islands and the Pillars of Hercules and the Tower of Bregon and the Isles of Gades any man who would fulfil the rules of fair play [3] for me with regard to it. Since you Ulstermen have distinguished yourselves," said he, " above the hosts of all those lands for the terror

---

[1] This certainly refers to the carl's bushy head of hair, as Zimmer was the first to understand.

[2] So called from his habit of sharp speech.

[3] The Irish phrase is *fír fer*, "the truth of men." On this technical expression ("das von Männern gegebene Wort, das unter allen Umständen eingelöst . . . werden muss "), see Zimmer, *Zeitschrift für celtische Philologie*, I, 101, apropos of the *Fled Bricrend*. He cites *Revue Celtique*, III, 184, and Windisch, *Irische Texte*, I, *Wörterbuch*, p. 550. Compare the kingly habit of granting requests or making pledges without knowing what is involved, common in romances and folk-tales (Campbell, *Popular Tales of the West Highlands*, II, 138).

[you inspire] and prowess and valor, for rank and pride and dignity, for justice and generosity and worth, find from among you one man who shall fulfil toward me the quest in which I am [engaged]."

"Verily, it is not right," said Fergus mac Roich, "for the honor of the province to be taken away for the lack of a man to make good their honor, and surely death would not be nearer to that man than to you!" "I am not avoiding that, then!" said he. "Then let us know your quest," said Fergus mac Roich. "If only fair play be granted me," said he, "I will tell it." "It is right also [for us] to fulfil [the rules of] fair play to you," said Sencha mac Ailill, "for it is not fair play for a great united host to attack one solitary stranger among them; and besides, we should have thought," said Sencha, "that even already you would have found one man to oppose you here." "I exempt Conchobar," said he, "because of his kingship, and I exempt Fergus mac Roig, because of his legal privilege; and whoever it is of you that is able," said he, "except these two, let him come, that I may [1] strike off his head to-night and he may strike off my head to-morrow night."

"It is certain now," said Dubthach, "that there is no one here who is a worthy warrior [a match for you?] . . . after those two." "Truly there shall be, this instant!" said Munremar mac Gerrcind. Thereupon he sprang out on the floor of the house. Now this was the strength of that Munremar: the strength of a hundred warriors in him, and the strength of a hundred . . . [2] in each of his two arms. "Stoop, carl, that I may strike off your head to-night and that you may strike off mine to-morrow night!" said Munremar. "I should have found *that* anywhere, if that were what I want," said the carl. "As we have agreed," said he, "so let us do — I to cut off your head to-night, you to cut off mine to-morrow night to avenge it." "I swear the oath of my people," said Dubthach Chafter-tongue [to Munremar], "death will not be more pleasing to you thus, if the man whom you shall kill to-night shall be ready to kill you to-morrow. It is given to you alone [i.e. it is your unique gift or privilege]," [said he to the carl,] "if you have the ability to be killed each night and to avenge it on the morrow." "Truly, I will carry out the plan which you all agree upon, though it seems wonderful to you," said the carl. Thereupon he exacted from the other a pledge . . . with regard to fufilling his tryst on the morrow.

[1] Here ends the *Lebor na hUidre* text. Our sole authority for the rest is the Edinburgh Gaelic MS. XL, except for the remainder of the sentence, which is preserved in Egerton MS. 93 and in the Leyden MS.

[2] Unintelligible word.

Then Munremar took the axe from the carl's hand. Seven feet,
now, between the two sides of the axe. Then the carl put his neck
across the block. Munremar dealt a blow with the axe across his
neck so that it remained fixed in the block so that he cut off the head
so that it was at the foot of the forked beam so that the house was
full of blood. Straightway he rose and picked [himself] up after that,
and gathered his head and his block and his axe in his bosom, and
thus went out of the house, and streams of blood from his neck so that
it filled the Red Branch on every side, and great was their horror as
they wondered at the marvel that had appeared to them. " I swear
the oath of my people," said Dubthach Chafer-tongue, " if the carl
comes to-morrow after having been killed to-night, he will not leave
a man alive in Ulster." However, the carl returned on the morrow
at night, and Munremar went away to avoid him. The carl began
to urge [the fulfilment of] his pact upon him: " Truly, it is not right
for Munremar to shirk the fulfilment of his bargain with me."

However, Loegaire the Triumphant was there that night. " Which
of the warriors that contest the champion's portion of Ulster," said he,
" will fulfil a bargain with me to-night ? Where is Loegaire the
Triumphant ? " said he. " Here! " said Loegaire. He took a pledge
from him in like manner, and Loegaire did not come. He came again
on the morrow, and took a pledge from Conall the Victorious in like
manner, and he did not come as he had sworn.

Again he came on the fourth night and anger and rage(?) was
upon him then. All the women of Ulster had come that night to see
the strange marvel that had come into the Red Branch. Cuchulinn
also was there that night. Then the carl began to upbraid them:
" Your valor and your prowess are gone, O Ulstermen," said he.
" Great is the desire of your warriors for the champion's portion,"
said he, " but they are unable to contest it. Where is that mad
wretched creature that is called Cuchulinn," said he, " [that I may
see] if his word is better than that of the rest of the host ? " " I have
no wish to bargain with you at all," said Cuchulinn. " Likely enough,
O miserable fly! Greatly do you fear death." Thereupon Cuchulinn
leaped toward him. He dealt him a blow with the axe so that he
sent his head to the top rafter of the Red Branch, so that the whole
house shook. Cuchulinn caught up his head again and gave it a blow
with the axe so that he made fragments of it. He rose up after that.

On the morrow the Ulstermen were watching Cuchulinn to see
whether he would avoid the carl, as the other heroes had done. The
Ulstermen saw that while Cuchulinn was awaiting the carl, very great
dejection seized him, and it would have been fitting if they had sung
a dirge over him, and they felt sure that his life would last but till the

carl should come. Then said Conchobar to Cuchulinn: "Avoid
him!" "By my shield and by my sword, I will not go until I fulfil
my pledge to the carl; for death is before me, and it is better for
me to have death than dishonor."

As they were there, then, at the close of day, they saw the carl
approaching them. "Where is Cuchulinn?" said he. "Here am I,
then," said Cuchulinn. "You are humble of speech to-night, poor
fellow; greatly you fear death. Though greatly you fear death, you
have not avoided it." The Cuchulinn went to him and stretched his
neck across the block. The size of the block was such that his neck
reached but halfway. "Stretch out your neck, wretch!" said the
carl. "You are torturing me!" said Cuchulinn, "kill me quickly;
verily I did not torture you last night," said he. "Verily, I swear,"
said Cuchulinn, "if you torture me, I will make myself as long as a
crane above you." "I cannot slay you," said the carl, "what with
the size of the block and the shortness of your neck and of your side."

Then Cuchulinn stretched out his neck so that a grown man's foot
would have fitted between each two of his ribs, and he stretched his
neck until it reached the block on the other side. The carl raised his
axe so that it reached the roof-tree of the house. The creaking of the
old hide that was about the carl, and the creaking of the axe, and the
force of his two arms raised aloft, were like the loud noise of a . . .
forest in a stormy night. It descended again . . . on his neck, and
its blunt side downward. All the nobles of Ulster were looking at them
meanwhile.

"Rise, O Cuchulinn! . . . Of the warriors of Ulster or of Ireland,
none is found to be compared with you in valor or in prowess or in
truth. The sovereignty of the warriors of Ireland to you from this
hour, and the champion's portion without dispute, and to your wife
precedence of the women of Ulster forever in the house of drinking!
and moreover," said he "whoever he may be who may contest it
against you from this time forth, I swear by what my people swear
that this shall be the length of his life. . . ."

Then the carl [departed]. And it was Curoi mac Daire who had
come in that guise to fulfil the promise that he had given to Cuchulinn.
From that hour the champion's portion was not disputed against
Cuchulinn, and thus ends the Champion's Portion of Emain, and
the Word-Battle of the Women of Ulster, and the Bargain of the
Champion in Emain Macha, and the Journey of the Ulstermen to
Cruachan Ai.[1]

---

[1] *Fled Bricrend*, edited by Henderson, 1899, chap. 16, §§ 91–102, pp. 116–
129. The translation given above makes free use of the renderings by
Henderson and Kuno Meyer (see p. 291, below).

No argument is needed to show that *The Champion's Bargain* is the same story as the Challenge in *Gawain and the Green Knight*. In both the Irish saga and the English poem we have a huge uncanny stranger visiting the court of a great national king on a high feastday and challenging the assembled company to an exchange of blows with an axe. In both, the stranger declares that he has come to test the valor of the court on account of its high reputation for bravery and other noble qualities. In both, the consternation of the warriors is dwelt on. In both, the stranger taunts the heroes when they hesitate, declaring that their fame is undeserved. In both, the king does not subject himself to the test: in the Irish he is expressly exempted by the challenger; in the English he resigns the adventure to Gawain. In both, one knight only is found who dares fulfil the compact, and he is the most distinguished of all. In both, the stranger spares this knight, proclaiming him the best of heroes. The contrast between the rude savagery of the Irish saga and the refined chivalry of the English romance is notable; but it is a difference of manners only — precisely such a difference as we should expect in a romantic French or English adaptation of an ancient Irish epic tale.

The close agreement between the stories cannot be fortuitous. Nor can it be due to the common utilizing of a casual bit of vagrant tradition. The Irish tale is carefully wrought out in detail with conscious art, and its correspondence with the English poem extends to certain minutiae which are not folk-lore, but literary elaboration.

Compare, for instance, the speech in which the challenger (in both the Irish and the English) celebrates the reputation of the court to which he has come. Says the Green Knight: — " Since the renown of the people is so exalted, and thy burgh and thy men are held the best, — stiffest under steel-gear on steeds to ride, the wightest and worthiest in the whole world, well-tried in all manner of games, — and since here, as I have heard tell, courtesy is shown, — *that* has brought me hither at this time. If thou art as bold as all men say, thou wilt grant me the game that I ask." So, in the Irish saga, the stranger declares: " The thing which I have come in quest of, I have found, neither in Ireland nor in Scotland, nor in Europe nor in Africa nor in Asia, as far as Greece and Scythia and the Orkney Islands and the Pillars of Hercules and the Tower of Bregon and the Isles of Gades, any man who would fulfil the rules of fair play for me with regard to it. Since you Ulstermen have distinguished your-selves above the hosts of all those lands for the terror [you inspire] and prowess and valor, for rank and pride and dignity, for justice and generosity and worth, find from among you one man who shall fulfil toward me the quest in which I am [engaged]." In the English poem, King Arthur replies: " Sir courteous knight, if thou crave battle here, thou shalt not fail to fight." Compare the words of Sencha in the Irish: " We should have thought that even already you would have found one man to oppose you here."

Further, we should note the upbraiding words of the stranger when he has specified the character of his proposal and the knights hang back. " What! " cries the Green Knight. "Is this Arthur's house that is so highly renowned in so many realms ? Where are now your pride and your conquests, your fierceness and your boldness and your great words ? Now are the splendor and the renown of the Round Table overcome by a word of one man's speech; for all cower for dread, though no blow has been given!" So in the Irish tale: — " Your valor and your prowess are gone, O Ulstermen! Great is the desire of your warriors for the champion's portion, but they are unable to contest it."

Further details might be cited, but these are enough for the present. Others will come out in abundance as we proceed.[1]

In the complete absence, then, of any indication to the contrary, we are forced to infer that the Challenge in *Gawain and the Green Knight* goes back, in some way, to an elaborate literary version of *The Champion's Bargain* in Irish. This literary Irish version, though it may not have been identical in all particulars with the text preserved in the *Book of the Dun Cow* and the complementary manuscript, cannot have differed much from that text.

However, the *Fled Bricrend* contains another version of the Challenge,[2] simpler in most respects than *The Champion's Bargain*, and apparently closer to the original form of the story. Here the three warriors who are contending for the hero's portion — Cuchulinn, Loegaire, and Conall — are sent for adjudgment to one Uath mac Imomain, that is, "Terror, the son of Great Fear." A full translation follows: —

Now this Uath mac Imomain was a man of great strength who used to form himself into whatever shape he pleased and perform tricks of magic and arts of wizardry. He was, indeed, the wizard after whom the Wizard's Pass is named, and he was called the Wizard from the extent of his forming himself into many shapes.

Then they went to Uath's loch, and a guide from Budi went with them. Then they told Uath the thing on account of which they had come to visit him. Uath said to them that he would undertake to judge them on condition only that they would abide by his decision. "We will abide by it," said they. He exacted a pledge from them. "I have a bargain [to propose]," said he, "and whichever it be of you who fulfils it with me, he it is who shall receive the champion's portion." "What kind of bargain is that?" said they. "I have an

---

[1] The analytical table of versions on pp. 66 ff. may be consulted if particulars are desired.

[2] The whole of this version is preserved in the *Lebor na hUidre* (see p. 292, below).

axe," said he, "and it shall be given into the hand of one of you, and he is to cut off my head to-day, and I am to cut off his to-morrow."

Then Conall and Loegaire said they would not make that covenant, for it would not be in their power to live after they had been beheaded, although perhaps it would be in *his* power. So Conall and Loegaire refused him the bargain; although other books say that they made that bargain with him, — namely, Loegaire to cut off his head the first day, — and that he [Loegaire] avoided him [i.e. did not appear to receive Uath's blow in return], and that Conall avoided him in the same way. Then Cuchulinn said that he would make the bargain with him if the champion's portion were given to him. Then Conall and Loegaire said that they would relinquish the champion's portion to him if he would make the bargain with Uath. Cuchulinn exacted a pledge from them that they would not contest the champion's portion if he should make the bargain with Uath. They also exacted a pledge from him that he would make the bargain. Uath laid his head on the stone for Cuchulinn,[1] and Cuchulinn struck him a blow with his [Uath's] own axe, so that he smote off his head from him. Then he [Uath] went off from them into the loch, with his axe and his head in his bosom.

On the morrow, then, he came to seek him, and Cuchulinn stretched himself out for him on the stone. He let the axe come down three times on his neck, back first. "Rise, O Cuchulinn!" said Uath. "The sovereignty of the warriors of Ulster to you, and the champion's portion without dispute!" The three champions then went to Emain, and the others [i.e. Loegaire and Conall] did not acknowledge the judgment that had been rendered him. The former dispute about the champion's portion continued. Then the advice of the Ulstermen to them was to visit Curoi for their judgment. Then they agreed to that.[2]

The presence of these two versions of a single adventure in the same Irish saga is due to the composite character of the extant text of the *Bricriu's Feast*. Old as it is, this text is well known to be a combination of two still older recensions, each of which contained a version of the Challenge. The combined text of the *Fled Bricrend* includes both ver-

---

[1] In the margin of the manuscript is added: "that is, after putting a spell on the edge of the axe."

[2] *Fled Bricrend*, edited by Henderson, chap. 14, §§ 75-78, pp. 96-101. The translation is based upon Henderson's rendering (see p. 292 below).

sions, — one (Uath) standing in the body of the saga, the other (called *The Champion's Bargain*) at the very end. The editorial activity of the combiner is easy to follow on a mere inspection of the extant text. The Uath sections are in a hand different from that of the scribe of *The Champion's Bargain* and somewhat later, but still of the early twelfth century.[1]

Of the two ancient Irish versions of the Challenge that are before us, the Uath version is the simpler and shows much less literary elaboration. The presumption is strong that it offers a more primitive form of the episode.

Two points of difference immediately appear. (1) In the Uath version, the three heroes visit Uath and request him to test their valor; in *The Champion's Bargain*, the uncanny creature visits the king's court, and the beheading game takes place in the presence of the assembled nobility of Ulster. (2) In the Uath version the game, as proposed by the giant, is to begin with his own decapitation: "'I have an axe,' said he, ' and it shall be given into the hand of one of you, and he is to cut off my head to-night and I am to cut off his head to-morrow.'" In *The Champion's Bargain*, on the other hand, the challenger begins with the opposite pro-position (" I will cut off his head to-night; he mine to-morrow "), but he reverses the order when this arrangement has failed to elicit a favorable response. This is an obvious, and rather clever, method of complicating the plot and heightening the suspense.

Though both Irish versions of the Challenge are asso-ciated with Cuchulinn, and, in their present context, pre-suppose the fully developed Ulster cycle of epic tales, yet there is no reason to infer that the story was originally told of that hero. On the contrary, it seems probable *a priori*

[1] See p. 292.

that it was in the first place a mere bit of floating folk-lore, ready to be attached to any famous warrior. However this may be, its association with the Cuchulinn saga must have taken place a long time before the two versions of the *Fled Bricrend* were amalgamated to make the text preserved in the *Lebor na hUidre*, — a text, we remember, that occurs in a manuscript of about 1100. Thus the Challenge, as a distinct Irish story, is carried back to a date at least as early as the tenth century.

The axeman belongs to a large class of supernatural beings whose heads return to their bodies after decapitation. Such creatures occur in popular tradition in almost every part of the earth — in Ireland, Scotland, the Færöes, Brittany, Holland, Germany, Hungary, Greece, Italy, Russia, India, the Philippines, Papua, and among many tribes of the American aborigines from the North Pacific coast to Salvador.[1] In origin they are doubtless serpent-monsters, or elemental water-demons with serpentine characteristics, and their peculiar ability to unite head with trunk may well come, in part, from that naïve scientific observation of the folk which is responsible for the widespread belief, well documented in the Scottish Highlands [2] and still common among American boys, that a snake's head will join its body again after being cut off. Ireland believed in such monsters in common with the rest of the world, though their serpentine origin had long been forgotten there, for obvious reasons, not unconnected with St. Patrick. The association of snake-men, *nāgas*, dragons, and other ophidian beings with lakes or tarns and, in general, with the element of water, is one of the most familiar of all traits of popular mythology. It can justly claim a scope as wide as the human race and an antiquity as venerable as the dawn of human thought. The

---

[1] See pp. 147 ff.   [2] See p. 192.

residence of Uath in a loch is manifestly a very archaic survival.

With these facts in mind, one can readily infer the most primitive form of the Irish tale of the Challenge: —

An elemental demon — a water-monster who inhabits a loch and is capable of human likeness — is in the habit of proposing to all comers an exchange of blows with an axe, granting them the privilege of the first stroke. To decline the challenge is death. To accept it is likewise death, for the monster's head returns to his shoulders and he instantly decapitates his mortal opponent.

The practice of exchanging buffets in regular succession, or of dealing alternate blows with a weapon, is an ancient and widespread method of duelling. Saxo Grammaticus comments on it in his account of the death of Agnerus (*Agnarr*) at the hands of Biarco (*Bjarki*). In their duel with swords there was a long dispute which had the right to strike first; it was settled in favor of Agnerus because of his higher rank. He cut through Biarco's helmet and inflicted a scalp-wound. Biarco, bracing his foot against a log of wood, cut Agnerus in two with a single stroke. Saxo remarks that " in ancient times " this regular succession of blows was the established custom in single combats. Other sources inform us that it was practised in the Scandinavian *holmgang*, the challenged party having the first stroke, as in modern duels he has the choice of weapons. In the *Helden-buch*, Wolfdietrich and the heathen engage in a game of knife-throwing on the principle of alternation, the host (though challenger) claiming the first three throws by virtue of the custom of his castle. Wrennok and Gandeleyn, in a very old English ballad, shoot at each other in turn. In a folk-tale from Madagascar there is a duel in which first one person, then the other, throws a dart. Such cases occur also in Philippine legend. Blows with the hand are given in like

succession in the game of pluck-buffet in the romance of
Richard Coer de Lion, in the *Gest of Robin Hood*, and in *The
Turk and Gawain*. In Chapman's *Alphonsus Emperor of
Germany*, two Dutch boors, Hans and Jerick, fight with
axes. The stage direction reads: " They must have axes
made for the nonst to fight withall, and while one strikes, the
other holds his back without defence." [1]

In view of the antiquity and the wide currency of this
method of duelling by alternate shots or blows, it would be
an easy step for popular superstition to ascribe to a supernatural creature the custom of challenging mortals to such a
combat. But we need not depend upon inferences. In
1827, Mr. P. Cunningham, writing of the blackfellows of
New South Wales, remarked: " Their common practice of
fighting among themselves is still with the *waddie*,[2] each
alternately stooping the head to receive the other's blows,
until one tumbles down, it being considered cowardly to
evade a stroke." [3] And in 1846, Principal Braim, of Sydney
College, in his history of the same colony, recorded the following superstition of the same aborigines with regard to an
"imaginary being named *Ko-yo-ro-wen* ": " His trill in the
bush frequently alarms the blacks by night. When he over-
takes a native, he commands him to exchange cudgels,
giving his own, which is extremely large, and desiring the
black to take a first blow at his head, which he holds down
for that purpose, after which he smiles and kills the person
with one blow, skewers him with the cudgel, carries him off,
roasts, and then eats him." [4]

The most skeptical critic of folk-lore would never think of
suspecting that this article of the Australian creed was in-

---

[1] See pp. 218 ff. for further details.

[2] A wooden club (see E. C. Morris, *Austral English*, pp. 491–492).

[3] *Two Years in New South Wales*, London, 1827, II, 22.

[4] T. H. Braym, *History of New South Wales*, London, 1846, II, 250.

fluenced by European tradition. The coincidence is purely fortuitous, or rather it results from the tendency of savage men to think in identical terms. It is therefore a precious bit of testimony to the primitive character of the Challenge story in its main features. Taken in connection with the worldwide belief in a class of supernatural monsters whose severed heads return to their bodies, the Australian testimony raises our inferential reconstruction of the earliest Irish form of the tale to the rank of an established fact.

In this earliest form, however, the Challenge is hardly a story at all. It is a mere belief, the result of misinterpreted observation and misunderstood experiences — a current superstition, attachable at will to any lonely tarn and not yet associated with the exploits of a particular hero. It becomes a tale when some hero, arriving at the loch by chance, or visiting it on purpose to try conclusions with the demon, emerges triumphantly from the encounter. This result he would achieve, of course, by outwitting the lake-man, either by destroying the head after he has severed it, or by keeping it away from the trunk until the creature is cold and dead. Examples of such methods abound in the folk-lore of Ireland and elsewhere.[1] At this stage of development, the story, after the manner of folk-tales, might well include three questers, only the last of whom succeeds. The adventure was now in a condition to be ascribed to almost any one — whether the anonymous or trivially named hero of a *märchen*, or some august personage of heroic saga who attracted folk-tales as a magnet attracts iron-filings; but there is no reason to suppose that it had yet joined the cycle of Cuchulinn.

A further development removes the challenger from the category of purely malevolent beings and also ennobles the

[1] See pp. 148 ff.

hero's character.   An interval is allowed between the original decapitation and the return-blow.   This gives the hero a
chance to escape if he is willing to show the white feather.
Three adventurers (the traditional number in folk-tales)
accept the challenge, but only the third returns to what he
supposes will be certain death.   Him the challenger spares,
striking him with the back of the axe, because of his valor
and his fidelity to his plighted word.   In this state the story
coincides to all intents and purposes with the Uath chapter
of the *Fled Bricrend*.   Probably, indeed, it was actually the
first author of this saga, or the first person that ever worked
it up in connected form, who thus modified the folk-tale in
the very process of attaching it to Cuchulinn as the conclusive test of his supremacy among the warriors of Ulster.

As we have seen, there were, as early as the eleventh century, two main versions of the complete Irish saga of the
Contention for the Hero's Portion, which were combined in a
text now actually extant in a manuscript written about 1100.
In one of these the Challenge was retained in the form in
which it now appears in the Uath chapter of the *Fled Bricrend*.   The other embodied the Challenge in a much more
elaborate form, represented by *The Champion's Bargain*.
Comparison shows at a glance that the Challenge in *Gawain
and the Green Knight* is much closer to *The Champion's
Bargain* than to the Uath episode.   Yet the Uath version
and *Gawain and the Green Knight* appear to agree in the
incident of the three harmless blows, which seems at first
sight not to be preserved in *The Champion's Bargain*.
Further scrutiny, however, shows clearly enough that *The
Champion's Bargain* does in effect afford this incident.
Cuchulinn lays his head upon the block, but the challenger
refuses to strike him until he has stretched his neck to fit it.
Cuchulinn makes the effort apparently, and calls for the

blow. A second time the challenger declines to strike because of the shortness of the hero's neck. Then Cuchulinn exercises his superhuman power of distortion and lengthens his neck to the necessary degree. Thereupon follows a blow with the back of the axe. Thus there are two refusals to smite in *The Champion's Bargain*, and one final blow. At a later stage of our study we shall take up the relation of the incident in this form to the three blows in the English romance.[1] For the moment it must suffice to remark that we shall find no reason to appeal to the Uath version to explain the three harmless blows in the *Gawain*.

The Irish tale of *The Champion's Bargain*, in a highly developed literary form, practically identical with that which concludes the *Fled Bricrend*, must have passed into French at an early date, for it was utilized by four romancers who wrote in that language, and none of them derived it from any of the others. The four romancers in question were the author of the lost French *Gawain and the Green Knight*, the author of the *Livre de Caradoc*, the author of *La Mule sanz Frain*, and the author of the *Perlesvaus*. Each of these documents embodies the story in a different combination. In the lost *Gawain* it was united with the Temptation, as we have seen; in the *Caradoc*, it was worked into a tale belonging to the cycle of The Faithless Mother; in the *Perlesvaus* it was made into an episode of the knight errantry of Lancelot; in *La Mule*, it was utilized in a tale that comes under the well-known type of a hero who is summoned by a messenger to the disenchantment of a waste city and the release of a princess. In none of these four romances, as I have said, does the author take the tale of the Challenge from any one of the other three. This is shown, in the case of *Gawain and the Green Knight*, the *Livre de Caradoc*, and *La*

---

[1] Pp. 40–41, 47–48, 72 ff.

Mule sanz Frain, by the fact that each of these three poems preserves features of the Irish story which the other two have lost.   In the case of the *Perlesvaus*, which departs more widely from the original than the rest, the evidence for independent derivation is equally cogent, though rather too complicated to be summed up in a sentence.   A fifth French romance, *Gauvain et Humbaut*, contains the incident in a very imperfect shape, so disordered as to make its immediate source a matter of conjecture.

Le Livre de Caradoc

Of the extant French versions of the Challenge that in the *Livre de Caradoc* is closest to *Gawain and the Green Knight*. The *Livre de Caradoc* is inserted in the first continuation of Chrétien's *Perceval*,[1] but it has no pertinency there, is clearly intrusive, and beyond question formed at one time an independent poem.   The facts are universally admitted and require no further discussion.[2]   We may without apology speak henceforth of the *Livre de Caradoc* as a work by itself, disregarding its position in the *Perceval*.

In the *Livre*, the Challenge is, of course, brought into more or less intimate relations with other events in Caradoc's career.   But it is easy to take it out of its frame, to isolate it, and to examine it as an independent unit.   This procedure is justified *prima facie* on two grounds: first, the Challenge is originally an Irish tale quite independent of Caradoc and his legend; and second, it is only in the *Livre de Caradoc* that the Challenge is associated with the other adventures therein contained, or with any of them.[3]   But this is not all.   The saga of Caradoc, as told in the *Livre*, belongs in its main outlines to a well-known type of *märchen* — that of the Faithless Mother (or Sister) whose love for a

---

[1] *Perceval li Gallois*, vv. 12,451–15,792 (Potvin, III, 117–221).
[2] See p. 297.   [3] See pp. 224 ff.

monster leads her to attempt her son's (or brother's) destruction, and in which the hero is saved by his dogs or his
amie.[1] The type is here modified by prefixing an account of
the hero's parentage which makes him the son of the uncanny lover — a motif best known in the Nectanabus portion
of the Alexander romance. To the whole is appended the
story of the Horn, which is applied to Caradoc's wife as a
glorification of her virtue. How far this complex represents
the saga of Caradoc (presumably Celtic) from which the
French author of the *Livre* mediately or immediately drew,
need not be determined. For one thing is abundantly manifest: the episode of the Challenge to the Beheading Game
does not properly belong in the tale of *The Faithless Mother*
and, indeed, it occurs in no other of the versions (about a
hundred) in which that *märchen* is extant. Finally, the
Challenge is so unskilfully worked into the main plot of the
Livre as to involve the romancer in a plain absurdity.[2]

We may therefore continue our study of the Challenge in
Old French literature, without pausing to discuss the peculiar
company into which the Caradoc poet has brought that story
by thrusting it into a plot with which it has nothing to do.

The Challenge in the *Livre de Caradoc* runs as follows:[3] —

King Arthur holds his Pentecostal feast at Carduel, summoning his
vassals from far and wide. The night before he has dubbed his grand-
nephew Caradoc knight. When the feast is ready, Kay announces it,
but the king refuses to begin until some strange news arrives or some
adventure happens, alleging a custom. While they are speaking, there
rides in at the hall door a very tall knight on a tawny steed; he is
dressed in a long ermine robe which reaches to the ground and

> En son cief ot un capelet,
> A un ciercle d'or de bounet.

He is armed with a very long sword. Riding up to the high dais, he
greets King Arthur courteously and asks " a gift." " Tell us what the

[1] See pp. 228 ff.   [3] Vv. 12, 592–885 (Potvin, III, 125–133).
[2] See pp. 225 ff.

gift is," Arthur replies, " and you shall have it." Then the stranger becomes more precise: " The boon is — to receive a blow on condition that I may give another."

> " Rois," fet-il, " ne vos voil deçoivre,
> Le don est colée reçoivre
> Por un autre colée prendre." [1]

The king still asking for particulars, the knight explains himself fully: — " If there is a knight here who can cut off my head with one blow of this sword, and if I can recover from the blow, he may be sure of having the blow returned a year from now if he dare await it."

> " Rois, je vos di tout a estrous
> Que, s'il a çaiens chevalier
> Qui la tieste me puist trencier
> A un seul cop de ceste espée,
> Et se repuis de la colée
> Apries saner et regarir,
> Seurs puet estre, sans falir,
> D'ui en .i. an d'ausi reprendre
> La colée, s'il l'ose atendre."

Then he dismounts, draws his sword, and holds it out; but the knights say that only a fool would risk such an adventure.[2] Then the stranger taunts them: " What is the matter, sirs ? Will none of you accept ? Now may King Arthur see that his court is not so mighty as everybody declares. I shall have a poor report to make of it."

> " Ha," fait li chevaliers, " signor,
> Et çou que est ? n'en feres plus ?
> Or puet veoir li rois Artus
> Que sa cours n'est mie si rice
> Comme cascuns dist et afice;
> N'i a nul chevalier hardi;
> Por voir le vos tesmogne ci
> Que jou dirai teles novieles
> Qui n'ierent ne plaisant ne beles."

He is departing in this mood when Caradoc springs forward and grasps the sword. The king tries to dissuade him: " Fair nephew, you can refrain without disgrace, for here is many a knight who could

---

[1] Montpellier MS. In the Mons MS. we have:
> Colée demanc, sans deçoivre,
> Por un autre errant a reçoivre.

[2] Kay makes this remark in the Montpellier MS.

strike better than you if he wished." Caradoc is resolved and raises
the sword. The stranger faces the dais, lowers his head, and extends
his neck. Caradoc decapitates him with a single blow and the head
falls on the dais. But the stranger picks it up by the hair with both
hands, puts it on his shoulders again, and stands up safe and sound.

> Caradeus fiert si durement
> Que la tieste voler en fist
> Desor le dois; cil le reprist
> Par les keviaus a ses .ii. mains,
> Ausi com s'il fust trestous sains;
> Si le ragointe en es le pas.[1]

" Caradoc," says the stranger, " you have struck me." " Truly,"
remarks Kay,[2] " you seem indifferent to the injury! A year hence I
would not be in Caradoc's place for all the gold in this land." The
stranger then departs, promising to return in a year and charging
Caradoc not to fail him. The king and the knights are sorrowful;
the court breaks up, to reassemble next Pentecost. Caradoc borrows
no trouble but remains in good spirits, passing the year in seeking
adventures and " les chevaleries dures."

The year is up and a very great court assembles to see Caradoc
lose his head. All the knights make heavy cheer. The strange knight
enters, as before, and rides up to the dais. He dismounts and draws
his sword. " Caradoc," he cries, " I do not see you. Come forward
and offer me your head, for I offered you mine! "[3] " Here am I,"

---

[1] Mons MS. The Montpellier MS. indicates that the head was replaced
with a rapidity almost too great for the eye to follow: —

> Si li a donné tel colée
> Que jusques el dois est coulée;
> Li chies li vole non pas pres
> Et li cors li suit de si pres
> Qu' ains que nus garde s'en soit prise
> R'a li cors sa teste reprise,
> Rasise l'a en son droit lieu.
> Li chevaliers saut anmi leu,
> Devant le roi, et saus et sains.

[2] Potvin reads " fait Caradeus," but the words are obviously meant to
be uttered by Kay.

[3] So in the Montpellier MS.: —

> " Carados, je ne te voi mie!
> Vien avant, si auras tel feste,
> Met me ci en present ta teste,
> Car ge i mis autant la moie."

The Mons. MS. has simply: " ' Caraduel,' fait il, ' u es-tu ? ' "

replies Caradoc, and prepares for the blow. King Arthur interrupts
with an offer of ransom, but the stranger rejects it. Caradoc grows
impatient at the delay: " Why will you not strike ? " he exclaims.
" You will make me die two deaths by aiming without striking. I
think you are a great coward! "

> Carados lí a dit par ire:
> " Porquoi ne ferez-vos, beau sire ?
> De .ii. mors me ferez morir
> Qui tant aësmes sans ferir.
> Moult vos en tieng ore a couart." [1]

Then he stretches out his neck and the knight raises the sword. At
this moment the queen comes out of her chamber with her ladies and
begs him to hold his hand. She tries to bribe him by offering him,
as his *amie,* any lady or maiden that he may choose, or all of them if
he wishes. He declines with courteous firmness, bidding her return
to her chamber and pray for Caradoc's soul. He then raises the sword
again but merely strikes Caradoc softly, flatlong. " Rise up, Caradoc," he says, " I do not wish to strike you any more, for you are a
valiant and faithful knight."

> " Caradoc, fait-il, lieve sus!
> Ne te voel ore ferir plus,
> Car moult es vallans chevaliers,
> Et hardis et seurs et fiers."

He then asks Caradoc to step aside with him, out of the king's hearing.
Caradoc does so, and the knight tells him a secret: —" You are my
son." " You lie," replies Caradoc, but the knight (who turns out to
be the enchanter Eliavrès) explains the facts in such a way that he is
convinced, though he still professes disbelief.[2] The stranger then
departs. The adventure is finished, and all sit down to dinner.

Since we have no critical edition of the *Caradoc,* nor even
a satisfactory report of the differences (which are consider-

---

[1] So in the Montpellier MS., but with *maus* by error for *mors* (it is *mors*
in the 1530 text). The Mons MS. has simply:

> " Chevalier, moult par es couars."
> Fait Caraduel. ' Fai erramment
> Çou que tu dois."

[2] The details are excessively curious, but they are not to our present
purpose, since they have nothing to do with the story of the Challenge (see
p. 225).

able) among the different manuscripts, we cannot be quite
certain of what the author wrote. Madden's summary
from the prose *Perceval* [1] differs from Potvin's verse text in
two important particulars. According to Madden, while
Arthur is awaiting an adventure at the Pentecostal feast,
" a knight hastily rides up, singing an air ' *bien doulcement*,'
whose appearance is thus described: — ' *et avoit dessus le
bonnet ung cercle, ou pendoit ung chapeau de fleurs, et estoit
vestu de satin* verd, *fourré de erminnes; et avoit une espée
saincte, dont puis eust la teste couppée, et en estoient ses
renges ou saincture de fine soie, batue en or, et force perles
semées par dessus.*' The knight comes to the king, and begs
to have a request granted, — to exchange blow for blow.
' How is that ? ' said Arthur. ' Sire, I will tell you,' replied the stranger, ' I will deliver my sword to a knight,
before your majesty and all the assembly, and if he is able to
cut off my head with it at a blow, in case I should afterwards recover, I will then return him the stroke.' " To
receive the stroke the challenger " lays down his head on a
block." And later, when the challenger returns after the
lapse of a year, we hear of the block again: " Carados lays
his head on the block, and tells the knight to do his worst.
Arthur and his queen both make an effort to save Carados
from what appears certain death, but in vain; and the
stranger having sufficiently kept them all in suspense, raises
his sword, and strikes the neck of Carados, but with the flat
side only of the weapon. He then tells him to rise, and
reveals to him that he is Eliaures, the enchanter, his real
father, and how it was brought about. He afterwards
mounts his horse and departs, leaving Arthur and his
knights to celebrate their feast in gladness."

[1] Edition of 1530, folios 76 v°–79 v° (*Syr Gawayne*, pp. 305–306). Cf.
Southey's summary from the same edition (*King Arthur*, 1817, I, xxxvi).

The old printed editions are not at present accessible to me, but Madden's report of their contents may be accepted without hesitation. In three particulars this report embodies traits which agree with some other version of the Challenge but differ from Potvin's text of the *Livre de Caradoc*: (1) the challenger wears *green satin*; (2) he wears a garland of flowers; (3) he lays his head down on a *block*, and the block is used for the return-blow likewise. Note, however, that the challenger does not bring the block with him, as he does in the Irish: it appears to be lying in the hall. I accept these three details as properly belonging to the *Livre de Caradoc* and use them accordingly.

A comparison of the Challenge in the *Livre de Caradoc* and *Gawain and the Green Knight* with the Irish story of *The Champion's Bargain*, shows instantly that neither the English poem nor its French source derived the incident from the *Livre de Caradoc*. For the *Gawain* retains several old features that the *Caradoc* has lost.

1. The description of the strange visitant in *Gawain and the Green Knight* resembles that in *The Champion's Bargain* much more closely than the French description does. In the Irish he is a huge and terrible giant; in the English he is tentatively called a "half-etin," and is the greatest of all men upon mould in his stature; in both, much emphasis is laid on his extraordinary guise. In *Caradoc*, on the contrary, no trace of his gigantic and savage appearance is preserved except the tame epithet "moult grant." [1] He is merely a tall knight, splendidly attired; there is nothing uncanny about his looks.

2. In both the Irish and the English, the stranger's eyes are particularly mentioned. In the Irish we have: —
" Fierce yellow eyes in his head; each of those two eyes

[1] V. 12642.

standing out of his head as big as a cauldron that would hold a large ox." In the English: " Fiercely his red eyes he rolled about; bent his rough brows, gleaming green." [1] The *Livre de Caradoc* has nothing to correspond with these passages.

3. In the French, the stranger greets Arthur " very courteously." [2] In the Irish, he stands silent until he is addressed by Dubthach. In the English, it is expressly stated that he greets nobody in the hall: [3] he rode straight up to the dais and called for " the governor of this troop."

4. The stranger's weapon is a monstrous axe in the Irish and the English, and its size and keenness are emphasized in both; in the French, the weapon is merely a " very long sword," [4] such as befits a tall knight.

5. In the Irish and the English there is an elaborate and striking passage in which the stranger, before telling what his wish is, celebrates the reputation of the king's court. The passages have already been quoted. [5] There is none of this in *Caradoc*. Immediately after Arthur has returned his greeting, the stranger says, in a single line: " ' Rois,' fait il, ' .i. don vos demanc ' "; the king replies, " You shall have it, whatever it may be "; the knight then issues his challenge.

6. In the Irish, the king is especially exempted by the stranger from the operation of the challenge; in the English, Arthur accepts the challenge himself, but transfers it to Gawain, at Gawain's request. In *Caradoc* there is no suggestion that the king could possibly become personally involved in the affair.

7. In the English and the Irish, the stranger goes out of the hall carrying his head with him. In the *Caradoc*, he

[1] Vv. 304–305.
[2] "Mout gentement" (v. 12651).
[3] V. 223.
[4] V. 12647.
[5] Pp. 15–16, above.
[6] V. 12655.

replaces his head as soon as it is cut off, and wears it on his shoulders when he makes his exit.

Several of these divergences are evidently due to polishing. The manner in which the *Livre de Caradoc* has toned down the rudeness of the original description is highly instructive with reference to current discussions on the Matter of Britaih. The *Livre* is as courtly as possible, in word and deed. The uncanny appearance of the strange visitant has vanished by sublimation, and the huge gisarm gives place to a sword. *Gawain and the Green Knight* stands midway between the Irish and the French in this regard. It does not so much soften the appearance of the stranger. He looks like a " half-etin," but, as we are at once assured, he is really a man and no giant. His language and manners are less conventionally courteous than in the French, and his weapon is still an unnaturally big axe. The French author of *Caradoc* has also done more or less condensing: he omitted the stranger's speech in praise of the court,[1] and he undoubtedly shortened the dialogue and cut out a number of details.

Evidently, then, the Challenge in *Caradoc* is not the source of the Challenge in *Gawain*. On the other side of the account, however, the French *Gawain and the Green Knight* cannot be the source of the Challenge in the *Livre de Caradoc*. For in some respects the English poem (in dependence, we may be sure, on its immediate French original) has lost old features which *Caradoc* has retained. This is due in part to changes in the Challenge story suggested or necessitated by its combination with the Temptation to make up the plot of *Gawain and the Green Knight*. Thus, in the Irish and in

---

[1] The taunt which the stranger utters in the Irish is, however, preserved in the *Livre de Caradoc* as well as in *Gawain and the Green Knight*, and this taunt certainly points to the presence in the immediate source of the *Caradoc* of the passage celebrating the reputation of the court.

Caradoc, the stranger returns to the king's court to exact the return-blow; the hero is not required, as in *Gawain*, to search out the stranger's dwelling and present himself there. This variation was of course occasioned by the necessity of bringing Gawain to Bernlak's castle, where the adventures included in the Temptation had to take place. The shift in the scene of the return-blow brings with it certain minor changes which need not be specified.

In its account of the return-blow the *Caradoc* is much closer than the *Gawain* to *The Champion's Bargain*. In the *Caradoc*, the challenger does not actually strike at the hero three times (as in the *Gawain*): he is twice ready to strike, but is interrupted by the king and the queen; the third time he deals a harmless blow with the flat of the sword (the back of the axe in the Irish). The interruptions by Arthur and Guinevere take the place of the byplay of the block and the short neck,[1] which was far too grotesque for the knightly feelings of the *Caradoc* poet (or for some predecessor of his in the direct line). But, except for this change, the Irish is followed closely enough. In *Gawain and the Green Knight*, we remember, Gawain " shrinks a little with his shoulders" as the axe descends for the first time. The challenger checks the weapon in full career, and upbraids him with cowardice. The second time Gawain stands like a rock, but the challenger similarly checks the axe, and, remarking that now he can properly hit him, since he is no longer in terror, brings the weapon down for the third time, cutting the neck slightly. This slight injury is then explained as due to Gawain's having failed to be absolutely true to his bargain — since he retained the magic lace that he ought to have

---

[1] The author's own text of the *Caradoc* probably had the block (see p. 32), but it certainly omitted the trait of the *short neck*, so much emphasized in the Irish. There is no block in the English romance.

given to Bernlak. This last change in *Gawain* is directly
due, of course, to the combination of the Challenge with the
Temptation. *Caradoc* is much nearer *The Champion's Bargain*. We shall return to this point by-and-by.[1]

The closeness of the *Livre de Caradoc* to *The Champion's
Bargain* in one significant detail not found in *Gawain and the
Green Knight* extends to actual similarity of phraseology.
When the stranger knight returns to Arthur's court to claim
the return-blow, he utters no greeting, but calls at once for
Caradoc:

> " Carados, je ne te voie mie;
> Vien avant, si auras tel feste,
> Met me ci en present ta teste,
> Car ge i mis autant la moie." [2]

" Here I am," replies Caradoc. Compare the Irish tale: —
" As they were there, then, at the close of the day, they saw
the carl approaching them. ' Where is Cuchulinn ? ' said
he. ' Here am I, then,' said Cuchulinn." Here, too, the
variation on the part of the English poem is due to the
amalgamation of the Challenge with the Temptation.
There is no possible place for any such passage in *Gawain
and the Green Knight*.

It is clear, then, that the Challenge in the *Livre de Caradoc*
is not taken from the lost French *Gawain and the Green
Knight*, and equally clear that the French *Gawain* did not
derive the incident from the *Caradoc*. The *Caradoc* version
(C) and the *Gawain* version (G) are mutually independent;
for each, as we have seen, preserves important details of the
Irish story that do not appear in the other.

---

[1] See pp. 40–41, 73–74.

[2] Montpellier MS. In the Mons MS. the passage runs:

> " Caraduel," fait il, " u es tu ? "
> " Vees me ci," fait Caraduel.
> " Dont vien avant," repont iluec.
> " Volentiers " (vv. 12776–79).

Yet the *Caradoc* version and the *Gawain* version resemble each other closely in noteworthy particulars in which both differ from the Irish tale. The two poems proceed side by side (except for the differences already mentioned) to the moment when the decapitated challenger leaves the hall. In both, Arthur will not eat till he has seen or heard of an adventure. While dinner is waiting a stranger enters and rides up to the dais. He is richly dressed *in green*. In Caradoc he wears a garland of flowers,[1] befitting the Pentecost season; in *Gawain* he carries a bob of holly, appropriate for Christmastide. He proposes the " game " in practically identical terms: he is to suffer the first stroke, and to exact the return blow a year hence. [*The Champion's Bargain* is very different. The stranger proposes to decapitate his opponent first and then to submit to having his own head cut off. When this arrangement is objected to, and the opposite procedure is proposed by Munremar, the stranger cavils, but at last consents. The return blow is to take place on the next day, not after a year.] In both *Caradoc* and *Gawain* the challenge is accepted and the challenger beheaded by one hero only, not (as in the Irish) by three. At parting, the challenger reminds his opponent of what is to be expected in a twelvemonth. The language in which, near the end of the story, Caradoc upbraids the stranger for slowness in striking is similar to that employed by Gawain on the same occasion:

> Carados li a dit par ire:
> " Porquoi ne ferez-vos, beau sire ?
> De .II. morz me ferez morir
> Qui tant aësmes sans ferir.
> Moult vos en tieng ore a couart." [2]

[1] See p. 32.

[2] Montpellier MS. The Mons MS. reads:

> " Chevalier, moult par es couars,"
> Fait Caraduel; " fai erramment
> Çou que tu dois," (vv 12802-4, III, 131).

Compare the English: " Why, thresh on, thou bold man! Thou threatest too long. I think thy heart grows cowardly at thy own self." A like speech is found in the Irish tale, but it is by no means so close to the English and the French poem as these are to each other: " It is torment that you are putting upon me, said Cuchulinn. Slay me quickly."

Since, as we have just seen, the version of the Challenge in *Gawain and the Green Knight* cannot be derived from that in *Caradoc*, nor the version in *Caradoc* from that in *Gawain and the Green Knight*, the special agreements between the *Caradoc* and the *Gawain* version over against the Irish story prove beyond question that the author of the *Caradoc* and the author of the French *Gawain* drew independently from a common source. This source was undoubtedly in French and in all probability was a brief episodical romance of Gawain, to whom it was natural for any French writer to attach such an adventure when it attracted his attention. This brief romance (which we may call R) is easily reconstructed. It was doubtless confined to the story of the Challenge, which it had derived (mediately or immediately) from an Irish literary version very similar to the extant *Champion's Bargain;* and it must have contained (1) all those features of the Irish which are preserved in either the *Caradoc* version or the *Gawain* version, and (2) all those features in which the *Caradoc* and the *Gawain* agree against the Irish.

THE FRENCH ROMANCE OF THE CHALLENGE (R)

The lost Old French romance of the Challenge (R), the common source of the Challenge in the *Livre de Caradoc* and in the French *Gawain and the Green Knight* may be reconstructed as follows: [1]

[1] I signifies *The Champion's Bargain*; C, the *Livre de Caradoc*; G, *Gawain and the Green Knight*.

King Arthur (CG) is holding high court (ICG) at Carduel (C, Camelot G) in the Pentecost season (C, at New Year G). The feast is ready, but he refuses to begin until some strange news shall come or some strange adventure happen, for such is his custom (CG). Then there rides (CG) in at the hall door a gigantic man (IG, very tall knight C) in green attire (CG) with a garland of flowers on his head (C, a bob of holly in one hand G). He is armed with a huge battle-axe (IG, a very long sword C). Riding up to the dais (CG), he challenges the court to the beheading game (ICG), declaring that he has come hither for that purpose on account of their brilliant reputation, which he celebrates in elaborate terms (IG). He will submit to the first stroke (CG, cf. I). If he survives it, he is to have the right to deal a blow in return (ICG) after a year's interval (CG). The knights are in consternation (ICG). One of them remarks that only a fool would accept such a proposition (C, cf. I). The visitor taunts the court: its reputation is lost forever (ICG). Arthur accepts the challenge, but gives way to Gawain (G; cf. I, in which the king is particularly exempted). The stranger dismounts (CG) and lays his head on a block (IC; he has brought the block with him in I but not in C). Gawain decapitates him with a single stroke (ICG) and the head falls to the floor (IG, the dais C). The stranger picks up his head (ICG) by the hair (CG), and departs without replacing it (IG; he replaces it in C). But before he goes, he rehearses the covenant (CG), promising to come back in a year (C) and warning Gawain not to fail him (CG). The knights are much concerned at their comrade's danger (ICG).

After a year (CG) the court assembles again (ICG). The challenger returns, as he had promised (IC). "Where are you, Gawain?" he cries. "Come forward and endure a

blow, as I did " (IC). " Here I am," replies Gawain (IC),
and extends his neck for the stroke (ICG). Twice the
stranger makes ready to smite but refrains (ICG), and
Gawain grows impatient (ICG). " Strike," he cries, " and
do not keep me in suspense! (ICG). I think you are afraid
to give the blow " (CG). At last the stranger strikes (ICG),
but with the back of the axe (I, flat of the sword C, cuts
Gawain slightly G). " Rise up, Gawain! " he cries (IC).
" I have no wish to strike you (C), for you are the best of
knights (IG, a very valiant knight C).

In one point our reconstruction of version R has been left
rather vague, — namely, in the matter of the two feints
that precede the final harmless stroke. The reason for this
vagueness is that here the *Caradoc* and *Gawain* versions do
not agree, and that neither accords with *The Champion's
Bargain*. In *Caradoc*, there is a block, but the weapon is a
sword. The challenger is about to strike, when Arthur interposes with an offer of ransom. This he rejects, and is
again on the point of striking, when the queen comes in with
her equally fruitless bribe — his choice of *amies*. This being
likewise rejected, he strikes Caradoc a harmless blow with
the flat of the sword. In the Irish, the challenger declines to
strike after Cuchulinn has laid down his head, and calls
upon Cuchulinn to stretch his neck across the block. The
hero makes an effort, but his neck is too short for the huge
block that the challenger has brought, and the challenger
once more refuses to deal the blow. Then Cuchulinn extends his neck stupendously, so that it fits the block, and
receives a harmless blow with the back of the axe.

In *Gawain and the Green Knight*, there is no block. Gawain
" shrinks a little with his shoulders " as the first blow falls,
and the challenger, checking the descent of the axe, reproves
him for cowardice. At the second stroke, Gawain remains

motionless, but this time too the Green Knight checks the axe, remarking that now it is proper for him to strike, since Gawain has recovered his courage. Then comes the third blow, which cuts a slight gash in Gawain's neck, but does no real injury.

Obviously, the episodical romance R, the common source of the Challenge in *Caradoc* and *Gawain*, retained the block, but either the author of R (or some predecessor) changed it from a huge tree-trunk that the challenger brought with him (" a load for twenty yoke of oxen ") to an ordinary log of wood that chanced to be lying in the hall. The change brought with it, of necessity, an abandonment of the challenger's reason for twice refusing to strike — the shortness of the hero's neck. Still, R must have retained the two refusals, in some form (for they occur in both *Caradoc* and *Gawain*), and must have accounted for them in some fashion. But *Gawain and the Green Knight* cannot here be true to R. In R, we remember, the events all take place at court, and its author would never have allowed Gawain to show a trace of fear in the royal presence and with the great Pentecostal assembly gazing at him. Then, too, the slight cut at the third stroke is a punishment for Gawain's venial fault in concealing the lace, — a talisman which only came into the story when the Challenge and the Temptation were combined in a single plot.

Caradoc, on the other hand, may well be pretty close to R. The two interruptions (by the king and the queen) are quite satisfactory and natural substitutes, in a chivalric French romance, for the grotesque incident of the huge block and the short neck. We may confidently accept them, then, as derived by the *Caradoc* from R, its source for the Challenge. The final blow is well preserved in the *Livre*. — with the trifling change from back of axe to flat of sword.

Indeed, we observe throughout that the *Caradoc* version is a tolerably faithful reproduction of R, and that the version in *Gawain* departs from R in important respects. Most of these changes are incidental to the process of welding together the Challenge with the Temptation and were undoubtedly made by the French author. The English poet elaborated details, but there is no likelihood that he modified the plot of his immediate original to any considerable extent.

LA MULE SANZ FRAIN

The importance of the version of the Challenge contained in *La Mule sanz Frain* (or *La Demoisele à la Mure*) by Paien de Maisières, makes necessary a somewhat full summary of that early thirteenth-century poem.

A damsel appears at Arthur's court, riding a mule without a bridle. She calls for a knight who will recover the bridle belonging to her mount. He is to ride the mule, which will convey him to the proper destination, and meanwhile the damsel is to remain at court. Kay essays the task, but returns in disgrace, as usual. Gawain then sets out, and of course succeeds.

The route is unknown to Gawain, who simply allows the mule to go its own way. The mule conveys him through a wood full of lions and other wild animals and a valley peopled by serpents and scorpions and fire-breathing monsters, but the wild beasts recognize and make obeisance to the mule and do the rider no harm and the serpents are likewise inoffensive. Then he passes through a kind of valley of the shadow of death, and enters a beautiful meadow, in which there is a delicious fountain. At last he comes to a deep and rapid river, spanned by a bridge consisting of a single bar of iron. Over this the mule carries him in safety, though the bar bends in a terrifying way. Beyond the river is a castle, well fortified, and surrounded with sharp stakes, on all but one of which is the severed head of a previous adventurer. The castle revolves incessantly. Awaiting his moment, Gawain urges forward the mule, which brings him through the castle gate at a bound, losing almost half its tail in the manœuvre. Within the walls is a town, which appears to be deserted; not a soul is to be seen in the streets. Soon, however, Gawain is greeted by a dwarf, and presently he is confronted by a *vilain*, who emerges from a cellar or underground vault. The *vilain* is bushy-haired; he is black and of frightful appearance, taller than St. Marcel, and carries on his shoulder a great battle-axe (*jusarme*). He conducts Gawain to a house, serves him with food, and makes a bed for him. Before Gawain goes to bed, however, the churl proposes a *jeu parti*: Gawain is to cut off his head with the axe and he is to retaliate next morning [or he is to behead Gawain first and Gawain may serve him in the same fashion next day].[1] Gawain of course prefers to begin the game. The churl then lays his neck on a block (*tronc*) and is decapitated. Instantly he leaps to his feet, picks up his head, and disappears in the cellar. Gawain sleeps sound. Next morning the *vilain* returns, with his head in place and the gisarm on his shoulder. Gawain extends his neck on the block. The churl raises his axe, but he has no wish to harm Gawain, for the knight had kept his covenant and was very loyal.

It now appears that the *vilain* is in the service of the lady to whom the castle belongs. Henceforth he is friendly to Gawain, whose troubles, however, are by no means over. Before he can win the bridle, he must fight with two lions. After this, he enters the castle proper where he encounters a knight, whom he overcomes. The knight then goes off and disappears from the story. Next Gawain kills two serpents which breathe blood and fire.

His perils are now past. The dwarf appears and conducts him into the presence of the lady of the castle, who, after jestingly reproving him for "killing all her wild beasts," entertains him at supper and offers him her possessions and herself. She is the mistress of thirty-eight castles besides that in which the scene is laid, and she informs Gawain that the damsel who visited Arthur's court is her sister. Gawain begs pardon: he wants only the bridle. Receiving this, he leaves the city, where, he says, he has already stayed too long. The streets are now alive with joyous citizens, who have all been in hiding for fear of the lions and serpents. Arrived at Arthur's court, Gawain gives the bridle to the damsel. The king and the queen beg her to stay with them and to take an *ami* from among the knights. She would remain, she replies, if she dared, but it is impossible. Her mule is brought and she mounts, — the king offers to conduct her on her way, but she says she wishes no escort.

> Congié prent, et si s'en depart;
> Si se remist en l'anbleüre.

---

[1] A lacuna in the text of *La Mule* is supplied from Heinrich von dem Türlin (see pp. 51–52).

De la damoisele a la mure,
Qui s'en est tote seule alée,
Est ci l'aventure finée.

Let us now examine the Challenge in the version afforded by *La Mule sanz Frain*. Though much condensed, this version exhibits remarkable agreements with *The Champion's Bargain* in points in which the *Livre de Caradoc* and *Gawain and the Green Knight* are at variance with the Irish tale.

1. The person who challenges Gawain is not a knight but a churl (*vilain*). His manners are better than those of the Irish giant, but in appearance he is very similar to that redoubtable axeman. He is frightful to look upon: " trestot herupé " (v. 506). Any one who had seen him would have said " qu'il eüst son oirre perdu " (v. 508).

Mout sanble estre li vilains fel;
Plus estoit granz que saint Marcel (vv. 509–510).

He resembles a Moor of Mauretania or one of these peasants of Champagne all tanned by the sun. [It is not said in the Irish that the Champion is black, but he wears " an old hide next his skin, and a black tawny cloak about him." His hair is bushy, like that of the *vilain*.]

2. There is a *jeu parti* offered. Gawain may cut off the *vilain's* head first, and take his turn on the morrow, or the *vilain* will cut off Gawain's head first, and give Gawain a chance next day.[1] In the Irish the giant's proposition is to cut off a man's head to-day and allow the man to return the stroke on the morrow; but Munremar suggests a reversal of the process, to which the challenger consents.

3. A highly significant agreement with *The Champion's Bargain* appears in the following lines:

[1] See p. 51, below.

Fors de laienz s'en ist Gauvains,
Lou col li estent sor lo tronc,
Et li vilains li dist adonc:
" Lesse col venir a plenté."
" Je n'en ai plus," fet-il, " par Dé,
Mes fier i, se ferir i viax " (vv. 620–625).

This is so condensed as to be barely intelligible, but comparison with *The Champion's Bargain* makes everything clear. In the Irish tale the block is so big that Cuchulinn's neck is too short for it. The giant insists that Cuchulinn shall adjust his neck to the block; otherwise, he declares, it is impossible to hit him squarely. Thereupon the hero, by the exertion of his superhuman strength, stretches his neck so that it fits the block perfectly.

These three points in which *La Mule* preserves features of the Irish original that are lost in both the *Caradoc* and the *Gawain*, prove that *La Mule* does not owe its knowledge of the Challenge to either of these poems. It might be contended that *La Mule* drew from the same lost episodical romance (R), reconstructed above, from which the *Caradoc* and the *Gawain* got the Challenge. On that hypothesis, the episodic French romance of the Challenge (R) must have taken over from its Irish source the *jeu parti*, the enormous block, and the grotesque incident of the hero's stretching his neck to the utmost; while the Caradoc poet and the author of the French *Gawain and the Green Knight*, acting independently of each other in adapting R to their purposes, must have dropped the block (*Gawain*) or its huge size (*Caradoc*) — and as a logical result, the neck-stretching — and must also have abandoned the *jeu parti*, all by mere coincidence of taste or judgment.

Such a coincidence in omission is by no means improbable *per se*, but there is an alternative hypothesis which avoids it. The author of *La Mule sanz Frain* may have known the

episodical romance in a version (which we will call O) somewhat earlier and ruder than R. In that case, we must suppose that O retained the incidents in question from its Irish
original; that *La Mule* got the Challenge story from O, and
kept these same incidents; that the author of R, in revising
and rewriting O, abandoned them; and that they are lacking
in the *Livre de Caradoc* and in *Gawain and the Green Knight*
because they had already been dropped in R, the common
source from which these two poems derived the story of the
Challenge. This hypothesis seems to me more probable
than the former; and it accords with the conclusion at
which we have already arrived[1] that R had dropped the
neck-stretching — an Irish incident that *La Mule* retains.
The hypothesis is farther confirmed beyond a reasonable
doubt by the fact that *La Mule* agrees with the Irish in
describing the challenger as a gigantic, ugly, shaggy-haired
churl, black or dressed in black, whereas in R (as represented by both *Caradoc* and *Gawain*) he is a knight magnificently attired in green. R cannot have been the source
from which Paien took the description, and, since there is no
likelihood that he went back to the Irish without an intermediary, the existence of O is raised to a practical certainty.

It is extremely probable, though not a part of the argument, that O was written in England in the Anglo-Norman
dialect, and that R was a *rifacimento* of O in some form of
Continental French. O and R, at all events, told the same
story (the Challenge) in substantially identical terms, and
their scope was limited to that single adventure.

In both versions of the episodical French romance of the
Challenge (O and R), the scene of the adventure must have
been Arthur's court, and both poems must have contained
the stranger's tribute to the fame of the royal *comitatus* and

[1] P. 41.

his taunting speech when he finds the warriors reluctant. Manifestly, then, if we accept R or O as the source from which *La Mule* derived the Challenge, we are required to account for the transference of the whole adventure, in *La Mule*, from the king's court to the castle where the gigantic challenger lives. An explanation is the more imperative because, in this particular feature, *La Mule* accords, not with *The Champion's Bargain* (and therefore with O and R), but with the other extant Irish version, in which the beheading game is proposed to Cuchulinn and his rivals by the water-giant Uath when they visit him, and the scene of the decapitation is the shore of Uath's loch.

At first sight, this agreement between *La Mule* and the Uath version seems to complicate our pedigree pretty seriously. One might argue, for instance, that the Challenge incident in *La Mule* goes back, somehow, to an Irish version considerably different from the Irish source of R-O; or even that it had two Irish sources, or two French sources (O and another) independently derived from the Irish. Either of these hypotheses would involve the assumption that the Irish tale of the Challenge made its way into French independently at two different times and in two different forms.

Fortunately, however, the required explanation is very easy to give, and involves no such complexities. *La Mule sanz Frain*, in its main plot, belongs to a well-defined and familiar type, abundantly represented in both *märchen* and romance: — A hero is summoned to an enchanted city, where he performs divers tasks or exploits which accomplish a reversal of the spells; thereupon the " waste city " becomes inhabited again, and the lady, released from her magical bondage, offers her hand and her possessions to the triumphant adventurer.[1] Now the story of the Challenge

[1] For a study of this type of *märchen*, see pp. 231 ff.

(or the Beheading Game) has no essential or original connection with a tale of this type. It existed, as we know,
quite independently of *La Mule sanz Frain* and long before
that poem was written. The author of *La Mule* derived the
Challenge story from O (a short episodical romance), and
utilized it to enrich his narrative, changing or omitting such
details as were inconsistent with his main plot. In this process, of course, he transferred the beheading game from
Arthur's court (its scene in O) to the Waste City, for only in
that way could he use it as one of the unspelling exploits
which his hero had to perform after passing through the
enchanted portal.

The agreement of *La Mule*, then, with the Uath version
(as against *The Champion's Bargain* and O-R) in locating
the Challenge at the home of the challenger, is not due to
any historical or genetic relation between *La Mule* and the
Uath form of the adventure. It is a chance coincidence, —
the purely fortuitous result of an alteration made by Paien
for his own immediate purpose. This change in the scene of
the Challenge of course necessitated the omission of the
stranger's laudatory address to the court, and of his jibes at
the backwardness of the knights, both of which, as we have
seen, were preserved in O and R.

Clearly, therefore, there is nothing in the evidence before
us that prevents our deriving the Challenge in *La Mule*
from O immediately, and, through O, from an Irish version
practically identical with *The Champion's Bargain*.

Further, we can even find a plausible reason for Paien's
insertion of the Challenge (or Beheading Game) into the
plot of his *Mule sanz Frain*. In the immediate source of this
poem, the enchanted city and its mistress were doubtless
held in subjection by a magician with whom the adventurer
had to fight, as in the similar tale of *Li Biaus Desconeus*, in

La Joie de la Cort in Chrétien's *Erec*, and elsewhere.[1] Now it is quite possible that this enchanter had the faculty of causing his severed head to return to his shoulders, — a well-known accomplishment in popular fiction.[2] Such a feature in the source of Paien's main plot would inevitably remind him of the story of the *jeu parti* of decapitation (the Challenge), which he certainly knew, as we have seen, in a form closely resembling *The Champion's Bargain,* and it would then be an obvious idea for him to insert it into his own composition. This conjecture derives some support from a story in the *Kathā-sarit-sāgara* which — though, of course, not the source of *La Mule sanz Frain* — is an excellent specimen of the type to which that source certainly belonged.

The hero Indivarasena received a sword in a dream from a goddess. " By the power of this sword," said she, " thou shalt conquer enemies hard to overcome, and whatever thou shalt think of thou shalt obtain." He awoke with the sword in his hand. After travelling (in company with his brother) a long distance, he found a splendid city, with golden houses. At the portal stood a terrible rakshasa, who told him it was the abode of the King of the Rakshasas. Indivarasena tried to enter, and decapitated the porter, who attempted resistance, with one blow of his magic sword.

Indivarasena entered the royal palace, where the King of the Rakshasas sat on his throne, with a lovely woman at his left hand and a beautiful maiden at his right. Indivarasena went up and challenged him to fight. The king drew his sword. " And in the course of the fight Indivarasena frequently cut off the Rakshasa's head, but it grew again. Seeing that magic power of his, and having had a sign made to him by the virgin at the rakshasa's side, who had fallen in love with him at first sight, the prince, after cutting off the head of the rakshasa, being quick of hand, again cut it in two with a stroke of his sword. Then the rakshasa's magic was baffled by contrary magic, and his

---

[1] On the *Joie de la Cort* and *Li Biaus Desconeus* see Paris, *Romania*, XX, 152 ff.; Schofield, *Studies on the Libeaus Desconus,* [*Harvard*] *Studies and Notes*, IV, 124 ff.; Philipot, *Romania*, XXV, 258 ff.

[2] Pp. 147 ff.

head did not grow again, and the rakshasa died of the wound." Both
the lovely woman and the princess were delighted. The hero asked:
" Why did this rakshasa live in such a city as this, guarded by one
warder only, and who are you two, and why do you rejoice at his
being slain ? " The virgin replied that the rakshasa had devoured
the rightful king of the city " by the help of his magic power." He
also ate up the attendants, but spared the queen and made her his
wife. The virgin was the younger sister of the rakshasa, and the hero
took her to wife.[1]

We may reasonably conjecture that, in the source of *La
Mule sanz Frain*, the enchanter who held the lady of the
castle captive and her city fast bound in chains of magic,
had the ability to play fast and loose with his own head.
Paien (or some predecessor in the direct line), being familiar,
as we know he was, with the Challenge to decapitation in an
episodic romance of Gawain (R or O), was reminded of it by
this accomplishment of his enchanter's, and so inserted it
into his plot. This made it necessary for him to change the
malignant magician of his source into a friendly person who
was glad to spare Gawain, and hence a knight had to be
invented to do the real fighting with the hero. No pains
were taken, however, to dispose of this knight, who simply
disappears from the story when he is overcome. No enchanter is left in the romance, which thus becomes irra-
tional and incomplete. The lady, who must have been glad
to have the lions and serpents slain and the city disenchanted, absurdly pretends to have ground of offence against
Gawain for " killing her beasts," and yet rewards him by an
offer of her hand and her extensive possessions. She is
nowhere said to have been under spells, though the condition of her city and the whole course of the plot show that
such must have been the case.[2]

---

[1] Book vii, chap. 42, Tawney's translation, I, 384–387.
[2] See pp. 242 ff. for an analysis of the plot.

Whether this conjecture as to the moving cause for the insertion of the Challenge is accepted or not, makes no difference in our main argument. That the Challenge is an insertion is, at all events, certain, for it is nothing but *The Champion's Bargain*,—condensed, but surprisingly well preserved, — and it existed long before *La Mule* was written.

Practically the entire *Mule sanz Frain* is embodied by Heinrich von dem Türlîn in his rambling and interminable romance *Diu Crône*,[1] thought to date from 1210 or thereabout. Heinrich makes a few changes in the episode of the Challenge; but these are not significant for our investigation, since they are the fruits of his own fancy. One of them, however, has a certain interest as showing how a contemporary understood the situation in the Waste City. Paien, we remember, says nothing of the spells to which the city and its inhabitants are subjected, and no enchanter figures in his narrative. We have entertained the conjecture that there was such a personage in the source of his main plot, and that the insertion of the Challenge disordered the story in this particular. Heinrich, it is agreeable to note, also felt that a magician was somehow missing in *La Mule*, and supplied one in his usual freehanded way. He did this by explaining that the *vilain* was really Gansguoter, " ein pfaffe wol gelêrt," who had taken a monstrous shape for the nonce. It was he that contrived the whirling castle, and he had done many other strange things. Heinrich's device is so lamely handled that his explanation raises more questions than it settles in the reader's mind; but, such as it is, it has a modicum of interpretative value.[2]

At a critical point in the story — the place where the *vilain* proposes the *jeu parti* — Heinrich had a better text of

---

[1] Vv. 12601 ff., ed. Scholl, pp. 155 ff.
[2] For further details see pp. 251 ff.

La Mule than ours. I have accordingly used his verses to
fill a lacuna in the French, which is unintelligible as it
stands in the unique manuscript. Let us speak well, then,
of the bridge that carries us safely over!

PERLESVAUS

In the conglomerate prose romance known as *Perlesvaus*
there occurs an excessively curious version of the Challenge.
It is told in two distinct chapters, separated by many pages
of miscellaneous adventure that have nothing to do with our
subject. The hero is not Gawain, but Lancelot, and the
story has been treated with great freedom.

Lancelot wanders into a waste country, where there is neither beast
nor bird, so poor is the land and so dry, and enters a great city. It is
empty of people; the walls and gates are crumbling with age, and all
the houses are ruinous. He draws rein before the finest and most
ancient of the palaces, and hears knights and ladies making their
moan: — " Alas! " they are saying to some knight, " alas that you
go to your death in such a way, and that there is no help for it! "
Soon Lancelot sees a young and handsome knight, richly dressed
and wearing a golden chaplet, come down through the hall with a
great axe in his hand. He dismounts at this knight's invitation and
asks his pleasure. " Sir," is the response, " you must cut off my head
with this axe or I will cut off yours."[1] Lancelot objects, but the other
says that it must be so, since Lancelot has entered the city. Lancelot
replies that he would be a fool who did not make the better choice in
such a *jeu parti*.[2] " You must promise to return in a year," continues
the knight, " and must then submit your head to the same danger to
which I expose mine." [3] Lancelot accepts the condition, since he had
rather die in a year than be killed on the spot. The young knight

[1] " Il couvient que vos me copez la teste de ceste hache, car de ceste
arme est ma mort jugiée, ou je vos an trancherai la vostre" (Potvin, I, 103).

[2] " Il seroit mout fox qui de cest jeu-parti ne panroit le meillor a son eus "
(I, 103).

[3] " Vos me creanteroiz, ainçois que je muire, que vos revendroiz dedanz
ceste cité antre ci et un an, et que vos metroiz vostre chief en autretel abandon
sanz chalonge conme li miens iert mis " (I, 103).

requires a solemn oath, rehearsing the terms of the compact.[1] Then he kneels down and stretches out his neck as much as he can (*estant le col au plus qu'il peut*). Lancelot begs the knight to change his mind and to have mercy on himself. " Then let me cut off your head," the knight answers, " for I can spare myself on no other terms." " In God's name! " says Lancelot, " I cannot consent to that." So Lancelot cuts off his head with a blow that makes it fly seven feet from the trunk. Then he throws down the axe, returns to his horse, mounts, and looks back; but he can see nothing of the body or the head; he hears a great cry of knights and ladies, afar in the city, who say that the dead man shall be avenged in a year or sooner. So Lancelot rides out of the town.[2]

The fulfilment of Lancelot's pledge and the conclusion of the incident come much later in the romance. Meanwhile he is occupied in knight-errantry, as usual.[3]

After a year of divers adventures Lancelot rides, at midday, into the Waste City, which he finds in the same desolate condition as before. Scarcely has he entered when he hears a great cry of ladies, complaining that one knight more has failed them by not returning according to covenant; "He has proved recreant," they say, " as all before him have done." Lancelot sees nothing of the ladies and wonders where they can be. He rides to the palace and dismounts. Immediately there comes down a tall and handsome knight carrying the same axe, which he is whetting with a hone (*d'une cueuz*). Lancelot asks him what he would do with the axe. The stranger recites the covenant, saying that it was his brother that Lancelot had killed a year ago, and that now Lancelot must kneel and stretch forth his neck as the knight had done and allow him to cut off his head. " If you refuse," he adds, " I will do it none the less. But I know that you will not refuse; else you would not have come hither." Then Lancelot kneels and stretches out his neck; but dodges the axe when it descends. " Sir," said the knight, " so did not my brother whom you killed; but he held his head and his neck still, and so ought you to do." Two damsels now appear at the windows of the palace. They recognize Lancelot, and one of them cries to the knight with the axe,

---

[1] " Ainssint me jurez-vos . . . que vos, d'ui cest jor an un an, a l'eure que vos m'aurez ocis, ou einçois, revenroiz ici meismes et metrez vostre chief an autretel peril conme li miens iert ja mis, sans desfans " (I, 104).

[2] Potvin, I, 102–104.

[3] The coming danger is once mentioned in the interval (I, 196–197).

who is about to strike once more: " If you desire my love, throw down the axe, and release this knight from his obligation." Instantly the stranger casts down his weapon and falls at Lancelot's feet, " et li crie merci conme au plus loial chevalier del monde." Lancelot, in reply, asks mercy of *him*, whereupon the knight declares that he will not slay him. Then the damsels descend from the palace and approach Lancelot. They inform him that they are the two sisters whom he saw in so poor estate in the Waste Castle where he lodged with their brother, and to whom he and Gawain and another knight had given the possessions of the robbers whom the three had killed. [This refers to an earlier adventure (Potvin, I, 91 ff.), which throws no light on the story that we are discussing. The author of *Perlesvaus* has worked the Challenge arbitrarily into his rambling plot.] They add that this city and the Waste Castle would never have been peopled, and that they should never have regained their lands, had it not been for Lancelot or some other equally loyal knight. At least twenty have lodged there as he did, and have each cut off the head of a brother or cousin of theirs, with the promise to return and submit to a blow in recompense, but Lancelot is the first to keep his word. Unless he had been true, they should have lost this city, without recovering the cities belonging thereto. Then the knight and the damsels conduct Lancelot into the palace, and looking out, Lancelot sees that the city is repeopled [and apparently reëdified as well.][1]

This version of the Challenge is oddly sophisticated. The mysterious knight is no longer able to pick up his head and replace it. He is actually killed by Lancelot, and it is his brother who deals the return-blow. An attempt to make credible a tale of supernatural marvels has betrayed the author into the grossest absurdity. He sacrifices knight after knight, brothers and cousins, in reckless fashion. The male kindred was nearly used up when Lancelot arrived in the nick of time. Only the two brothers were left, and one of them Lancelot had to kill. Clearly, then, it was the last chance. If Lancelot had not returned, the country would have been forever lost to its rightful owners, for it required

[1] Potvin, I, 231–234. For the Challenge see also the Welsh translation of *Perlesvaus*, chaps. 139, 189, 199–201 (Robert Williams, *Selections from the Hengwrt MSS.*, Vol. I, *Y Seint Greal*, pp. 258–260, 327, 347–350 (English translation, pp. 605–606, 649–650, 663–665).

two knights (besides Lancelot) to fulfil the conditions of the enchantment — one to be beheaded, the other to survive! Again, though the result of Lancelot's return is to disenchant the city and its inhabitants, as well as the surrounding country, the author says nothing of spells. His description enables us to recognize the causes that have reduced the Waste City to its dismal plight, — for we have waste cities enough in romances that express themselves clearly, — but he carefully refrains from any mention of enchantment. We simply learn that, if Lancelot h'ad been untrue, the territory would have passed out of the hands of the family for good: why, we are not informed. As our author tells the tale, it is impossible to see how Lancelot's fulfilment of his promise could restore the country to its true possessors. But he prefers to leave this question unanswered rather than to include statements about enchantment if he can avoid them. The repeopling of the Waste City is apparently accomplished, not by surcease of spells, but merely by the return of the inhabitants from the surrounding forest where they had been hiding [from what ?]. There is no mention of the land's becoming fertile again, nor is it said that the ruinous dwellings returned to their pristine splendor. Contrast the way in which the waste city behaves in *Li Biaus Desconeus*, whose author is not afraid of supernatural incidents. In *Li Biaus* we are expressly told that the city was reduced to ruins by enchantment and that the inhabitants fled in terror.[1] After the spells are dissolved, the denizens, lay and clerical, return, and holy water is sprinkled in the streets.[2]

> Que vos feroie longes noveles ?
> Tot fu la cité restorée
> Et de boene gent bien puplée.[3]

---

[1] Ed. Hippeau, vv. 3293 f., pp. 117–118.
[2] Vv. 3428 ff., 3452 ff.　　　[3] Vv. 3627 ff.

The attempt to take the supernatural out of the Challenge in the *Perlesvaus* has made the episode altogether inconsequent.

Yet in spite of sophistication and absurd false-reasonableness, the *Perlesvaus* keeps a number of old features in its version of the Challenge, and shows remarkable similarities now to one of the versions already studied, now to another.

The *Perlesvaus* version offers a striking resemblance to *La Mule sanz Frain* in certain old features not preserved in either *Caradoc* or *Gawain*, and inferentially absent from their common source — the episodical romance that we have called R.

1. *Perlesvaus* and *La Mule* are the only versions, except *The Champion's Bargain* and *Humbaut*,[1] that keep the *jeu parti*. This is well preserved in *La Mule*,[2] less satisfactorily (but with sufficient clearness) in *Perlesvaus*; and both texts apply the term *jeu parti* to the proposition made by the challenger.

2. There is also a similarity between Lancelot's and Gawain's reply. In *Perlesvaus* the knight tells Lancelot to cut off his head, adding that if Lancelot refuses, *he* will cut off *his*. This appears to be a mere threat of death, but observe what follows: Lancelot answers that in such a *jeu parti* only a fool could hesitate, and Gawain says the same thing in *La Mule*.

" Sire," fet Lanceloz, " il seroit mout fox qui de cest jeu-parti ne panroit le meillor a son eus " (*Perlesvaus*, I, 103).

> " Mout sauré," fait Gauvains, " petit,
> Se je ne sai louquel je preigne.
> Je prendré conment qu'il aviegne:
> Anuit la toie trencherai,
> Et lou matin te renderai
> La moie, se viax que la rende."
>
> (*La Mule sanz Frain*, vv. 580–585).

---

[1] See p. 62.

[2] When the text has been corrected by the aid of Heinrich (see pp. 51–52).

3. The emphasis that *Perlesvaus* puts on the knight's " extending his neck as far as he can " looks like a weakened form of the incident in *La Mule*, which, as we have seen, is itself a reminiscence of Cuchulinn's extraordinary feat in the Irish story.

These correspondences might be explained by supposing that *Perlesvaus* drew from *La Mule*; but since that would involve a dubious question of dates, it is safer to account for them by referring *Perlesvaus* to O (the common source of *La Mule* and R). *Perlesvaus* also agrees with O in making the respite a year, a period which in *La Mule* is changed by the conditions of the main plot to a single night.

So far, so good, but there is trouble ahead; for when we compare *Perlesvaus* with *Gawain and the Green Knight*, we are struck by three points of resemblance in details not occurring elsewhere.

1. In *Perlesvaus* the second knight, when he descends from the hall to give Lancelot the return blow, is whetting his axe with a hone. So the Green Knight at the Green Chapel, before he strikes at Gawain, whets his axe noisily. The detail is made much of in the English romance.

> Thene herde he of that hyƷe hil, in a harde roche,
> BiƷonde the broke, in a bonke, a wonder breme noyse.
> Quat! hit clatered in the clyff as hit cleue schulde,
> As one vpon a gryndelston hade grounden a sythe.
> What! hit wharred and whette as water at a mulne.
> What! hit rusched and ronge rawthe to here (vv. 2199 ff.).

2. Lancelot dodges the first blow in *Perlesvaus*. So Gawain " shrinks a little with his shoulders " as the Green Knight's axe descends the first time.

3. The knight in the *Perlesvaus* reproves Lancelot for dodging, exactly as the Green Knight upbraids Gawain. The terms of the reproof are almost identical: —

Sire chevaliers, ainsint ne fist mie mes freres que vos oceistes, ainz tint le chief et le col tout quoi, et ausint vos couvient-il feire (I, 233).

> Nawther fyked I, ne flaȝe, freke, quen thu myntest,
> Ne kest no kauelacoun, in kyngeȝ hous Arthor;
> My hede flaȝ to my fote, and ȝet flaȝ I neuer (vv. 2274 ff.).

The first of these three matters — the whetting of the axe — gives us no trouble. It is a mere trifle, which may have been independently added to the story more than once. Only when the Challenge and the Temptation were combined in a single plot, came the opportunity to develop this detail in verses so weirdly impressive as to tempt one to exaggerate its value as testimony. And, after all, the derivation of *Perlesvaus* from O accounts for the whetting in both *Perlesvaus* and *Gawain*: it stood in O, we may suppose, but was dropped by *La Mule*; R took it from O, and the *Gawain* from R (though the *Caradoc* dropped it). So much for the first special agreement between *Perlesvaus* and *Gawain and the Green Knight*.

The dodging and the reproof, however, are not so easily disposed of. These form a single incident, the reproof being the logical result of the dodging, and its very terms growing out of the situation. There was no such incident in O or R. It was invented by the French author of *Gawain and the Green Knight* to replace the interruptions of Arthur and Guinevere, which were no longer available to account for the two feints or abortive blows, now that the scene had been shifted from the court to the challenger's abode. The incident, then, was either borrowed by the author of the *Perlesvaus* from the French *Gawain*, or was his invention likewise. The former alternative would give the *Perlesvaus* version of the Challenge two distinct sources, — the French *Gawain* as well as O. This is possible enough in nature, but not very likely. It is far more probable that the author of

Perlesvaus used his own intellect in what, after all, is no astonishing flight of fancy. He had the same impetus thereto that the *Gawain* poet had, — necessity. His source (O) furnished him with nothing that he found available to account for the two feints or abortive strokes. The block and the neck-stretching, which O had retained from the Irish, he abandoned as grotesque and unchivalrous. Something had to be substituted, and what is more instinctive than to duck one's head as a blows descends ? In his story, as in *Gawain and the Green Knight*, the scene had been shifted to the challenger's abode, and there were no spectators visible. Thus even a model knight might be allowed to betray a little human weakness. So long as the scene of the whole story remained (as in the Irish and in O) the king's court, no dodging could be allowed. The rebuke, as we have seen, follows with inevitable logic form the dodging, and its terms are a matter of course. Nothing yet hinders us, then, from continuing to derive the Challenge story in *Perlesvaus* from O, the common source of *La Mule* and R, as we have already done on the strength of its agreement with *La Mule* and the Irish.

Still, if the reader prefers to derive the episode in *Perlesvaus* from *La Mule*, there is no conclusive evidence to prevent, unless indeed the *Perlesvaus* is the older work — a point that cannot be determined. One argument in favor of that theory would be the coincidence of the two texts in applying the adventure to the disenchantment of a waste city; but waste cities are common things in romance.[1] Again, we have nothing that proves beyond question that *Perlesvaus* drew from O rather than from R. For all three of the points above mentioned (p. 56) in which *Perlesvaus* agrees with *La Mule* and the Irish against *Caradoc* and

[1] P. 238.

Gawain may be explained away. These are, it will be re-
membered, (1) the *jeu parti*, (2) the remark of the challenged party that anybody would be a fool who did not
take the easier horn of such a dilemma, and (3) the neck-
stretching. As to the neck-stretching, that is but ambigu-
ously preserved in *Perlesvaus*. The *jeu parti* may have
stood in R and undergone simplification in *Caradoc* and
Gawain independently. The remark of the challenged
party may also have stood in R. In that case it was modified in *Caradoc* and transferred to the knights in general or
to Kay: —

> Ains dient li boin chevalier
> Que fols seroit qui çou feroit
> Qu'en aventure se metroit
> Se n'i aroit pris ne honor (vv. 12674 ff., Mons.MS.).

> Fet Kex: " Ge nel feroie mie
> Por tot l'avoir de Normandie!
> Sire chevaliers, fox seroit
> Qui en tel maniere feroit (Montpellier MS.).

There is also one slight point of possible agreement be-
tween *Perlesvaus* and R (as represented by *Caradoc* and
Gawain) in something that was certainly not found in O.
In Potvin's text of *Caradoc* the challenger —

> En son cief ot un capelet
> A un ciercle d'or de bounet (vv. 12645–46).

In the prose *Perceval* as quoted by Madden [1] there is an
additional detail which doubtless belongs to the authentic
text of the poem: the challenger " avoit dessus le bonnet
ung cercle *ou pendoit ung chapeau de fleurs.*" [1] This decora-
tion is preserved not only in *Caradoc* but also in *Gawain*,
where the garland of flowers for Whitsuntide is changed to a

[1] P. 31, above.

bob of holly for Christmas. In R, then, the challenger wore
a garland and perhaps also a golden circlet. Now in *Perlesvaus* he " avoit un grant chapel, an son chief, d'or." [1]
In and for itself such a comparison is trivial enough, but in
so nice a balance it may count for something.

On the whole, therefore, though I am convinced that
Perlesvaus did not borrow the Challenge from *La Mule sanz
Frain*, I cannot make up my mind postively between O and
R. I incline towards O, however, and shall assume that
derivation henceforth, though without dogmatism. Fortunately, the question affects our pedigree at no vital point.
It concerns merely the individual history of the *Perlesvaus*,
and its settlement one way or another would not modify our
reconstruction either of R or of O in any significant fashion.

HUMBAUT

In the Old French romance of *Humbaut* of the first half of
the thirteenth century, the Challenge story appears in a
curiously altered form. I summarize not only the incident
itself, but enough of the setting to show the connection.

Gawain is Arthur's messenger to the King of the Isles. His errand
is to demand the submission and allegiance of that powerful monarch,
who has hitherto acknowledged no overlord. Gawain enjoys the com-
panionship of one Humbaut, a wise knight of the Round Table, who
is well acquainted with the route and its perils, as well as with the
peculiarities of the insular realm, from which, indeed, he has just
returned. After some miscellaneous adventures, including one with
an Imperious Host,[2] the two knights reach the Kingdom of the Isles
in a ship.

On the shore they encounter a knight whose duty it is to joust with
every armed knight who arrives by sea; but Humbaut persuades him
to wait for their return. Gawain and Humbaut ride up to the city
gates, which stand open. Close to the road, but not (it seems) across
it, lies a deep ditch, spanned by a single plank only a foot and a half

---

[1] Potvin, I, 103.　　　　[2] Vv. 490–850 (see pp. 99 ff., below).

in breadth. At midpoint of the plank sits a fierce fellow, who claims his privilege (*droit*): namely, to fight (rough-and-tumble, apparently) with every foreign knight who passes. Gawain dismounts, walks gingerly out on the plank, and kicks the fellow into the fosse. They ride into the city without further opposition. It is quite clear that they are not obliged to cross the plank. The author has utilized the well-known incident of the Perilous Bridge in an eccentric and not very felicitous fashion.

The streets are full of people, and everything looks prosperous and merry. As they ride toward the castle, a vagabond (*pautonniers*) calls after them, and just misses them with a shot from a sling. Arrived at the castle gate, they find a *vilain* sitting at the left of the portal, and an attendant is just handing him an axe. He demands his " rights," and springs to his feet.

> " Hunbaus," fait il, " qui qui me hace,
> De cestui vel avoir mes drois."

" Tall and black, ugly and hideous," he stands looking at the two knights and bars their way. Humbaut asks him to postpone the affair until they return, but he does not seem to hear. Gawain remarks that something must obviously be done before they can proceed: "What *is* this *vilian's* right that he demands ? " Humbaut replies: " He proposes to you a *jeu parti*, which I can explain fully; but it is a savage bargain to accept, for both alternatives are bad. You can cut off his head with this axe first; he offers you his neck freely, on condition that immediately after you hold out yours to him. And he will remain close by, will hold the axe in his hands, and will strike but one blow. [Or, if you prefer, he will behead you first, and then submit to a stroke in return.[1]] This is the *jeu parti*. Take whichever alternative you please." " I shall ask nobody's advice," replies Gawain with some humor, " for in such a choice I am quite capable of deciding for myself. Give me the axe first. I will make no mistake, since I am risking my life." [Some further conversation follows, which is fragmentarily reported in the manuscript. All that is certain is, that Gawain repeats his determination to strike first.] Then the *vilain* gives Gawain the axe and stretches out his neck, feeling quite safe as to the issue. Gawain, amazed at his cheerful demeanor, puts strength to the blow, and makes the *vilain's* head fly more than ten paces away. The *vilain* open his two fists and thinks to go after it; but Gawain, detecting enchantment, catches him by the garments,

---

[1] The unique text is defective here.

and so the *vilain* is thwarted and the enchantment comes to naught, for he falls dead on the spot, and never after was there any *jeu parti*.[1]

Gawain and Humbaut pass into the courtyard. More than ten squires run up to take their horses. Discarding their shields, for greater ease, but retaining their swords, they enter the building, where they find a dwarf, the ugliest creature Gawain had ever seen, sitting by the door. He, like the others, is clamorous for his right. "What does this devil want?" asks Gawain, and Humbaut explains that his privilege is to engage in four word-combats (*quatre fois tencier*) with every strange knight. Gawain avers that, for his part, he never had any skill in railing, but the dwarf begins without further ceremony and exhibits considerable talent. "Verily," replies Gawain, "I will vie with him in such railing as befits him," and he cleaves his head with his sword. Then Gawain and Humbaut enter the presence of the King of the Isles, and Gawain delivers Arthur's message, calling upon him to do homage and pay tribute, and summoning him to Arthur's court before New Year's day. The two knights then make good their escape.[2]

The resemblance between *Humbaut* and *La Mule sanz Frain* in the Challenge is remarkably close until the very end, but the two conclusions are utterly at variance.

The Challenge is a part of the machinery of an enchanted (or otherworld) realm. The thing happens in the enchanted city to Gawain, who has gone thither on a quest under expert guidance. The challenger is a *vilain*, tall, black, and hideous. He offers a *jeu parti*. Gawain protests that he cannot hesitate which alternative to accept. He beheads the *vilain*.

Up to this point, the summary will serve for either *Humbaut* or *La Mule*, so closely do the two agree. But here the author of *Humbaut* abandons the proper conclusion of the Challenge. Instead of submitting to the return-blow, Gawain causes the *vilain's* death by preventing head and body from joining.

[1] The Challenge story occupies vv. 1460–1539 of *Humbaut* (ed. Stürzinger and Breuer, Dresden, 1914, *Gesellschaft für romanische Literatur*, XXXV).

[2] *Humbaut*, vv. 418–1764.

This state of things is easily explained by supposing that the author of *Humbaut* borrowed the Challenge from *La Mule*, but changed the *dénouement* to suit himself. One circumstance, however, must give us pause: the *dénouement* in *Humbaut* is good orthodox folk-lore. In fighting with any foe who has the faculty of recalling his head to his shoulders, alternative methods of procedure are well established: you must either destroy the head before it has time to go back, or keep head and trunk apart until death ensues. Both tricks are abundantly reported in folk-tales, and either is held to be creditable to a hero's skill and wisdom.[1]

Now it is true that *Humbaut* is a skimble-skamble sort of romance, but the first half, which narrates the mission of Gawain to the King of the Isles (vv.1–1775), hangs together well enough, and conforms in the main to an established type of *märchen*: — An adventurer makes his way into the realm of an other-world potentate (or an enchanter), where, coached or assisted by a wise companion (often a helpful animal), he surmounts the magic obstacles, thwarts or destroys his demonic opponents, and kills or subdues the ruler (or, at all events, comes off unscathed). In such a tale, a head-recovering monster is eminently in place among the terrors of the other-world *ménage*, and a prodigy of that kind may well have stood in the main source of this portion of *Humbaut*. If so, he was certainly (as in *Humbaut*) a purely hostile figure, and was certainly thwarted and slain (as in *Humbaut*) by some trick of keeping head and trunk apart. This *dénouement*, then, was not invented by the *Humbaut* poet. He simply retained it from his main source, though he modified the rest of the adventure by substituting a part of the Challenge story in a form closely resembling

[1] See examples, pp. 148 ff.

that in *La Mule*. This was a natural thing for him to do, since he certainly knew the Challenge, and must have been struck with the similarity in appearance and actions between its gigantic axeman and the head-recovering *vilain* in the tale that he was working up. He rejected the *dénouement* of the Challenge for an obvious reason: it did not suit his plot to make the *vilain* friendly to Gawain. The attempts of the *Humbaut* poet to enrich his plot with features from the Challenge result in a violation of good faith on the part of the matchless Gawain, who does not fulfil his compact with the axeman. But the author was not fussy about trifles, and probably thought *nulla fides* a satisfactory principle. Compare the treatment accorded to the railing dwarf.

Where the author of *Humbaut* found the Challenge story cannot certainly be determined. Perhaps in *La Mule*, but quite as likely in O. In either case, he omitted the block, but retained the *jeu parti*.

In the source from which Paien derived the main plot of *La Mule sanz Frain*, there was, we have seen reason to believe, an enchanter whose head returned to his shoulders whenever it was cut off. With this personage Gawain had to fight as a part of the process of relieving the city from spells. In the combat, he cut off the enchanter's head, and baffled the magic either by splitting it before it had time to return to the trunk or by keeping the two apart till the marrow was cold; in either case, the enchanter was effectually killed. This trick was, of course, quite justified, for there was no *jeu parti*, and no promise on Gawain's part to submit to decapitation in his turn.

This incident of the enchanter, we conjectured, reminded Paien of the Challenge story, which he knew in version O, and he accordingly substituted that story at the appropriate place in *La Mule*.

To the numerous examples which folk-tales, from India to North America, afford of this class of supernatural creatures with returning heads, and of heroes who baffle them by a trick,[1] we are now able to add an Arthurian romance, the *Humbaut*. The importance of the testimony afforded by the *Humbaut* does not depend upon any particular view of the relation between this romance and *La Mule*. The thwarting trick is not derived by *Humbaut* from *La Mule*, for it is no part of the latter and cannot have stood in any version of it which the *Humbaut* poet knew. For the trick he was indebted either to the main source from which he derived his story of the Embassy to the King of the Isles, or to his own general knowledge of popular fiction. On either of these alternative suppositions, his document gives evidence not only of the usability, but of the actual use, of this thwarting *motif*, along with the hostile creature with the returning head, in Arthurian romance, and thus increases the probability that Paien found such an incident in the main source from which he drew the plot of *La Mule*. Thus far, and no farther, is the thwarting *motif* in the *Humbaut* of immediate significance for our investigation. But even so, its testimony is not unwelcome.

The Anglo-Norman Romance of the Challenge (O)

We may now venture to reconstruct version O,[2] presumably Anglo-Norman, and to point out in footnotes the relation of that version to its derivates, the Challenge in

[1] See pp. 45–47, 148 ff.

[2] The existence of a common source for the various French versions of the Challenge (or Beheading Game), including that preserved in the English *Gawain and the Green Knight*, was recognized by Gaston Paris (*Histoire Littéraire*, XXX, 72): " un poème français épisodique, qui avait pour sujet principal ce qui dans les autres textes ne forme qu'un incident au milieu d'autres."

La Mule (M), in *Perlesvaus* (P), and in R — the common source from which the *Livre de Caradoc* (C) and the French *Gawain and the Green Knight* (G) derived the Challenge. This reconstruction, with the commentary, will serve as a recapitulation of our results up to this point.

King Arthur [1] is holding high court (IO) [2] at Carduel [3] one Pentecost season,[4] and knights and ladies have assembled in great numbers (IO).[5] The feast is ready, but he refuses to begin until some strange news comes or some adventure happens, for such is his custom (O).[6] Suddenly there enters the hall (IO) [7] a huge giant, ugly and black, with fierce eyes and bushy hair (IO).[8] He advances to the high

[1] Conchobar in I. [2] I signifies Irish (*The Champion's Bargain*).

[3] Emain Macha, the Ulster capital, in I.

[4] Time and place preserved in R, and hence in C and the French G; changed by the English author to New Year (Christmastide) and Camelot.

[5] The ladies come in later in I. The fact that it is a full court was dwelt on in O, and therefore in R (whence it is kept in C and G). In M the scene of the Challenge is transferred to the Enchanted Castle, to which Gawain is conducted by a guiding animal, and in P the scene is similarly shifted, to suit the author's purposes. Hence the opening incidents of O are dropped in M and P. The full court at Carduel at Pentecost time, which does occur at the beginning of M, is not there taken from O, but belongs to the main plot of *La Mule* (see p. 42), being a conventional starting point for many Arthurian romances.

[6] Preserved from O by R, and hence by C and G. This is a convention (see p. 5).

[7] Lost in M and P, of course, on account of the changed setting. Kept from O by R (CG).

[8] Fully described in I and thence, though perhaps less grotesquely, in O. From O the gigantic and frightful traits are well preserved in M, but P abandons them, making the challenger a tall and handsome knight. R kept at least a part of the description from O, but dropped the ugliness and attired the challenger magnificently in green (green attire kept in C from R, but C dropped all grotesqueness and made him simply a very tall knight; G also kept the green attire, but doubtless retained more of the description from R than C did; the English author made the knight and horse both green, with green hair and mane: see p. 142). In R he wore a garland of flowers (kept in C; in G he carries a bob of holly).

dais (O) [1] on horseback (O ?),[2] but greets nobody in the hall (IO).[3] He carries a huge axe in one hand and an enormous block in the other (IO).[4] There is consternation among the knights (IO).[5] The stranger announces that he has come to challenge some knight to a game which he has never found anybody willing to play with him; here, however, he hopes to meet with better success, because of the renown of the court, which he celebrates in a more or less formal speech (IO).[6] Arthur assures him that he is not likely to fail of his request, and asks for particulars (IO).[7] The stranger then offers a *jeu parti*: " I will cut off the head of one of your champions to-day, and he may cut off mine a year hence; or he may cut off my head now, and I shall have the right to cut off his in a year " (IO).[8] The champions all

[1] Kept in R (CG).

[2] Perhaps he walked in O (cf. M and P), and the riding came in with R (so in CG), which had greatly modified the clumsy grotesqueness of the visitant (well preserved in M from O). However, a horse would be out of place in M and P, even if O had said that the stranger rode.

[3] Kept from O by R (hence in G; C modified R, making the stranger greet Arthur " very politely ").

[4] Axe retained from O in M and R and from R in G (changed in C to a long sword). Block seems to be stationary in M, but its huge size is implied by the retention of the neck-stretching. Size of block reduced to the ordinary in R, in which it is merely a log that happens to be lying in the hall (the same in C from R; block dropped altogether by G).

[5] Kept from O by R (and from R by G; dropped at his point by C in the process of condensation). Dropped, of course by M and P (change of setting).

[6] Very formal and elaborate in I; less so, no doubt, in O, but still identical with I in substance. Kept from O by R and hence found in G (though dropped by the condensing author of C). No place for it in M or P.

[7] So, practically, in I, though in much greater detail than was preserved in O. Kept from O by R (and hence in G and, in condensed form, in C). No place for it in M or P.

[8] I has the *jeu parti* in effect; in O the stranger's proposal was probably called a *jeu parti* and stated in alternatives. *Jeu parti* retained from O (both in name and terms) by M and (with the name, but some modification of detail) by P. R abandoned the *jeu parti*, and made the stranger offer his

hesitate (IO).[1] Somebody remarks that he would be a fool
who did not take the more favorable alternative in such a
choice (O).[2] The stranger taunts the court, declaring that
its renown is lost because of cowardice; it by no means
deserves the reputation it enjoys (IO).[3] Arthur, in shame
and wrath, springs forward and grasps the axe, but Gawain
begs the adventure and the king resigns it (O).[4]

The challenger lays his neck on the block and Gawain
beheads him with a single blow (IO).[5] The challenger picks
up his head (IO) [6] and departs, carrying it with him, as well

own head on condition of returning the blow a year hence if he survived
(so, therefore, in C and G). The interval is one night (not a year) in I,
but it was probably increased to a year by O (so in P from O). M agrees
with I in exacting the return-blow overnight, but this is due to the setting
of the Challenge in M, not to survival from O. At all events, the interval
was a year in R.

[1] Kept from O by R (hence in CG). Lancelot shows reluctance in P
(where, however, there is so much sophistication that the evidence is worth-
less). In M Gawain of course has no chance to hang back.

[2] I contains some conversation with the challenger that suggested this
remark (see p. 12, above). O probably gave it to Gawain. From O the
remark is kept (as made by the person who accepts the challenge) in M and
P. R omitted the *jeu parti*, but kept the remark in part, whence it came
into C (though lost in G).

[3] Kept from O in R (hence in C and G).

[4] Probably in O (for there are traits in I that may have suggested it),
but preserved in G alone, and therefore perhaps first in R (lost in C). The
traits in I that may have suggested the incident in O are Munremar's
springing forward and grasping the axe (which is of no great consequence)
and the formal exemption of King Conchobar by the challenger (which
seems significant). At all events, Gawain was certainly the hero who
accepted the Challenge in O, and hence in M (P transfers it to Lancelot)
and R (whence G kept the hero, though C substituted Caradoc).

[5] Kept from O (with block) in M (a trace, perhaps, in P, where the
challenger " stretches out his neck as much as he can," though the block is
lost). Block kept in R (see p. 70, note 6, below).
(CG), and holds out his neck (CG).

[6] Kept from O by M (but not by P, in which the challenger is really
killed) and by R (CG). R added the detail of picking up the head by the
hair (CG).

as the block and axe (IO).[1] Before he leaves the hall, the
challenger's head speaks, promising that he will come back
at the year's end and warning Gawain to be ready for
him (O ?).[2]

Gawain spends the year in knight-errantry (O).[3] When
the day comes round, a great court assembles to see Gawain
fulfil his compact (O, cf. I).[4] All are sorrowful for Gawain
(IO).[5] The giant enters, as before, with axe and block
(IO),[6] his head standing safe and sound on his shoulders
(IO).[7] " Where are you, Gawain ? " he cries out (IO).[8]
" Come forward and offer me your head as I offered mine to
you! " (O).[9] "Here am I!" replies Gawain (IO).[10]   The

[1] Kept from O by M, substantially (though the block seems to have been
stationary in M), but modified in P (where, however, the body and the
head disappear mysteriously). For block in R see p. 68, note 4. In R, as
in IO, the challenger certainly left the hall without replacing his head on
his shoulders'(so G; in C he puts it back before he goes).

[2] Perhaps first in R (hence in G, and with a slight change, in C). Not in
M (and of course not in P).

[3] Kept from O by P (with change of hero; dropped of course in M).
Kept also from O by R (hence in C, omitted in G).

[4] Kept from O in R (hence in C, and, with the necessary change, in G).

[5] Kept from O in R (hence in CG).

[6] Axe kept from O in M and R, and from R in G (changed to a long sword
in C). Block seems to be stationary in M, but its huge size is implied in the
retention of neck-stretching. Size reduced in R, in which it is a log that
chances to be in the hall (the same in C from R; block dropped altogether
in G).

[7] Kept from O in M and P (though in P it is the challenger's brother),
also in R (CG).

[8] Kept from O by R (hence in C). Lost in M (from O) but retained (in a
manner) by P (in the lamentation of the ladies for the supposed faithlessness
of Lancelot).

[9] Kept from O by M (in effect) and P (with changes). Kept fully by R
(hence in CG).

[10] Kept from O by M (with change) but dropped in P. Kept from O by
R (hence in C, but modified by change of setting in G, in which Gawain
announces his presence without being called for).

challenger commends him for keeping his word (IO).[1] Then
Gawain lays his neck on the block, (IO),[2] but it is too wide
for him, and the challenger, after preparing to strike (or
making a feint or half-stroke), bids him stretch his neck
that he may hit him properly (IO).[3] Gawain tries to obey,
and another refusal or feint or half-stroke follows; but the
challenger still bids him stretch his neck to fit the block
(IO).[4] " This is the best I can do," replies Gawain (O),[5]
making another effort (IO).[6] He upbraids the challenger
for tormenting him (IO),[7] calls him coward (O),[8] and urges
him to strike without more delay (IO).[9] Thus there are two
feints or half-strokes or refusals before the challenger
actually hits Gawain (IO).[10] The third time the challenger
raises the axe, but brings it down on Gawain's neck in a

[1] Kept from O (with changes) in P, but dropped by M. Also kept by R
(hence in G, but lost by condensation in C).

[2] Kept from O in M (dropped in P, in which he kneels and holds out his
head); kept from O by R (hence in C, dropped in G).

[3] Condensed from O in M; dropped in R (hence lacking in (CG). In R
the failure to strike was due to Arthur's interrupting. In P (from O) there
may be a trace of the neck-stretching.

[4] Condensed from O in M; dropped in P; also dropped in R (hence
lacking in CG). In R the failure to strike the second time was due to interruption by the queen (kept in C; changed in G).

[5] Kept from O in M; lost elsewhere. This speech is not in I, but I contains a vivid account (which might well suggest it) of the superhuman efforts
of Cuchulinn.

[6] Condensed from O in M (dropped in P, in which there is only one blow,
which Lancelot dodges; the knight is about to strike a second time, but
throws down the axe at the request of his *amie*). Dropped in R (hence
wanting in CG).

[7] Kept from O by R (though lost by condensation in M). Kept from R
by G and C.

[8] Kept from O by R (CG); or perhaps first in R.

[9] Kept from O by M (not by P) and R (CG).

[10] Feints or half-strokes lost in M by condensation (but traces left); one
wasted stroke in P (Lancelot dodges). Two interruptions (by king and
queen) and one harmless blow in R (kept in C; changed in G).

harmless blow, back uppermost (IO).[1] The challenger then bids Gawain rise (IO),[2] and hails him as the best of knights for his valor and loyalty (IO).[3]

The matter of the feints or half-strokes is not quite easy to make out. In *The Champion's Bargain*, the challenger twice declines to smite on the ground that Cuchulinn's neck does not fit the huge block, and then, when the hero has stretched himself superhumanly, strikes one harmless blow with the back of the axe. So the incident probably stood in O, with the huge block and the neck-stretching (though not so grotesquely described). M drew from O, but condensed the narrative, so that we cannot make out two feints (or refusals to strike), but only one, indicated, after Gawain has laid his neck on the block, by the *vilain's* saying " Lesse col venir a plenté " (v. 623). Gawain replies: " This is all the neck I have," and urges the *vilain* to strike if he is going to strike. Then the *vilain* raises his axe, but does not touch him with it, because of the knight's loyalty. After all, M is surprisingly close to I, merely reducing two preliminary refusals and requests to stretch the neck to one (by a telescoping process), and changing the final blow in a slight detail (the *vilain* refrains from touching Gawain with the axe, instead of hitting him with the back of it). We may feel tolerably safe, then, as to our conjectural reconstruction of O. P (which drew from O) handled its material with great freedom throughout. The author found the block and the

[1] So, at all events, in I. Probably retained in O (but not kept in plain terms in M, and much changed in P). R, too, doubtless kept the incident in this shape (hence the flat of the sword in C; in G, Gawain is slightly cut by the third blow, but that is a special change due to a new motif).

[2] Kept from O (though dropped in MP) by R (whence it is retained by C; in G, Gawain springs up and away after the third stroke, declaring that he has fulfilled the covenant).

[3] Kept from O (in effect) in MP and (fully) in R (whence it appears in G and, in part, in C).

neck-stretching too rude for his taste; he discarded the block altogether, retaining, however, a trace of the stretching in the sentence, " si se met a jenoillons et estant le col " (I, 233); compare the place where the challenger submits to the blow, " atant s'ajenouille li chevaliers et estant le col au plus qu'il peut " (I, 104). Having abandoned the short neck as a reason for declining, the author of P nevertheless wished to keep one feint (or declined stroke), and he accordingly accounted for it, very naturally, by making Lancelot dodge, so that the axe missed him. Then, of course, the axeman protested, contrasting Lancelot's conduct with that of the knight whom he had beheaded, and calling upon him to hold his head still. The final stroke is then prepared for, but as the axeman is in act to strike, he is adjured to desist by his *amie*, and throws down the weapon. The author of P, then, departs from O considerably, but in a perfectly intelligible way, and from motives easy to grasp. His changes are due merely to his own preference, and in no way invalidate our reconstruction of O on the basis of I and M.

When we come to R, we naturally expect the retention (from O) of two declined or unexecuted strokes preceding a harmless blow with the back of the axe. R discarded the huge size of the block, and it therefore could not explain these by shortness of neck. C gives us some information as to how R actually accounted for them — by having Arthur interrupt and try to bribe the challenger the first time, and Guinevere repeat the interruption when the challenger is about to strike the second time (she offers him his choice of *amies*). This clever substitution for the neck-stretching doubtless stood in R. It can be made out with sufficient clearness in our present text of the *Livre de Caradoc*. After the first interruption, Caradoc upbraids the challenger and exhorts him to strike in language similar to I, and furnishing additional support to our reconstruction of O. When the author of the French *Gawain* combined the Temptation with the Challenge and shifted the scene of the return-blow by this combination to the challenger's own abode, he had to give up the explanation of R for the two harmless or declined blows, since Arthur and Guinevere were not present. He therefore made Gawain " shrink a little with his shoulders " the first time, and represented the second blow (or feint) as a necessary result of this shrinking. Since Gawain holds still the second time, the Green Knight is ready to proceed, and strikes a real blow the third time, cutting his neck slightly. This last slight injury and the two feints are then explained by Bernlak on moral grounds (with reference to Gawain's fidelity to his agreement to exchange winnings) in a way that was impossible in I, O, or R, — that could not come into the tale, indeed, until the Temptation was combined with the Challenge. There is a coincidence between G and P — the dodging or shrinking and the reproof that follows, but these are mere coincidences, and not to be explained as retentions from a common source. The exhortation to the axeman to strike quickly and not torment his victim (which stood in I, and was kept by O, and from O by R) was quite available, and the author of *Gawain and the Green Knight* kept it (as did C).

RECAPITULATION

We may now sum up the results of our study of the Challenge.

Of the two versions of the Challenge contained in the Irish *Fled Bricrend*, one (the Uath version) had no effect on French literature, and is of interest only for the earlier history of the tale. The other (*The Champion's Bargain*), a highly developed literary version, passed into French and was worked up in an episodical romance of Gawain (O), probably composed in England in the twelfth century in the Anglo-Norman dialect. O is lost, but we may feel sure that its plot was confined to the story of the Challenge, and that it followed the Irish with reasonable fidelity, retaining (for example) the grotesque features of the block and the neck-stretching. From O the Challenge was taken independently (1) into the plot of another Gawain romance, *La Mule sanz Frain*, in a condensed form, (2) with many alterations into the prose *Perlesvaus*, in which the adventure was transferred from Gawain to Lancelot, and (3) apparently into the *Humbaut*, in which it appears in a singular shape. About 1200 or a little earlier, O was revised or rewritten by some Frenchman, probably in a dialect of Continental French. This reworking (which we call R) was more courtly and polished than O, but did not depart from it in any essential feature, remaining an episodical romance of Gawain with its plot confined to the Challenge. Its chief single difference from O consisted in the abandonment of the byplay with the block and the neck-stretching, for which the author substituted courtly interruptions by the king and queen. From R the Challenge was inserted, with slight modifications but with a change of hero, into the story of Caradoc, and was thus a part of the *Livre de Caradoc* when that romance was put into the first continuation of Chrétien's *Perceval li Gallois*. Another French poet combined the Challenge as told by R with an entirely different tale of Gawain (the Temptation), and thus constructed a highly ingenious plot in honor of that hero. His work is preserved to us in an English version, our *Gawain and the Green Knight*. This, however, is in no sense a translation, but rather a highly original retelling of the combined story, in a new style and with many new details of description and the like. In mere plot, however, it is improbable that the English poet departed much from his immediate source, for most of the variations from R that we find in *Gawain and the Green Knight* are such as would inevitably result from the combination of the Challenge with the Temptation.

La Mule sanz Frain, Perlesvaus, and the *Livre de Caradoc* all come very early in the thirteenth century. It is safe, therefore, to refer the French poem O (doubtless Anglo-Norman) to the twelfth century and the French R to about 1200. As for the French *Gawain and the Green Knight*, its earlier limit is the date of R, its later limit the date of the English version. We may reasonably refer it, therefore, to about 1250.

III.   THE TEMPTATION

As the Temptation appears in the English poem, it is a trial of Gawain's fidelity to his host and of his loyalty to the chivalric ideal of " truth." Primarily, however, the Temptation is a story of quite a different character — not ethical at all, but connected with a long chain of folk-lore. For we may unhesitatingly recognize its central incident as one of those tests or proofs to which supernatural beings are wont to subject mortals who venture into their other-world domain. Such tests are of many kinds, are inspired by all sorts of motives, and serve the most various purposes in story-telling. Their object may be to destroy the hero who has intruded into the supernatural realm or to eject him from it. On the other hand, they may be merely terms to be met — conditions precedent to the hero's entering upon the life of the Other World and enjoying the love of the *fée* or goddess. Sometimes they are used to deter or exclude the unworthy and ensure the selection of the matchless hero. Not infrequently they result from an enchanter's spell, and their fulfilment reverses the charm and puts an end to his usurpation, restoring the land to its legitimate ruler and the bespelled inhabitants to their normal shape or condition.[1]

The actual origin of any particular detail among these multifarious bits in the kaleidoscope of folk-lore and romance may be difficult, or even impossible, to discover. An incident springing from a definite custom, or from a specific and consistent article of popular belief, may drift far away from its primary *milieu* in creed or code, and attach itself now to one story now to another, in total oblivion of its first use or its initial purport. Supernatural creatures of the most various kinds exchange rôles with bewildering nonchalance, or are reduced to the status of robbers, knights, ladies, or other classes of ordinary mortals. The Other World may appear as an island, or a castle, or a cave, or an orchard, or a fair meadow, or even as the Christian hell. New varieties of *märchen* — developing from such shifts, misunderstandings, and substitutions, or from contamination — become established as independent traditional types, and not only propagate their kind, but are ever ready to slide into fresh combinations. It was neglect of facts like these that vitiated the results, and has finally discredited the science, of the once-flourishing school of comparative mythologists.

In investigating the Temptation, then, our task is not to ascertain its absolutely primal meaning — to discover, in short, the purpose of the man who first devised, imagined, or practised such a thing in the backward and abysm of time. This primal meaning may or may not emerge from

[1] See pp. 237 ff.

our study. That is a matter of small concern. What we shall attempt is much simpler and much more hopeful of accomplishment. We have to ask ourselves *in what shape, and in what context, and with what meaning, the Temptation story came into the hands of the clever Frenchman who amalgamated it with the Challenge to make the plot of Gawain and the Green Knight.*

For this inquiry we have plenty of documents. Let us note at the outset what to exclude. First, our story of the Temptation has nothing whatever to do with the cycle of tales known, from its most distinguished example, as Potiphar's Wife — not the remotest connection with the *motif* of Phædra and Hippolytus. This proposition is self-evident. In our story, the lady is not in love with the hero whom she wooes, and has no intention to be false to her lord. Consequently she takes no offence at the hero's offishness and brings no false accusation against him. Everything is lacking that makes the story of Potiphar's Wife what it is. Secondly, the Temptation in our sense must be sharply distinguished from that class of stories in which a visiting hero receives the favors of his host's wife (or daughter) or of the lady paramount of a castle. In this class, there is no temptation in any sense: we have simply an epic *bonne fortune*, which the hero accepts without demur. Finally, our Temptation story should not be equated with that type of myth or *märchen* in which a *fée* or goddess entices her chosen hero to her other-world abode, eager for his love, but impelled to test his worthiness before she accepts it. It is, to be sure, quite possible that one or more of these three types or situations may have shared in the genesis of our Temptation story, or may have influenced its history. That is a point which we shall consider in due season. Here we are concerned, not with the possible origins or formative elements of the Temptation or its *dramatis personae*, but with the tale itself, in its habit as it lived, — with the individual story, fully formed, and characterized by its own peculiar plot. For in this shape it had a definite existence before it came into the possession of the Frenchman who combined it with the Challenge.

We observe, then, one differentiating feature which distinguishes our story from all other tales in which a woman wooes a man, — and that is, the part that is played by the husband. In our Temptation, the wife loves her husband alone, and it is in obedience to his instructions that she tempts the hero. Our Temptation, as we have already remarked, is a test-story, and the test is applied by the husband, the lady serving merely as his agent or instrument. And among the great variety of test-stories that crowd the collections of oral literature, the central incident of our Temptation has a definite place: it belongs to the large and varied category of *conditions for disenchantment*.

In a well-known kind of popular tale, a stranger is entertained at the house (or castle) of a magician or supernatural being, where he can escape death or disgrace only on certain rigidly pre-ordained terms, which are the same for all comers. The test may be complicated, it may be simple, but it is always difficult. Many have failed to fulfil it, — in fact, all men have failed until such time as the hero of the story is subjected to the trial. The very fact that the tale is told at all presupposes failure on the part of every one who has hitherto made the attempt.

Sometimes the tests are well-known, and the adventurer treads wittingly in the path of scores of unsuccessful predecessors. Examples of this, from the folk-lore of ancient and modern times and of all peoples, will occur, in abundant measure, to every reader. In a special class of these stories,

however, the interest is heightened by a peculiar and ingenious provision of fate which seems to assure the failure of
the quester: *he does not know in what the tests consist.* There
is a pre-arranged law which he must follow, — either doing
something in particular or refraining from doing something,
— or take the consequences; but the law is so illogical,
so capricious, that the chances are overwhelmingly against
his conforming to it.   Or perhaps the test is simple and
obvious enough, so that, when once it has been fulfilled,
everybody wonders that it had so long defied solution.   In
this case, the difficulty consists in the fact that the adventurer is not only ignorant of what he must do, but that *he
does not know there is any test at all.*   In this category, doubtless, belongs the famous Grail-question, which Gawain
neglected to ask and which Perceval did not think of till he
had once missed his opportunity.

The multiplicity of these tests needs no demonstration to
any one who has the slightest familiarity with " popular "
fiction.   That the romances of the Round Table abound in
similar incidents is likewise well known.   Such instances are
of course usually attired in the conventional chivalric cos-
tume, but their true nature is easily discernible.   One of the
accretions which they have received from chivalric fiction is
noteworthy and pertinent here: it is often fated that only
the best knight in the world shall ever succeed in meeting the
exigency.   This feature could find no place in an isolated
story or *märchen*, the hero of which is anonymous, or has a
commonplace name, or at all events is no more associated in
the teller's mind with other *märchen* heroes than if the tale
which is being told at the moment were the only one in the
world, such is the charmingly improvident, hand-to-mouth
way of the muse of folk-lore.   When, however, many stories
have been associated together and brought into connection

with a brotherhood of knights, and when it is realized that anybody and everybody may essay the test and that there are good knights and bad, the element of mere chance is deliberately eliminated and the proviso that only the best shall have grace for the trial — be it simple or complicated — is imposed as a reasonable restriction.

The fulfilment of the trial brings safety or good fortune to the adventurer. What does it bring to the enchanter or supernatural being who operates it ? This question must be answered in two ways, which, though at first they appear inconsistent, are by no means out of harmony. (1) The fulfilment of the test puts an end to it forever. The riddle of the Sphinx is guessed, and no man need worry over it in the future. What was to be done, was to be done once, and that once is once for all. The enchanter or supernatural being, then, who is probably conceived as malevolent, or at any rate as dangerous and disagreeable, loses all his power and disappears, or perhaps he is killed and troubles men no more. This is no doubt the primitive conception, so far as such an adjective may be used in considerations of this nature. But (2) another conception easily develops: the operators of the test are not properly malevolent beings; they are, on the contrary, themselves the victims of enchantment. They have been bewitched or put under spells, from which they can be released only by the successful fulfilment of the tests, as described above. Under these circumstances the inhabitants of the enchanted castle (if castle it be), though in fact they are friendly to the guest, for in him they recognize a possible deliverer, are constrained by the terms of the spell to conduct themselves as if their main purpose were to entrap him. If he succeeds, however, in coming through in safety, they rejoice with him, for with his success comes their release. In this form of the story the bespelled persons (or some of them) often wear a monstrous or terrible guise, and disenchantment transforms them to their human shape.

In a weakened or disguised form of a test-story of this kind, the fact that the dwelling is enchanted or that the owner of it is a supernatural being (originally malevolent) is lost sight of, and we have simply " the custom of the castle." Whoever lodges here must do so and so, or he is slain or ejected with contumely. In nearly every case of this sort we may recognize the old kind of story, though the writer at the moment may have had no idea that he was dealing with a supernatural being. The host acts as he acts — absurdly or otherwise — because it is his " custom," and a reason for the custom need not be asked any more than in the case of a thousand other customs which people observe without understanding them or even realizing that they need an explanation. Sometimes it is merely the humor of the castellan to do as he does, and, when he is overcome (his test being met), he is persuaded, or forced, to forego his peculiar institution. In this last form the whole situation was probably not distinguished by the romancers themselves from the ordinary case in which a knight keeps a ford against all comers or refuses hospitality to all who do not overcome him in a joust. That all such incidents go back to definite tales of supernatural beings it would be folly to maintain. That many do, and that the *genre* was established under such influence, it would be equally venturesome to deny.

One very special form of test, — which may work either for the safety of the adventurer merely or at the same time for the disenchantment of the person who imposes the task, — takes shape in an odd kind of story, which must have been a great favorite in the middle ages — that in which an imperious host maltreats or kills all guests who demur to his orders, however curious, absurd, or difficult these may be.

In the full extremity of this test, the guest does not know that unquestioning obedience to his savage and whimsical host is the sole means of safety. Hence it is only by happy chance, or by virtue of instinctive courtesy, that the test is gone through with. The host may be under spells, and in that case the story becomes a tale of disenchantment.

In Arthurian romance these various test-stories are sometimes utilized in a peculiar but very natural way. As the household of King Arthur is recruited from hostile knights who have been overcome by his paladins, so it occasionally happens that knights released from an enchantment that has given them a churl's form and made them disagreeable and terrible, join the company of the Round Table.

The application of these remarks to the Temptation in *Gawain and the Green Knight* remains to be made. We may begin by considering the *Ider*.

IDER

The Old French romance of *Ider* (of the first half of the thirteenth century) contains a curious episode, the striking parallelism of which to the Temptation in *Gawain and the Green Knight* needs no emphasis.

Ider is in search of somebody to give him arms and dub him knight. He falls in with a king named Ivenant, who is ready to meet his wishes under one condition: — "Go to my castle and wait for me in the hall. My wife will offer you her love, though in fact she cares for me alone. She is irresistible; but if you can withstand her wiles, my arms and armor shall be yours. If you yield, your head is to be shorn like a fool's (*en crois*)." Ider accepts the bargain, confident that his love for his own *amie*, Guenloie, will protect him from the lady's blandishments. He enters the hall, where he finds many knights and squires playing chess and other games, and, fatigued as he is, he falls asleep on a couch (*faudestué*). The queen, who is in her chamber, learns of his arrival from one of her maidens. She descends to the hall immediately, wakes Ider, and wooes him ardently. Harsh words and threats not sufficing to discourage her, Ider gives her a kick " al ventre," which causes her to fall over backward. " I cannot blame him," remarks the author, " for he could not defend himself [otherwise]." All the company hear the words and see the blow. The incident amuses and delights them vastly, for they are familiar with the custom of the castle.

> Cil qui sont as gieus en la sale
> Voient le cop e les diz oënt;
> Mult s'en rient, mult s'en esjoënt,
> Bien sevent la costume tute.

The queen rises from the floor and returns to her chamber, exacting from Ider a promise to grant her another interview before he receives Ivenant's arms. King Ivenant arrives and learns from one of his retainers that Ider has resisted the queen. The queen would have kissed her husband, but he calls her harlot, and gives her a kick which knocks her down again. Ivenant then offers his arms to Ider, remarking that he has previously made the same bargain with a thousand men [all of whom, it is clear, have found the test beyond their strength]. Ider remembers his promise to talk with the queen again before taking the arms; but he is careful to speak at the chamber door, without entering and without seeing the lady, and loud enough for the king to hear. His words are harsh, even insulting:

> " Je ne vos voi, mes je vos oi,
> Si ne vos quier veer ja mes,
> Mes pur fole dame vos les."

The king laughs when he hears it.[1] He then gives Ider arms and the accolade. The young knight takes his leave and rides away.[2]

Here we have the Temptation, deprived of all supernatural setting and reduced to a mere " custom." The savagery of manners and the brutal frankness of the whole adventure are especially noteworthy as showing how primitive the romance is at this point. In fitting the incident into the history of Ider, certain changes have no doubt been made.

---

[1] It looks as if the author of *Ider* had not quite grasped the significance of the incident he utilizes. Certainly he leaves us surprised at the brutality of Ivenant toward his wife.

[2] *Ider*, ed. Gelzer, Dresden, 1913, vv. 185-512.

Thus the young knight's confidence that his love for Guen-loie will protect him against the queen's advances is a manifest modification. So is Ivenant's disclosure of the nature of the test. But it is easy to detach the incident from all accretions, and to recognize therein the resistance (for whatever reason) to the powerful charms of a lady as the test imposed — without his knowledge — on a wandering adventurer. Nobody has stood the test before, but he is successful. It seems quite clear that his exploits bring about the discontinuance of the " custom." Whether disen-chantment followed, we cannot say, and need not con-jecture. Only the central incident is preserved, but that has fortunately come down to us in a marvellously primitive shape. It is rude enough to form part of the Ulster heroic cycle, and it is all the better evidence on that account.

THE CARL OF CARLISLE

A second instance of the Temptation, in which the super-natural setting is fully preserved, and which illustrates almost everything that has been preliminarily said about these matters, is found in the extraordinary Middle English romance of *The Carl of Carlisle*. This piece is preserved in the Porkington MS. (about 1450–60) and Bishop Percy's Folio MS. (about 1650). Comparison of the Porkington version with that in the Percy Folio shows that we have to do with two texts of a single English poem, not with two independent compositions on a similar theme or two inde-pendent renderings of a common original. The identity of phraseology is sufficient to prove this beyond a shadow of doubt. The Porkington text is in tail-rhyme stanzas, the Percy text is in short couplets. Clearly one is a redaction of the other.

It is usually held that the Percy version is a ballad made out of the Porkington version by rejecting the *rimes couées*. But the assumption is not justified. The Percy version is not a ballad, though Madden prints it in quasi-ballad stanzas. It is simply a romance in short couplets, and is not stanzaic. The Porkington MS. is about two hundred years older than the Percy Folio, but that is no reason for inferring that the version which it contains is later than the Porkington version. Nor is there any antecedent probability that a romance in *rime couée* is older than a romance in short couplets: on the contrary, couplets were in earlier use in such poems. Indeed, the Percy MS. itself preserves the couplet-version of Marie's *Lai de Lanval* which was utilized by Thomas Chestre as the basis of his tail-rhyme romance of *Launfal*. It was long held that Chestre's stanzaic romance (which happens to be preserved in an older MS.) was the original of the *Launfal* in short couplets, but this view is now given up. The presumption, then, is that the Percy version of the *Carl of Carlisle* is the older. At all events, the Percy version preserves an important part of the romance which the text afforded by the Porkington MS. has lost.[1] In most regards, however, the Porkington MS. furnishes a better text.

The *Carl of Carlisle* was probably translated or adapted from some French poem. The extant French version of a similar story, however, which forms a part of the *Chevalier à l'Épée*, is certainly not the source of the English romance. The two go back to a common source, which the English *Carl* represents much more faithfully than the French. The brutalities of the English poem must not lightly be regarded as debasements. They should be compared with the tone of the incident just quoted from *Ider*. A summary of the

[1] See pp. 88–89, 301–302.

English romance will show how significant it is in the present investigation. I follow the Porkington text, except as indicated, usually disregarding trivial variations of the Percy MS.

King Arthur is sojourning at Cardiff [the Percy MS. says simply in Wales] with many knights (including Sir Raynbrown, " the knight of arms green ").[1] One day, in the course of a hunt, Sir Gawain, Sir Kay, and Bishop Baldwin follow a reindeer (red deer, Percy) into a wide forest. A thick mist rises, and they give up all hope of rejoining their companions that night. The Bishop knows of a possible harborage. There is a " Carl in a castle " near-by; he is called the Carl of Carlisle. But no one ever put up with him without being beaten, and, if he got off with his life, he had only God's grace to thank. Kay blusters: he should like to visit the Carl; they will beat *him* if he is not complaisant. Gawain, on the contrary, says he will try what fair speech can accomplish. They ride to the Carl's gate, and Gawain sends in the porter with a courteous request for lodging. The porter warns them that they will be sorry for their coming, as *he* is, — his lord is an evil man.

The three guests are promptly admitted, and enter the hall, while their steeds are taken to the stable. The Carl is described as a giant, dreadful to see, with wide mouth, gray beard, long locks, and a hooked nose. It is a large span between his eyebrows and two (three, Percy) tailor's yards across his shoulders; he is nine yards (fifty cubits, Percy) in height. Four strange " whelps " are lying by the fire, — a wild bull, a felon boar, a lion, and a huge bear. They are about to attack the guests, but creep under the table at a word from their master. The Carl receives his guests politely enough, and offers them wine out of a nine-gallon bowl.

Baldwin, Kay, and Gawain, one after another, go out to look after their horses. Baldwin and Kay, finding that a little foal of the Carl's is feeding by the side of their palfreys, turn him out, with contumely, and are rewarded by the Carl with a tremendous buffet. Gawain sees the foal standing in the rain, puts him in, and covers him with his own green mantle. The Carl thanks him for his courtesy.

Supper is ready by this time, and seats are assigned to the Bishop and Sir Kay. The Carl's wife has a place opposite Kay at the table.

[1] The Percy text does not say that the " Knight of armes green " is present, but mentions him (with no personal name) in connection with his father Sir Ironside.

She is very lovely and gloriously arrayed. " Alas," thinks Kay, " that so fair a lady should be matched with so foul a wight! " The Carl reads his thought and rebukes him. Gawain is still standing in the hall floor, not having been bidden to sit. The Carl tells him to dart a spear at him, and to hit him " even in the face " if he can. The spear is well aimed, but the Carl dodges. He then gives Gawain a place at table opposite his wife, with whom the knight at once falls so deeply in love that he can neither eat nor drink. Observing his abstraction, the Carl tells him to drink his wine — the lady is not for him. The Carl's daughter, a very beautiful girl, richly attired, then appears; she harps and sings. Then the Bishop and Sir Kay are conducted to their chamber. But Gawain is led to the Carl's own chamber, and bidden by the Carl to go to bed to his wife, take her in his arms, and kiss her [thrice, Percy]. Gawain obeys, and when the situation becomes critical, the Carl interferes, but, in reward for the knight's obedience, lodges him with his daughter, to their mutual satisfaction.

Next morning [1] the Carl takes Gawain to a room in which there are the bones of fifteen hundred men (ten cartloads of bones, Porkington) and many a bloody sark. " All these," says the Carl, " I and my whelps have slain." After dinner the Carl conducts Gawain to an armory and, selecting a sword, commands Gawain to smite off his head. Gawain is reluctant, but his host threatens to smite off *his* if he declines, and the deed is done. Instantly the Carl " stands up, a man of the height of Sir Gawain " [no longer a monstrous giant]. He thanks Gawain for delivering him from the witchcraft under which he has suffered so long. Forty years ago he was thus transformed by necromancy, and since that time he and his whelps have slain every guest who did not do his bidding. Gawain is the first who has stood this test, and now the evil custom is abolished. " God reward you, for all my bale is brought to bliss! " The three guests are dismissed with rich presents, Gawain taking with him the Carl's daughter, to whom he has been married by the good bishop. Next day Arthur dines with the transformed Carl, and makes him a knight of the Round Table, establishing him as lord of Carlisle.

For the conclusion of the romance I have based the summary on the Percy MS., which is clearly right in almost every detail. The Porkington text omits the disenchantment by decapitation. The Carl, after inviting his guests

---

[1] For the rest of the story the Percy MS. is followed.

to dinner, tells Gawain that for twenty years [1] no man has lodged with him without being slain. The condition of the exemption was that his guests should do his bidding in every particular, and Gawain is the first who has stood the test. "Now," says the Carl, "my bale is brought to bliss," and he prays God to reward his deliverer. Then he shows Gawain the ghastly remains of the victims, and promises to forsake his wicked customs, and to practise true hospitality hereafter for Gawain's sake. Dinner follows. Then the guests depart with splendid presents, Gawain taking the daughter with him. Next day King Arthur and his knights dine with the Carl and are nobly entertained. Arthur dubs the Carl knight, makes him one of the fellowship of the Round Table, and grants him the country of Carlisle as a fief. Gawain weds the daughter, and there is a fortnight's festival.

Not only is there no beheading in the Porkington text, but the Carl says nothing about being under a spell. However, the situation is clear enough without express words, and his intense feeling of relief at being able to abandon his evil ways is proof enough that he had been acting under magic compulsion. There is also not a word about the Carl's losing his monstrous shape, though that is clearly a *sine qua non* for his being made a knight of the Round Table — an incident that the Porkington text retains.

LE CHEVALIER À L'ÉPÉE

The *Chevalier à l'Épée* has not preserved the story so well as the English romance (whether in the Percy or the Porkington version), and has appended an incident which originally had nothing to do with the matter. A summary of the French poem will make its relation to the *Carl of Carlisle* so clear that further discussion is hardly necessary.

[1] This is doubtless better than " forty " (the Percy reading).

The introduction to the adventure is not so well managed in the French. Gawain loses his way in the woods and comes to a great fire, by which a chevalier is sitting. He spends the night by the fire, and the next morning his new acquaintance invites him to his castle, which he says is not far off. Gawain consents. [There is no such reason for guesting as in the *Carl*.] On their way thither, the stranger excuses himself and rides on ahead, ostensibly to prepare for Gawain's coming. [This incident, otiose in itself, is inserted to make possible the scene which immediately follows.] As Gawain proceeds, he overhears certain shepherds lamenting his probable fate. Questioning them, he learns that many knights have visited this castle but that none have ever come back. The belief of the neighborhood is that the castellan kills every guest who does not fulfil all his commands, be they good or ill. Gawain scorns to decamp in obedience to the word of common fame.

As here told, this incident almost spoils the story. It is proper that Gawain should be warned of danger[1] — and such a warning undoubtedly stood in the common original of the *Carl* and the *Chevalier* — but he should not receive advance information (and in the *Carl* he does not) of the only method of escape. His deliverance should be due (as in the *Carl*) to his innate courtesy. Besides, it is ludicrous that the lord of the castle should ride ahead merely to give the shepherds a chance to block his game.

Arrived at the castle, Gawain is well received. He takes pains to agree with his host in everything. [The poverty of the story at this point shows its variation from the older form. Certain tests in the way of bizarre orders which Gawain is to fulfil or the like (even if these are not the same as the spear-throwing in the *Carl of Carlisle*) ought to be found, especially since we learn later that it has been difficult for previous adventurers to pass the day without opposing their host in something. Throughout the day the host (in this poem) requires naught of Gawain which the knight cannot easily and agreeably do, — nothing, in short, but to stay in the castle, eat dinner, and pay court to a charming young lady.] The host introduces Gawain to his daughter and instructs her to be in all ways agreeable to the knight. He leaves them together while he goes to the kitchen to give orders

---

[1] The warner is a traditional figure (see p. 104).

for dinner. [Apparently the author forgets that the host had ridden ahead with the express intention of seeing that everything was ready.] Gawain and the maiden fall in love. She tells Gawain of her father's evil ways and cautions him not to contradict or oppose him. [This is a feeble repetition of the warning already uttered by the shepherds, and is certainly not wanted.] After dinner the host goes out " to view his woods." He bids Gawain stay indoors and talk with the maiden. Nothing of importance passes between them, but she takes occasion to caution him yet again not to oppose her father in any way!

At night the host returns and has Gawain put to bed in his own bed along with his daughter. Gawain would have had his will, but the maiden warns him that if he attempts this a magic sword which hangs near-by will dart from the sheath and pierce him through the body, as it has done to every knight who has so far been submitted to this test. Nevertheless Gawain — thinking death better than ridicule — twice approaches the damsel, but is both times slightly wounded, and finally remains quiet. Next morning the lord of the castle is disappointed at finding his guest alive. Discovering how the sword has behaved, he asks and learns Gawain's name, and learning it, hails him as the best knight in the world. The bed and the sword, he says, were a test for the discovery of this nonpareil. He now offers Gawain his daughter and his castle. Gawain accepts the former but not the latter. The next night Gawain and his *amie* sleep together undisturbed. Gawain remains some time at the castle, but at last, wishing to return to his kindred, departs, along with his *amie*.

The narrative of Gawain's first night at the castle is certainly not in its original form, for it includes the incident of the Perilous Bed, which is foreign to this story and is not very skilfully introduced into it here.[1] We should particularly note that the host is not acting squarely. Gawain has every reason to make the damsel his *amie*. It is really disobedience not to do so.[2] We observe, too, that throughout the *Chevalier à l'Épée* there is no mention of the host's wife. Comparison with the *Carl*, with *Gawain and the Green Knight*, and with *Ider* justifies us in inferring that the missing lady has been supplanted by her daughter. Note that

[1] See p. 303, below.
[2] See vv. 286–291, 364–365, 501.

the couple are lodged in the host's own chamber and bed.[1] The sword is intrusive. Gawain should refrain out of courtesy, and loyalty to his host — this being the supreme test. It is not beyond the bounds of legitimate guessing to conjecture that in one form of the story Gawain placed his drawn sword between the lady and himself as a proof of continence. Perhaps the adventure in the *Carl* should be changed, too, so that the test may occupy not a few minutes but all night. The author of the *Chevalier à l'Épée* found the test too incredible, for more reasons than one, and so substituted the daughter for the wife and, borrowing the adventure of the *lit périlleux* from Chrétien, made the sword a magic weapon which actually ensured chastity. The author of the *Carl* (or one of his predecessors) for a similar reason reduced the night to a short time and kept the husband standing near, thereby making the test ridiculous, from the point of view of a test, but at the same time equating it with what he supposed to be the limits of human fortitude.

The end of the *Chevalier à l'Épée* is quite a different story, added merely to separate Gawain and his new *amie*, for Gawain can have no enduring *liaison*. He must take the daughter, for he has won her, and the winning of her is a necessary part of the tale; but the *conteur* wishes to get rid of the lady, and he accordingly substitutes for the proper conclusion (doubtless preserved in the English) a well-known cynical parable that contrasts the fidelity of dogs with the faithlessness of women.[2]

The French poet gives no reason for the strange custom of the castle except that the sword was to pick out the best knight in the world.[3] There is no suggestion that the castellan is under spells. It is not even said that he abandoned his evil ways. In this, as in so many other points, *The Carl of*

---

[1] Vv. 456 ff.   [2] See p. 304.   [3] Vv. 746–766.

Carlisle is nearer the original form of the story. Observe, also, that the frightful shape of the lord of the castle has disappeared in the French poem. He is, to all seeming, an ordinary knight. This modification of the savagery of the tale is parallel to the treatment which the Irish story of the Challenge has experienced in the *Livre de Caradoc*,[1] and is highly significant.

THE CANZONI AND THE EXEMPLA

The essentials of the story which we are examining are preserved in two short Italian poems of the fourteenth century, one of them anonymous, the other by Antonio Pucci.[2] The anonymous poem tells the following tale:

Gawain (*il buon messer Chalvano*), in a strange country and in need of food and drink, sees a castle (*rocha*) and asks a peasant (*vilano*) to whom it belongs. " To the most courteous of knights," is the answer, " who receives all comers honorably, but beats them soundly when they depart." Gawain laughs: " Let me once have enough to eat, and he may break my neck if he wishes." The castellan meets Gawain, attends him into the castle, holds his stirrup as if Gawain were his lord, seats him at table, and serves him in person. Gawain makes no objection to all these courtesies. After supper the guest is conducted to a rich bed. Next morning the owner of the castle is as ceremonious as ever. He holds Gawain's stirrup again, escorts him some miles on his journey, and takes his leave. Gawain soon recollects what the peasant had told him. He turns back, calls after his host, and asks him why the customary beating has been dispensed with. " My father left me this castle," the gentleman replies, "and a competent estate. Everybody who comes to my house acts as if he were the master of it. That is, he wishes to give me what is my own. If I say, ' Drink,' he says, ' Drink *you*! ' For this reason I treat him as he deserves. You have not attempted in this fashion to deprive me of the mastership in my own house. Hence I have not beaten you." The poem closes with a plain statement of the moral: We should never contend in courtesy with our entertainer, but should accept his hospitality without ceremonious protest.

---

[1] See pp. 33–34.   [2] See p. 304, below.

Pucci's poem tells the same story in almost identical terms and appends the same moral. The two *canzoni* resemble each other closely in length, in metrical and rhetorical structure, and even in phraseology.[1] Yet neither of them is a *rifacimento* of the other. The anonymous *canzone* cannot be derived from Pucci, for it preserves the Arthurian framework which Pucci has rejected: the adventure happens " in the time of the Round Table " and the hero is Gawain (*Chalvano*); in Pucci, the hero is merely a " gentleman of Rome " who is travelling " alla ventura," and the Round Table is not mentioned. On the other hand, Pucci retains the very important incident of the test by means of the host's wife, which the anonymous *canzone* has discarded: —

> Mangiato ch' ebbon con suo piacimento,
> Vennono al tempo poi a un ricco letto.
> Disse il signor perfetto:
> " O gentiluomo, entrate in questa sponda! "
> Ch' era dall' altra sua sposa gioconda.
> Ed ei v'entrò, nè fe al dir diviso:
> Ma quel signor da poi nel mezzo entrava,
> E così si posava (Carducci, p. 462).

The anonymous poem says merely: —

> Quando fu tenpo, fu mosso a dormire
> In u leto richisimo e adorno (vv. 27–28).

Pucci's preservation of this important episode shows his independence of the anonymous *canzone*. We are forced, therefore, to derive both poems from a lost original. That this was in Italian, and that it did not differ much in form or phrase from the two poems as we now have them, is shown by the close similarity between the metrical structure and the language of the poems themselves.

The lost Italian original of course went back to some French romance of Gawain. But this French romance can-

[1] See Rajna, *Zeitschrift für romanische Philologie*, I, 385.

not have been *Le Chevalier à l'Épée*, as Rajna was inclined to think. For Pucci has the characteristic episode of the test with the wife, which is preserved in *The Carl of Carlisle*, but for which the author of *Le Chevalier à l'Épée* has substituted the daughter and the *lit périlleux*.

The Italian poem which Pucci and the anonymous rhymster worked over must, then, go back to a French poem from which both the *Carl* and the *Chevalier* are somehow derived. Thus the existence of the two Italian poems raises the French origin of *The Carl of Carlisle* from an inevitable probability to a complete certainty, since there can of course be no direct connection between the English romance and the Italian *canzoni*. It also confirms our inference that the *Carl* is in some ways a more faithful reproduction of its original than the *Chevalier*. The common French original of the *Carl* and the *Chevalier* must have had both the temptation with the wife and the winning of the daughter. The *Carl* has preserved both incidents; the *Chevalier* has omitted all mention of the wife, but has kept the winning of the daughter, transferring thereto an essential part of the Temptation and adding the *lit périlleux*. This transference accounts for the contradiction which the French poem shows. It was proper for Gawain to spare his host's wife, but he had every right to make the daughter his *amie* — in fact he had been ordered to do so by his host, whose commands he was bound to obey to the letter. Hence the host ought not to expect him to refrain. There is no such contradiction in the *Carl*.

The two *canzoni*, as we have seen, resemble each other so closely that we can form an exact idea of their immediate Italian original. This must have differed considerably from its French source, for it was no longer a romance of magic and marvels, but a mere anecdote, intended to enforce a familiar lesson in manners — in short a *versified exemplum*. Indeed, Pucci's *canzone* is entitled " Dà un esemplo," etc., and the anonymous *canzone* is headed " Morale."   Clearly, then, the lost Italian poem did not draw its material from the lost French poem directly, but through some inter-mediate version in which the tale had already been stripped of its marvels and clothed in the sober garb of a brief moral anecdote, — in a word, through a Latin *exemplum in prose*.

Such a Latin text is fortunately preserved in Harleian MS. 3938, a collection of fables and miscellaneous *exempla* made in Italy.   The manuscript is of the sixteenth century, but the contents are much older, and a comparison of the *exemplum* with the two *canzoni* shows that it cannot be a reworking of either of them.   Since the text is brief and inedited, I print it entire.

Legitur in nouis Artusii de Britagna, quod dominus Galuanus nepos regis Artusii, audiens de quodam castellano qui ultra modum honorabat milites forenses in domo sua et in recessu faciebat eos uerberari, iuit ad curiam ejus. Et dum ille qui erat custos hoc uidisset, dixit castellano de adventu militis: castellanus iuit ei obuiam cum multis dominabus et domicellis alacriter suscipiens eum; et cum veniret ad plateam, aliae ex dominabus ceperunt frenum equi, aliae lanceam, aliae clipeum, aliae galeam, aliae stapidem tenuerunt, aliae calcaria, aliae destrarium miserunt ad stallum. Et ductus ad prandium, multis ferculis ei datis, alia dedit aquam ad manus, alia bacile tenuit, alia manutergium; et posito eo ad mensam, alia fercula presentabat, alia panem, alia carnes ei incidebat, alia uinum propinabat. Et sero positus honorifice ad dormire, et a domicellabus spoliatus et discalciatus, passus est sibi fieri omnia. Mane autem facto, audita missa et sumpto prandio, accepit lanceam. Et castellanus faciens ei scortam bene duabus miliaribus eum licentiauit. Et cum ille ab eo longius recessit dixit intra se: " Ego sum uilis, quia recedo nec sciam causam quare alii verberati sunt et ego non." Et reuersus ad castellanum, quesiuit quare milites in recessu suo verberarentur, et ipse tantum honore[m] receperat. Cui castellanus respondit: "Cum milites veniunt ad domum meam, ego nitor eis honorem facere, ipsi uero in contrarium faciunt et dicunt: ' Domine, domine, ego nolo, hoc non faciatis!' et nolunt in domo mea mihi dominari.   Et propterea eos uerberari facio in recessu. Vos quidem non sic fecistis; immo quicquid uobis facere uolui passus fuistis.   Vnde nihil dico uobis et aliis nisi in recessu." [1]

This copy does not transmit the precise text that our Italian versifier had before him, for it lacks certain incidents that he must have found in his immediate source, — in particular, Gawain's conversation with the warning peasant, and the test with the wife, though it has a trace of both: of the warning in the fact that Gawain had heard of the *châtelain's* custom; of the test, in the fact that he is waited upon so elaborately by women.   Still, the Harleian copy does undoubtedly represent, with condensation and other changes, the Latin *exemplum* which the Italian versifier used, — and it appeals expressly to a written source in Arthurian romance, that is, as we now understand, to the lost Old French original of the *Carl of Carlisle* and *Le Chevalier à l'Épée*.

A similar *exemplum* is recorded by Étienne de Bourbon, the celebrated Dominican preacher and inquisitor of the thirteenth century, in his work entitled *De Septem Donis Spiritus Sancti*.

DE TIMORE HUMANO

Qui vero preponunt carnem spiritui similes sunt illi qui preponit asinum suum sibi et plus de eo cogitat.   Et similes sunt illi militi, qui elegit hospicium ubi provideretur equo suo et ipse negligeretur.   Unde dicitur quod tres milites condixerunt ad invicem (ad hoc facit exemplum quod audivi a fratre Matheo, primo Fratrum Predicatorum Parisius priore, qui dicebat vel parabolice vel in veritate) quod quererent fortunam (que dicitur *fortune aventure*); et cum ingrederentur civitatem quamdam, dictum est eis quod non erant ibi nisi tria hospicia: in uno equi bene procurabantur et equites fame moriebantur;

---

[1] Harleian MS. 3938, fol. 121 (see Herbert, *Catalogue of Romances*, III, 710). I have regulated stops and capitals.

in alio erat a contrario; in tercio autem equus et eques bene, sed vix erat quin in exitu eques bene verberaretur. Tres ergo tria hospicia acceperunt, et invenerunt ut eis dictum fuerat, tercio excepto, qui non fuerat verberatus. Et cum quereret causam quare non fuerat verberatus, dictum est ei quod domino domus bene obediens in omnibus fuerat.

Civitas est mundus, in quo sunt tres hospites: quidam sunt qui nimiam curam gerunt de equo procurando, neglecto milite (equus corpus, miles anima sunt) . . .; alii sunt qui indiscreto animo corpus atterunt, et spiritus et spiritualium curam tantum gerunt; tercii sunt qui utrique discrete intendunt, et ut per omnia Deo obediant: hii sine flagello, cum recedunt a mundo, pertranseunt.[1]

Étienne, we observe, heard the story from Matthew, prior of the Friars Preachers at Paris, and he was not sure whether Matthew told it as a fact or *parabolice*. Étienne's *exemplum* has been so elaborated in a spiritual sense that it cannot find any certain place in our pedigree. There is, however, nothing to show that it was not ultimately derived from the source of *Le Chevalier à l'Épée*, though it would be rash to undertake to prove any such proposition.

Another version of the same story is current as a folk-tale in Russia.

There was once a countryman named Damian who was very fond of fighting. One day he invited another peasant to his house, and, having bidden his wife prepare a meal, told his guest to be seated. " Don't give yourself any trouble for me, Master Damian," he replied; whereupon Damian gave him a good sound slap in the face, with the remark that " in another's house one ought to obey the head of the family." They took their places at table and Damian applied himself to serving his guest. The latter fell to, but protested again when he saw Damian cut the bread: " Why cut so much bread, Master Damian ? " Damian dealt him another buffet, and repeated the performance at every contradiction, always making the same remark— that in another's house one should do as the owner bids.

Then there arrived in the courtyard another guest, ill-clad, but shrewd and subtle. "Welcome, welcome!" said Damian, saluting him

---

[1] Ed. Lecoy de La Marche, pp. 17–18. For other copies see pp. 271 ff., below.

from the doorstone, and already anticipating the pleasure of a new affray. " Pray excuse me," said the newcomer, " for entering your courtyard without an invitation." " No excuse is necessary. Walk in! " The stranger entered, took his seat at the table, accepted what was offered him, and did whatever he was bidden, so that Damian had no chance to quarrel with him. Then Damian thought of other expedients. He produced the best suit of clothes he had and said to the stranger: " Strip and put on these," thinking that he would certainly decline. But the guest obeyed, and continued to comply with all the commands of his host. Finally Damian told him to mount a good horse he had, and to leave in exchange his own sorry nag. The stranger obeyed, while Damian thought he must be dreaming. Then Damian told him to depart, and off he went; but when he was out of the courtyard, he put spurs to Damian's horse, calling out, as he rode away: " Blame yourself, Damian, for the devil isn't here for nothing! " [1]

Here the moral has been quite distorted, and the *exemplum* becomes a humorous anecdote of " The biter bit," but the story is still recognizable.

HUMBAUT

The Old French romance of *Humbaut*, already drawn upon for the Challenge,[2] contains an episode that involves an *Imperious Host*. It is not brought into connection with the Challenge, but occurs at least a day's journey on the hither side of the harbor where Gawain must embark for the city of his destination.

Gawain and Humbaut are riding to the King of the Isles to claim his allegiance for Arthur. Humbaut informs Gawain that they are to take hospitality that night with a rich and powerful lord, who gets very angry with anybody who violates his commands in the least particular. Hanging is the penalty for the most trifling disobedience. " Take special pains," he warns him, " that our host may find nothing to criticise in your conduct. Before he sits down at table himself, he

---

[1] Afanasief, new ed., III, 521–522, as reported by Wesselofsky, *Rivista di Filologia Romanza*, II, 227.

[2] Pp. 61 ff.

will assign you to a place above all the others, and you and his daughter
will sit together. She is the fairest creature in the world, and she has
confessed to me that she loves you and would gladly be yours, but she
lives in deadly fear of her father's wrath. Be very careful how you
bear yourself in your conversation with her. I have spent more than
thirty-one weeks at her father's, and I know his ways." Gawain
promises to walk circumspectly: their host shall find nothing to
object to.

They arrive at the castle, which is on a harbor, and includes a fine
town, with a flourishing commerce. More than twenty knights come
to meet them. Humbaut presents Gawain by name to the rich lord,
who is playing draughts in his hall. He springs up and greets him as
the best knight in the world. Gawain sits by his side and tells of their
journey. The table is laid. The daughter enters, and her father
makes her sit above all the others, and himself conducts Gawain to a
place by her side. Humbaut sits with the host.

Gawain asks the maiden for her love, and she grants his suit. She
has often heard of his renown, she declares, and has never wished to
love another. They pledge their faith, and are so enamored that they
forget to eat. Gawain loses all memory of Humbaut's warnings, and
the damsel all thought of her father's anger. Humbaut sees that they
are in love and he is much alarmed [but their host pays no attention
and shows no displeasure]. At bedtime, the maiden retires to her
chamber. Her father follows, detains her at the chamber door, and
reproves her for impoliteness in taking such short leave of the wisest
and most courteous of men. He bids her give Gawain one kiss by way
of leave-taking. Gawain promptly kisses the maiden four times.
The lord is furious: " He makes no account of my commands! He
has kissed my daughter three times more than I said! Have his eyes
put out, and let him be thrown into my prison! "

All the knights protest in concert: "You have committed many
outrages, but none that touches *this*! We shall all be hanged or burned
wherever we are taken! Messire Humbaut does not come hither to
pay the eyes of the king's nephew as scot ! " The lord is [unaccount-
ably] placable, and accepts Gawain's apologies, — " but let him be
more careful another time." That night the damsel visits Gawain
secretly. Early next morning he and Humbaut leave the castle
without let or hindrance, and apparently without seeing their host
again. Whether Gawain returned to the castle at some later time
cannot be determined, for the romance is not finished in the unique
manuscript.[1]

[1] Vv. 490–850, ed. Stürzinger and Breuer, pp. 15–26.

The episode of the Imperious Host, as told in *Humbaut*, makes a pretty good story, but has been so freely handled by the author (or by some predecessor) that it helps us in only a general way. On the whole it comes nearest to *Le Chevalier à l'Épée*. As in that poem, there is no wife, and the Temptation is transferred to the daughter. But the damsel becomes Gawain's *amie* secretly, and not (as in the *Carl* and the *Chevalier*) by the father's orders as a reward for Gawain's obedience. Gawain, in fact, is not obedient, and escapes cruel punishment only by the strenuous exertions of the host's retainers.

As in the *Chevalier*, Gawain is forewarned of his host's requirements with complete particularity. His informant, however, is a companion, not a peasant whom he falls in with. Thus, by a coincidence, we have a slight agreement with the *Carl of Carlisle*, in which Bishop Baldwin tells Gawain of the danger of lodging at the castle. But the resemblance is purely fortuitous and does not indicate any special connection with the *Carl*. Baldwin's warning, indeed, is very different from Humbaut's, for it gives Gawain no information how to avoid the danger.[1]

In general, however, the episode in *Humbaut* is helpful, for it serves as one more indication of the popularity of the Temptation in mediæval literature; and besides, it illustrates the readiness with which the story might be modified to suit a fresh context.

THE PRINCIPLE OF MANNERS

It would be possible to regard some *exemplum* enforcing the lesson that a guest should obey his host in everything without ceremony — such a didactic anecdote as Étienne's — as the kernel of the special group of Arthurian romances

---

[1] P. 104.

that we are considering, — the *Carl-Chevalier* group. Such an hypothesis will doubtless seem attractive to those students who are anxious to explain away all the Celtic material as a mere outgrowth of mediæval ethical formulas or social conventions. Ammunition for a campaign of this nature might perhaps be found in the burlesque romance of *Ralph the Collier* (*Rauf Coilyear*), which belongs to the group of poems and tales in which a king who has lost his way is hospitably entertained by a rustic who has no suspicion of the exalted rank of his guest.[1]

Charlemagne has got separated from his retinue in a great storm. He falls in with Ralph the Collier, who offers him a lodging. When they are about to enter the house, the collier " puts the king before him," but Charles steps back to let his host enter first. Ralph resents this extremely. He seizes Charles by the neck and forces him in, upbraiding him with his discourtesy. The guest ought to obey the host, he intimates. The host should be allowed " to be lord of his own " (v. 128). When supper is ready, Charles is bidden to take the collier's wife by the hand and " begin the buird," i.e. sit at the head of the table. Unmindful of his recent lesson, Charles replies that it would be unseemly for him to take his place before his host is seated. Thereupon Ralph hits the king under the ear and makes him stagger half across the room. " Thou shouldst have better manners," he cries. " Do as I bid thee! The house is mine and all that is in it." The king obeys, and has no more trouble. The residue of the story does not concern us.

Ralph's views of politeness, it will be seen, are precisely like those of the hospitable gentleman in the *canzoni*, and he expresses them in very similar language. His method of instruction, too, resembles that of the lord of the castle in Pucci and the anonymous Italian poem. We are obviously in the presence of a mediæval commonplace lesson on this subject. And, in fact, the principle of manners involved is well-known apart from its illustration in tale-telling. Thus

[1] See p. 305.

in *Le Castoiement d'un Père à son Fils* we find the precept
clearly stated:

> Beau père, dit li filz, comment
> Doit on respondre à la gent,
> Quant aucuns m'envie à mengier ? . . .
> Fai ce que il commandera,
> Qui que soit qui t'enviera.
> S'il est preudon de grant affaire,
> Tu ne t'en doiz mie retraire.[1]

Similarly, in *Les Contenances de la Table*, we read:

> Enfant, se tu es en maison
> D'autrui, et le maistre te dit
> Que te sees, sans contredit
> Faire le peulz selon raison.[2]

The proverbial remark, when a guest contends with one in
courtesy, was, in Elizabethan England: " Let me rule you
in my house, and you shall rule me in yours." [3]

To infer, however, that a romance like the *Carl* or the
Chevalier was evolved from a mere principle of manners
would be a real *hysteron proteron*. It would be to ignore the
marvellous, which is the gist of the matter. For the *Carl*
and its group turn unquestionably on disenchantment, and
obedience to the savage host is a condition precedent. No
doubt the proverbial didactics of the middle ages lent a
certain coloring to the romance.[4] Or we may even grant
that the *Carl* shows a combination of two stories: an old

---

[1] Barbazan-Méon, II, 163 (quoted by Wesselofsky, *Rivista di Filologia
Romanza*, II, 226).

[2] Vv. 25–28, Furnivall, *The Babees Book*, Part II, p. 9.

[3] Deloney, *Gentle Craft*, ed. A. F. Lange, p. 70; the play of *Sir Thomas
More*, act iv, scene 1, vv. 106–107 (Tucker Brooke, *The Shakespeare Apoc-
rypha*, p. 404).

[4] In the *Roman van Walewein*, Gawain meets the courtesy of his host, who
bids him sit by the queen at dinner, with the remark: " You are my host;
I will do as you bid; but I am not worthy of the honor " (vv. 2562 ff., ed.
Jonckbloct, p. 87).

disenchantment tale in which the charm could be unlocked only by a quester who should obey his host in all things; and an exemplary anecdote enforcing the lesson of courteous deference.   Such an admission probably goes farther than need be, but if it is made, will in no wise affect the issue. For the true kernel of the romance still remains that of disenchantment by performing strange requirements.

The Version used in the French Gawain and the Green Knight

We have not yet exhausted the information to be derived from the *canzoni*.   In some respects these poems show closer resemblances to the *Chevalier* than to any other poem that remains to us.   Thus in both the Italian and the French the intending guest is warned by a peasant (in Pucci, by a *donzello*) of the disagreeable custom of his host.   In the Italian he is informed that all strangers are beaten soundly when they depart; in the French, he learns that they never get away alive.   This assuredly traditional figure of the warning peasant [1] is lacking in the *Carl*, but has left a trace behind.   When the three companions, — Gawain, Kay, and Bishop Baldwin — are at a loss for a night's lodging, it is Baldwin who informs his friends of the whereabouts of the castle, and the good bishop is acquainted with the Carl's reputation: —

> Was ther nevyr barun so bolde,
> That euer myȝt gaystyn in his holde,
> > But evyll harbrowe he fonde;
> He schall be bette, as I harde say,
> And ȝefe he go wtt lyfe a-way,
> > Hit wer but goddes sonde (vv. 145–150).

[1] Cf., for example, *Kulhwch and Olwen* (Loth, 2d ed., I, 291); *Ivain*, vv. 5105 ff.; *Erec*, vv. 5716 ff.; *Perceval*, vv. 8969 ff.; *Vengeance Raguidel*, vv. 580 ff.; *Eger and Græme* (Laing), vv. 101 ff., 1441 ff.

Pucci's *canzone* confirms our conjecture [1] that the test with the wife lasted all night in the original, as it does (with substitution of daughter for wife) in the *Chevalier*, and also our inference that in the original of the *Chevalier*, Gawain laid his sword between himself and the lady. In all cases in which the hero is brought into such circumstances, — whether as a test or a reward, or merely as a *bonne fortune*, — the duration should not be less than a night and the pair should be left alone, as in *Wolfdietrich* [2] and in a large number of examples cited by Child in his comments on the ballad of *The Broomfield Hill*. [3]

The incident of beheading the host to disenchant him is preserved in the Percy version of the *Carl*, but is omitted in the Porkington text and the *Chevalier* because of its grotesque improbability. It is the final act in the unspelling process and is done, as it should be, at his own request. The excision of the incident in the Porkington version has left its mark: [4] the redactor omits too much, — he does not explain how the monstrous Carl could become a knight of the Round Table with no change of shape. We observe, too, that the Porkington version is not very clear as to the host's being disenchanted at all, and that the *Chevalier* has suppressed all reference to his being under spells. Disenchantment by decapitation is an ancient and widespread theme, [5] and is unquestionably in place in this group of romances. Thus we may now recognize in the common source of the *Chevalier à l'Épée* and *The Carl of Carlisle* a short romance in which the Temptation was used as the supreme trial to which an adventurer is subjected. The outcome being favorable, the enchantment which kept the host in his hideous gigantic shape and forced him to act as a destructive monster was

---

[1] P. 92. [2] Pp. 218–219. [3] P. 263, below.
[4] Paris, *Histoire Littéraire*, XXX, 68. [5] Pp. 200 ff.

dissolved; one final ceremony (decapitation) restored him to his human shape, and he was then made a knight of the Round Table.

By comparing the *Ider* [1] with the poems which we have just been considering, and by bearing in mind the English *Gawain and the Green Knight*, we are enabled to reconstruct, beyond a reasonable doubt, that form of the Temptation which the author of the lost French *Gawain and the Green Knight* combined with the Challenge to make up his plot. It had some such shape as follows: —

Gawain has lost his way and is in need of shelter. He is harbored in a castle or manor, the lord of which is a giant or a huge carl with a fair and seductive wife. This carl is under spells which force him to put to death all guests who do not successfully submit to certain tests. He has already slain great numbers. Gawain knows nothing of the tests, or even of their existence, though he has been warned against his host; but his innate courtesy and loyalty carry him in triumph through even the hardest of them, — temptation by the beautiful lady of the castle, who pretends to be enamored of him but really loves her husband alone. On the accomplishment of this last test, the host bids Gawain cut off his head. He obeys, reluctantly, and the enchantment is dissolved, the knight rising up in his true shape. Gawain then takes his host to court, where he is made a knight of the Round Table.

This reconstructed version is no fancy sketch. It is preserved to all intents and purposes in the group of poems to which the *Carl of Carlisle* belongs. Indeed, except for the active temptation on the lady's part, it might serve as a reconstruction of the French romance to which all the poems of the *Carl* group (the *Carl*, the *Chevalier*, and the *canzoni*) have been shown to go back, and this feature, does survive in the *Ider* in a very primitive form.

[1] See pp. 83 ff.

IV. THE COMBINED PLOT OF GAWAIN AND THE GREEN KNIGHT

WE have now studied in detail the two stories — the Challenge and the Temptation — which the author of the French *Gawain and the Green Knight* fused or amalgamated in constructing his plot. Each of the two, as we have seen, has an origin and a history quite independent of the other. Nowhere do they occur combined to make a single narrative except in *Gawain and the Green Knight*. Our next business is to examine the method and the result of this process of combination.

At the outset we must be on our guard against a mistake too often made by students of this romance. *Gawain and the Green Knight* is by no means a mere version of the Challenge modified by the insertion of an additional adventure. On the contrary, the Temptation with its attendant circumstances occupies, in actual space, rather more than half of the English poem and claims considerably more than half the reader's interest. Indeed, it would be quite as correct to say that the author takes the Challenge as a mere frame in which to put the story of the Temptation. In fact, however, the poem as we have it is a skilful combination of two entirely independent adventures so managed as to produce a harmonious unit. No reader who was ignorant of the parallels which we have been discussing would think of taking it apart, or would suspect that it had been put together out of elements that originally had nothing to do with each other, any more than a reader of King Lear would imagine that the story of Gloster and his two sons had originally nothing to do with the Lear story but was first combined with it by Shakspere himself on the basis of an anecdote in Sidney's *Arcadia*.

The gigantic axeman of the Challenge, who visited Arthur's court and proposed the beheading-game, and the monstrous carl of the Temptation, who subjected his guests to a crucial test with his wife, are now merged in a single character. This was easy and natural, for both the challenger and the host were huge uncanny creatures, of strange appearance and supernatural powers, who survived decapitation. Bernlak de Hautdesert,[1] the personage resulting from this merging of the challenger and the host, is a shape-shifter: he appears first as a half-etin at Arthur's court, afterwards as a comely knight at his own castle, still later as a half-etin once more at the Green Chapel. Here again, the French poet was proceeding by an easy and natural method. The axeman of the Challenge was manifestly a being with strange powers, and shape-shifting might readily be credited to him, while the host in the Temptation actually shifted his shape from giant to knight at the end of the story. From this shape-shifting quality there results, in the combined plot, the inability (on the part of both Gawain and the reader) to suspect that the knight who entertains him is identical with the challenger. Their identity is revealed after the return-blow is given. In the English poem, Bernlak is left in his half-gigantic guise, but we may conjecture that in the French original he resumed his knightly appearance, somehow, at the moment of the *éclaircissement*. We shall return to this question presently.

In the Challenge, Gawain was subjected to a single test for valor and fidelity to his word; in the Temptation (in the form in which that story came into the hands of the French author whose craftsmanship we are considering) he was tested for courtesy when a guest. In the combination,

---

[1] This name may be used for convenience, though it may first have been given to the character by the English poet.

Bernlak tests *all* his knightly qualities, — the Challenge and the Temptation fitting together admirably for this purpose. The scene of the return-blow is transferred to a place (called the Green Chapel in the English) near Bernlak's castle. Thus Gawain's presence is ensured on the spot where the Temptation must be carried out; for the castle is the only place in the vicinity of the Green Chapel where a traveller can find hospitality, or, indeed, at which the exact whereabouts of the Chapel can be ascertained. In the combined plot, then, Gawain can never find the Green Chapel without calling at the castle, — so that, if he keeps his appointment (as he did in the Challenge story), his presence at the place of the Temptation is made absolutely certain. Here the French author is proceeding in accordance with *données* of romance and *märchen* that he certainly knew well. For there are many stories in which a hero, having submitted himself to the terms of a game or adventure, must, as a part of the bargain, present himself within a given term at a place of which he has never heard and whose whereabouts are quite unknown to him. It may well have been his knowledge of such stories that first suggested to our combining Frenchman the union of the Challenge and the Temptation which he carried out so felicitously.[1]

We should here remember that at least two other romancers, working quite independently of the French Gawain poet, and utilizing the Challenge in combinations quite different from his, shifted the scene of the return-blow to the residence of the challenger as a necessary result of their combinations, — the author of *La Mule* and the author of *Perlesvaus*.[2] In their case, however, the opening scene of the Challenge had

[1] See pp. 196–197.
[2] Perhaps we should add the author of *Humbaut* (p. 62); but he may have been indebted to *La Mule*, though I hardly think so.

to be shifted also. Not so in the case of our poem. *There* it could remain at Arthur's court, and remain it did. Incidentally, the shifting of the scene of the return-blow by the combination greatly increases the honor due to Gawain for keeping his word. A less valorous and faithful knight might have returned to Arthur's court with a lie on his lips to claim credit for achieving an adventure which he had avoided. No such avoidance was possible so long as the return-blow was to be dealt by the challenger in full sight of the assembled court at the Pentecostal feast.

In the Temptation, Gawain was warned on his approach to the castle that nobody could put up there and escape with his life, or without bodily harm.[1] This incident, of course, the French combiner dropped, leaving his hero to seek hospitality at Bernlak's castle with no thought of danger. The omission raises the test involved in the Temptation to the very highest conceivable power — for Gawain has no suspicion that anybody is testing him at the castle, or that his conduct there has any bearing on the issue of the beheading-game. In the *Carl*-group he comes through the tests by innate courtesy, and so he does in *Gawain and the Green Knight*, but in the *Carl* he has reason to walk circumspectly, for he is aware that he is on dangerous ground. In the romance, he is quite at his ease, and his good qualities manifest themselves with pure spontaneity.

Yet the figure of the warner, so conspicuous in the Temptation, was not dropped by the author of *Gawain and the Green Knight*. He kept that character in mind and utilized him in a highly felicitous manner. On New Year's morning, we recall, Gawain leaves Bernlak's castle under the conduct of a servant who is to guide him to the Green Chapel some

---

[1] So in *The Carl of Carlisle*, *Le Chevalier à l'Épée*, both of the Italian *canzoni*, and (in effect) in the Latin *exemplum* (pp. 96, 104).

two miles distant. As they draw near, the attendant beseeches Gawain to abandon his purpose. "The place is held to be full perilous. It is inhabited by the worst man upon earth, — he is stiff and stern, and loves to strike. He is bigger than the best four of Arthur's retainers. None passes the Green Chapel that he does not kill. If you go there, you may be sure of death, though you had twenty lives, for you cannot defend yourself against his blows. Therefore, good Sir Gawain, let the man alone! Go away in some other direction, and I will return to the castle; and I swear to you by God and all his saints that I will keep your flight a secret!" Gawain thanks his guide warmly, but declares that to shun the danger would be inexcusable cowardice.[1] In details, no doubt, this incident owes much to the English poet. In substance, however, it unquestionably stood in his immediate French original, which obviously derived it from the Temptation.

How far the details of the Temptation in the English *Gawain* reproduce those in its French source can never be determined, for the English poet was a man of genius and lavished his powers on this part of the romance. In the main outlines, however, the Englishman probably changed nothing. This probability is strengthened by a consideration of that form of the Temptation story which his French predecessor worked with, a form that we can reconstruct pretty well by comparing *Ider* with the *Carl*, the *Chevalier*, and the Italian *canzoni*.

In this version, we may conjecture, Gawain was not actually put to bed with the host's wife, as in the *Carl*, in Pucci, and in the source of the *Chevalier*. The lady, we may be sure, was not merely passive, as in the *Carl*: like Ivenant's wife in *Ider*, she must have done her best to win

---

[1] Vv. 2087 ff.

the love of her guest, though she cared for nobody but her husband. Probably, however, the coarseness and bald simplicity of manners which mark the episode in *Ider* had been a good deal refined before the author of the French *Gawain* received the incident,[1] though much of the delicacy which distinguishes the English romance may be unhesitatingly ascribed to the English poet. In *Ider* the lady approaches her guest in the hall, in the presence of a multitude of knights and squires. In the English, Bernlak's wife visits Gawain when he is alone. In both she finds him asleep. This detail of awaking the hero may have been in the version of the Temptation used by the author of the French *Gawain*.

In the English romance, Bernlak (like Ivenant) is absent from the castle when the test takes place: he has gone out very early in the morning to hunt, leaving Gawain, exhausted by his toilsome journey, to lie abed as late as he wishes. This reminds one of the conduct of the castellan in the *Chevalier à l'Épée*, who leaves Gawain all day in his daughter's charge while he goes out " to view his woods." In the original of the *Carl* and the *Chevalier* we may probably infer a similar situation. In any case, the husband's absence, whether it was in the source used by the Frenchman or was invented by him, accords with popular fiction. In folk-tales in which a hero seeks entertainment at the castle of a giant or ogre or enchanter and is well received by the monster's wife or daughter or captive, whose love he wins,[2] it is often the habit of the proprietor to spend the

---

[1] It is not maintained that the *Ider* was the source, mediate or immediate, from which the author of the French *Gawain* drew, but only that the *Ider* contains the incident in a ruder form than that in which it occurred in the French *Gawain* or its source.

[2] See pp. 232 ff.

day away from home, hunting or seeking for prey.[1] This feature, then, may well have stood in the source from which the French *Gawain* derived the Temptation.

In the Temptation there was also a daughter (so in the *Carl* and the *Chevalier*) who became Gawain's *amie*; but this character was quite useless to the French combiner (indeed, worse than useless), and he dropped it.

In the fully developed *Gawain and the Green Knight*, — the result of a combination of the Challenge with the Temptation on the part of some French romancer and of much elaboration in details by the English poet, — the proofs which Gawain must undergo include that of his host's merry bargain: he must faithfully deliver to the lord of the castle (Bernlak, now identified with the challenger of the old story) all that he wins on each of three successive days of his sojourn there, in return for the avails of Bernlak's hunting. No such compact occurs in any other version of the Temptation, nor have I found it elsewhere. Its object is to test the truth of Gawain further. Bernlak's bargain is to all intents and purposes a wager. He pays his stakes at nightfall, and Gawain should regard the fulfilment of the compact as a debt of honor. The skilful way in which the bargain is interwoven with the whole plot is noteworthy. Gawain gets nothing but the kisses which the lady bestows in her efforts to win his love, and the green lace which she gives him both as a token of affection and as an amulet to protect him from wounds. He delivers up the kisses to his host, but keeps the lace, moved by the danger to which he is so soon to be exposed. The offer of the lace is incidental to the lady's wooing, its acceptance is due to Gawain's concern about the

---

[1] Examples are countless. A good one may be found in the Panjâbi story of *The Princess and the Ogres* (Swynnerton, *Indian Nights' Entertainment*, pp. 360–364).

return-blow. The whole transaction depends upon a state of things which could not exist until the Challenge and the Temptation were combined in a single plot. There was, then, no magic lace in the version of the Temptation that the French author used; neither was there, in all likelihood, an agreement to exchange winnings. At all events, the happy thought of explaining the two harmless blows with the axe as due to Gawain's fidelity on the first two days, and the slight cut at the third stroke as a punishment for withholding the lace — this must be credited to the combiner, for it was impossible until the combination was made. Some of these details, indeed, may be the work of the English poet. In particular, one is inclined to ascribe to him the extraordinary delicacy with which the principle of the climax is employed in the three temptations to which Gawain is exposed.

If the exchange of winnings was, as seems probable, inserted when the Challenge and the Temptation were combined, then perhaps it takes the place of ruder tests that stood in that version of the Temptation which the combiner utilized. In any case, the general principle remained the same: Gawain must do as his host bids, or he is lost. He does not know the importance of such obedience, but (as in the *Carl*) his courtesy prompts him to yield in all things to his entertainer, on the mediæval principle that a man is master in his own house and that his guests owe him unquestioning complaisance. " Truth " does the rest, and the tests at the castle are triumphantly met.

There is a very plain trace of the traditional insistence of the host on obedience remaining in *Gawain and the Green Knight*. When Gawain learns that the Green Chapel is but two miles from Bernlak's castle, he accepts the invitation to lengthen his visit in the following terms: " I will remain, as you wish, and will do in other respects whatever you think best." Bernlak takes instant advantage of the courteous phrase: "You have declared that you will do what I bid. Will you keep this promise?" "Yes, indeed!" replies Gawain. "While I remain in your castle, I will submit to your commands."[1]

What motive, according to the French combiner, had Bernlak in desiring Gawain's presence at his castle and in subjecting him to the Temptation? Doubtless to be released from enchantment, for it seems likely that, in merging the challenger and the host in one personage, the Frenchman would retain for this personage the characteristic trait that he was under a spell and could be released only by some knight who should come successfully through the Temptation as well as the other tests. All the host's strange actions in the Temptation story which the French combiner used, were explained by the enchantment under which he labored and from which he hoped one day to be relieved. This enchantment (taken over by the French poet) was now made to account for all the actions that Bernlak performed with reference to the beheading game as well as with reference to the Temptation. The beheading game was thus no longer a mere test of the hero's valor and honor (as it was in the Irish story, and hence in the episodical French romance R used by our poet): it became not only a means of getting Gawain to the castle, but also a part of the fore-ordained machinery of disenchantment. Bernlak owes his strange shape to hostile magic, and none can set him free but the best of knights who shall (1) respond to his challenge at Arthur's court, (2) keep his word and seek the Green Chapel, (3) call at the castle on the way (as he must do if he is to find the Chapel at all), (4) resist the lady's wiles, and

[1] Vv. 1079–1092.

(5) accept the return-blow. Thus the combination of the
two tales to make the plot of the French *Gawain* resulted in
an elaborate disenchantment story retaining the main features of both its component parts and bringing them all into
line as consistent incidents subservient to one ruling purpose.
Here again we may profitably compare the craftsmanship of
Shakspere in constructing the plot of *King Lear*. Confirma-
tion for this theory may be found in the English poem, for
there Bernlak is certainly under spells when he visits the
court, though the English author has abandoned the
dénouement of his French original, as we shall see in a
moment.

What was the concluding incident in the French *Gawain
and the Green Knight* ? If we are not quite off the track in
the foregoing paragraph, the question answers itself. For
the Temptation story that the French combiner was using
afforded him (with hardly any modification) a perfectly
satisfactory catastrophe: having fulfilled all the tests, the
Host asks Gawain to behead him (as a regular means of destroying the enchanted body). When this is done, he stands
up in his true shape as a comely knight, thanks his deliverer,
explains his extraordinary actions, and accompanies Gawain
to court, where Arthur makes him a knight of the Round
Table.

No doubt the French combiner omitted the final unspelling decapitation, for to retain it would have caused a
ludicrous multiplication of beheadings, and, though common
enough as the last act in an unspelling process,[1] it was by no
means indispensable. Probably, after Gawain had accepted
the (harmless) return-blow, Bernlak, freed from enchantment, at once resumed the shape which he had worn at the
castle, explained the whole matter, and returned to his

[1] Pp. 200 ff.

castle with Gawain.[1] Then, doubtless, after receiving the thanks of the lady as well as of her lord, Gawain returned to court, taking Bernlak and his wife with him. There Bernlak was received into the fellowship of the Round Table, and consented to hold his lands as Arthur's vassal.

For an ending of this sort we have not only the direct evidence of the *Carl*, but the concurrent testimony of almost countless examples — in a word, we have the support of a convention as solidly grounded as any that is prevalent in Arthurian romance. Instances from the *Perceval* alone are Guiromelant,[2] Brun de Branlant,[3] Le Riche Sodoier,[4] Ambioris,[5] Li Biaus Mauvais,[6] and Garsalas.[7] In some of these cases, moreover, there is unquestionably disenchantment — notably in the story of Li Biaus Mauvais and Rosete, his hideous *amie*, who afterwards became one of the loveliest ladies of the court.

We may, then, feel pretty confident, (1) that in the version of the Temptation used by the author of the French *Gawain and the Green Knight*, Gawain's entertainer was (as in the *Carl of Carlisle*) under spells which transformed him to a huge and monstrous shape, and that the final act in his disenchantment was (as in the *Carl*) decapitation by Gawain; (2) that, in this same version, the unspelled giant, returning to the form and stature of a normal man, was (as in the *Carl*) recruited to Arthur's company; (3) that the author of the French *Gawain* preserved both the disen-

---

[1] We are at liberty to imagine, if we wish, that Bernlak vaulted over the brook again after the final blow, returned to the cave, and came forth in his proper guise. But this is a detail of which nobody can be certain; for immediate transformation before the face and eyes of the hero is a common incident in unspelling stories. Besides, it is quite possible that the hollow mound is the English poet's addition to the tale (see p. 142).

[2] Vv. 11560 ff.   [4] Vv. 19411 ff.   [6] Vv. 25607 ff.
[3] Vv. 12437 ff.   [5] Vv. 23554 ff.   [7] Vv. 27699 ff.

chantment and the recruiting, but dropped the unspelling decapitation near the close; and (4) that the English poet omitted both the disenchantment and the recruiting.

The English poem, indeed, shows plain traces of innovation in the *dénouement*. The catastrophe leaves Gawain, in a manner, discomfited. He returns to court full of shame, and Arthur comforts him by decreeing that all the knights of the Round Table shall wear the green lace as part of their insignia. Such touches are delightful, but contrary to custom, for the old French poets are loath to let Gawain come off from any adventure without the highest credit. It would have been far better, from their point of view, to send him home in triumph with the emancipated Bernlak in his train. Other changes introduced by the English author at the close will be mentioned presently.

The substantial accuracy of the inferences just enumerated is further supported by the testimony of an extremely curious Middle English romance, *The Turk and Gawain*, which has never had the attention it merits.

The Turk and Gawain

The Turk and Gawain is preserved in the Percy Folio only. The text is poor, and the poem has suffered sadly from the mutilation of the manuscript. These facts may partly account for the neglect which so interesting a piece has experienced at the hands of scholars, but they create no presumption against the age or significance of the story. Gaston Paris vouchsafes it but six lines (in a footnote), and ascribes it to the sixteenth century.[1] There is, however, absolutely no reason for assigning so recent a date except the lateness of the manuscript, and we should remember

---

[1] *Histoire Littéraire de la France*, XXX, 68.

that the Percy Folio contains, amongst other old material, a copy of the short version of *Launfal*, a poem used by Thomas Chestre in the fourteenth century. We need not hesitate, despite the condition of the extant text, to push the date of *The Turk and Gawain* itself back into this same century, or to the beginning of the fifteenth, at the latest.

Despite the mutilation of the manuscript, the plot is easy to follow, for the context and the general run of the narrative enable us to fill the *lacunae* with confidence. In the following summary, these gaps are indicated by brackets. Each gap is of half a page — about six stanzas, or thirty-six lines.[1]

A dwarf (*Turk*), " not high but broad," enters Arthur's hall while the king is at meat, and asks if there is any one present so hardy as " to give a buffet and take another." Kay replies insultingly and is reproved by Gawain. The Turk calls upon " the better of you two " to come on. [Gawain gives the buffet, apparently on the understanding that he shall go away with the Turk and receive the return blow elsewhere.] The Turk promises that the buffet shall be well paid, and that (to boot) ere Gawain sees the court again, he shall be as well frightened as ever man was. Gawain protests that he is quite ready to go with the Turk; he will never flee, he declares, from any adventure.

They ride [2] northward two days and more, and Gawain has great need of meat and drink. At length the Turk leads Gawain into a hill, which opens to receive them and closes behind them. They experience frightful weather. [After a time they come in sight of a castle. As they approach, the Turk gives Gawain certain instructions, among them an injunction that, if addressed, he is to] make no answer except to him alone.

They enter the castle, which is splendidly furnished. Nobody is to be seen, but a board stands ready spread with " all manner of meats and drinks." Gawain, quite famished, is on the point of falling to, but the Turk restrains him, and brings forth safe food. Gawain eats and drinks, and then begs the Turk to give him the buffet and let him go. [The Turk refuses, and they continue their journey. They come to the seashore], embark in a boat, and sail to a place where they

[1] See pp. 296–297.   [2] In v. 79 it is said that the Turk has no horse.

see a fine castle, in which dwells, says the Turk, a heathen soldan, the King of Man, and with him a hideous rout of ugly giants. He foretells strange adventures, but promises to stand by Gawain.

[They enter the presence of the king himself, who is feasting in the hall.] He makes a speech, expressing hatred for Arthur and all his company, but invites Gawain (by name) to take his seat at the table. Gawain declines: it is not proper for a knight errant to be seated in a king's hall before adventures are seen. The king then calls for his tennis-ball, and with it come a hideous rout of seventeen giants, who think to beat out Gawain's brains. The ball is of brass and there is no man in England able to carry it. [Gawain is challenged to play at tennis, but the Turk, who is called his " boy," undertakes the game and worsts the giants. The second game is casting] the axle-tree, at which the giants are likewise discomfited by the Turk. A great brazier stands in the hall. One of the giants lifts it and sets it down Gawain's boy then seizes it and swings it round his head, so that the coals and red brands [fly about. . . . The king declares that] he has slain many a knight who has come hither, — none ever went back to tell the tale, — and now he will slay Gawain.

The Turk is wearing a garment of invisibility (though apparently he has hitherto been in plain sight). The king leads Gawain to a place where there is a boiling cauldron, tended by a giant with a fork. The Turk seizes the giant and throws him in, holding him down with the fork until he is scalded to death. Then Gawain gives the king his choice between death and Christianity, but he spits upon the knight, and the Turk throws him into the fire. " Now," says the Turk, " all the peril is past." [The Turk then gives Gawain the buffet, but so lightly as not to hurt him.] The Turk brings forth a golden basin and takes a sword, bidding Gawain strike off his head and let his blood run into the basin. Gawain demurs, but the Turk insists and he beheads him. As soon as the blood lights in the basin, the Turk stands up a stalwart knight, sings *Te Deum*, and thanks Gawain warmly. Gawain and the transformed Turk set free many captives, including seventeen ladies. [Gawain and Sir Gromer (for this is the Turk's name) return to Arthur's court with the ladies], who are restored to their husbands. Sir Gromer asks Arthur to make Gawain King of Man, but Gawain declines the office and Arthur grants the island to Gromer.

However much our text of *The Turk and Gawain* may have suffered from slovenly copyists and the accidents of time, the plot is immediately recognizable as belonging to a well-known type of popular tale. A *märchen* (perhaps Celtic) has been, doubtless at an early date, fitted out, like so many others, with the paraphernalia of Arthurian romance. The tone is simple and uncourtly, and the poem shows no trace of the refining hand of Chrétien's school. Some of the rudeness may be due to the English author or redactor, who was certainly addressing a rather humble audience, but, if this is the case, his changes merely restored the romance to a closer likeness to its original form. For we know that even the most carefully polished Arthurian romances retain traces enough of the ruder material out of which they are wrought — material which, whatever its origin, was quite consonant with the state of society depicted in Middle Irish literature. It is not necessary to maintain that the source of *The Turk and Gawain* was a Celtic tale. For our present purposes this is a matter of indifference. Yet such a contention would be hard to oppose, and I have little doubt of its correctness. There is no reason to postulate an intermediary French version.[1]

In the general type of tale to which *The Turk and Gawain* belongs, the hero, visiting a giant or the like, is forced to undertake a number of impossible tasks, but comes off in triumph by the aid of one or more supernaturally gifted companions. Specifically, the little romance belongs to the more limited type in which the companion or companions perform the tasks instead of the hero himself. A further limitation consists in the fact that the attendant is bespelled to an ugly shape, and that the accomplishment of the adventure effects his disenchantment. All these varieties are abundant in popular fiction. The introductory incident, with the challenge to a game of pluck-buffet, serves to embark the hero on the adventurous journey which is to free

[1] P. 274.

the enchanted person. In this point, too, the story is true-bred, for a match of some kind which the hero loses to a supernatural opponent, is often the occasion of his setting out on a perilous adventure.[1] The beheading at the end is the final act in the unspelling process.

In such *märchen* the hero usually gets a reward for himself: the treasures of the giant or enchanter fall to his lot, and he wins a wife as well. Traces of these features may still be detected in the English romance. Sir Gromer wishes Arthur to grant Gawain the kingdom of Man, after the death of the " soudan," but Gawain magnanimously declines it. Among the ladies who are freed from captivity may well have been, in the source, the sister of the hero's bespelled companion. She disappeared, perhaps, when the story was attached to Gawain, whom, as we have already observed, the romancers were disinclined to involve in any permanent *liaison*. Compare the way in which the author of the *Chevalier à l'Épée* contrives to get rid of the damsel whom Gawain has won at the castle.[2]

The *Turk and Gawain* is particularly interesting in the present investigation. The Turk, like the Carl of Carlisle, is a knight condemned by enchantment to wear a hideous figure; like the Carl he is freed from the ban by decapitation at the hands of the hero after previous tests have been fulfilled; like the Carl he becomes Arthur's vassal. In these points the *Turk and Gawain* also resembles that form of the Temptation story which was used by the author of the French *Gawain and the Green Knight*. All this, however, would add little to the strength of the contention that these three features formed a part of the Temptation story in question, were it not for the fact that the *Turk* shows a special resemblance to *Gawain and the Green Knight* in a very

[1] See pp. 137–138, 196–197.   [2] P. 92.

remarkable matter: the Turk appears at Arthur's court with a challenge to an exchange of buffets.[1] He is to stand a buffet on this occasion, and his smiter is to allow him to repay it. The course of the story shows that the return-blow is not to be given on the spot, but that Gawain is to leave the court with the Turk and receive it at some place to him unknown. This incident is identical to all intents and purposes with the Challenge. Now, we have seen that the Challenge was utilized by the author of the French *Gawain and the Green Knight* as a means of getting Gawain to the castle of Bernlak, where the [unspelling] Temptation was to be undergone. Similarly, in *The Turk and Gawain*, the challenge to pluck-buffet is the means used by the bespelled Sir Gromer (the Turk) to get Gawain to the castle where the tasks preliminary to his own disenchantment must be performed. The mutilation of the Percy MS. — to light fires — has deprived us of an account of the return-blow. The natural place for it is just before the Turk brings out a basin and asks Gawain to decapitate him, and there is a gap in the manuscript there. We must suppose that, after the King of Man is dead, the Turk claims the return-blow from Gawain, that Gawain immediately assents, and that the Turk spares him or strikes him gently. The danger is quite as great as in *Gawain and the Green Knight*. The buffet, if given in earnest, would certainly have dashed out Gawain's brains, for the Turk is far stronger than any of the Manx giants. Gawain's faithfulness to his word is a condition of the disenchantment, and the Turk is now ready for the final act. Accordingly, he asks Gawain to cut off his head, and when this is done, immediately stands up a fair knight.

We have, then, in *The Turk and Gawain*, a disenchant-ment story containing a close parallel to the Challenge to

[1] See p. 221.

decapitation, utilizing that incident for the same purpose for which *Gawain and the Green Knight* utilizes it, and winding up with disenchantment by decapitation and with the reception of the unspelled monster as one of Arthur's vassals.

Professor Hales believed that the author of *The Turk* derived the incident of the Challenge from the English *Gawain and the Green Knight*,[1] but I see no reason for supposing that he drew from that poem rather than from its French original. Indeed, it is quite possible that he picked up the Irish story in traditional circulation in his own half-Celtic neighborhood. If he did have recourse to the French *Gawain*, his poem is more or less usable as evidence that in that version, as we have already inferred upon other grounds, the *dénouement* consisted in the disenchanting of Bernlak and his reception into the fellowship of the Round Table or among the number of Arthur's vassals. If, on the other hand, we prefer to think that the author of *The Turk* drew from one of the episodical French poems of the Challenge (O or R) or from current tradition in his own locality, we have at least a tolerably good instance of the same procedure that we have observed in the construction of the plot of *Gawain and the Green Knight*. The Challenge, originally Irish, is combined with another story to frame an Arthurian romance in which the challenger is under spells, in which he uses the " game " as a means of getting his rescuer to the place necessary for disenchantment, and in which, finally, he becomes Arthur's vassal as soon as he is released from spells. In this case, the parallelism between the *Turk* and our reconstruction of the lost French *Gawain and the Green Knight* shows that we have used a sound method in that reconstruction.

[1] *Bishop Percy's Folio Manuscript*, I, 88.

Everything seems to point, then, to the conclusion at which we had arrived, on the evidence of the *Carl of Carlisle*, before we began to examine *The Turk and Gawain*. If the French *Gawain and the Green Knight* is ever discovered, we may expect it to represent the challenger as released from enchantment by Gawain's successful adventure, as accompanying his rescuer to Arthur's court, and as becoming a vassal of the king.

With these facts in mind let us examine another remarkable romance contained — in a sadly corrupt and disordered state — in the Percy MS. This piece is entitled simply *The Green Knight*. It extends to only about five hundred lines, but is almost identical in plot with the English *Gawain and the Green Knight*, of which, indeed, it has ordinarily been regarded as a condensed and enfeebled *rifacimento*, with all the poetry left out.[1]

The Green Knight in the Percy Manuscript

The Green Knight's name is Sir Bredbeddle and he dwells in the West Country. His wife, as he is well aware, loves Gawain though she has never set eyes on him. Her mother, Agostes, is a witch who can change men's shapes, and she has taught Bredbeddle how to apply this art to himself. She advises her son-in-law to visit Arthur's court at Carlisle in quest of adventures; but the suggestion is really made for her daughter's sake, with the purpose of procuring Gawain's presence at the castle. Bredbeddle is delighted to go, for he feels some eagerness to test Gawain's "three points," which appear to be valor, courtesy, and truth. He sets out accordingly, in green armor, with a green weapon, and, on a green horse. [This, by the way, seems to

---

[1] See p. 296.

be the full extent of the " transposition " that he undergoes
in our text, but there was doubtless more in the version of
which the Percy MS. is a poor copy.[1]] His weapon is styled
a " long fauchion " in v. 77, nor is anything said of an axe
until v. 188, when Gawain seizes " the axe " to cut off the
stranger's head in response to the challenge. The Green
Knight's ability to replace his head is ascribed, like his
" transposed " appearance, to the arts of his mother-in-law:
" All this was done by enchantment that the old witch had
wrought." When the return-blow is dealt, the weapon is
again a " fauchion " (v. 452.) The Percy text is, as this
instance shows, much confused and somewhat defective.
Other signs of corruption are not lacking. Thus, when the
Green Knight issues his challenge he names the Green
Chapel as the rendezvous (vv. 148–150), and afterwards the
head repeats this mention of the place: —

> Saith: " Gawaine! thinke on thy couenant!
> This day 12 monthes see thou ne want
>   To come to the greene chappell! " (vv. 196–198).

It is certainly better to have the Chapel mentioned but
once, and accordingly we find in the longer English romance
no locality specified in the initial challenge. Again, the
bargain between Gawain and Bredbeddle is not to exchange
their winnings, but to share them. This results in an
absurd contradiction at the end,[2] for Gawain certainly does
share his gains with his host, even if he retains the lace, so
that it is unjust to accuse him of not keeping his word. The
three hunts are reduced to one, from which Bredbeddle
brings home hinds, does, wild swine, foxes, " and other
ravine." By a similar process of telescoping, Sir Bredbeddle

---

[1] See vv. 49–60, 73–84, 92–105, 337–342, 442–444.

[2] Noted by Furnivall, *Bishop Percy's Folio Manuscript*, II, 77.

is made to deal but one return-blow, inflicting a slight wound. The two preliminary feints or interrupted strokes are omitted. This corresponds with the fact that Gawain's stay at the castle lasts only one day, and that he has there-fore been tempted by the lady but once. It was on that occasion that he received the three kisses and also the lace. After smiting Gawain, Sir Bredbeddle accuses him of dodg-ing, ("shunting"), though the narrative says nothing of Gawain's having shown any fear. There are other minor instances of corruption or disorder, and in general, it is evident that the Percy text is a faulty transcript, perhaps written down from memory.

Most of the errors and inconsistencies just noted are chargeable to careless copying and the casualties of trans-mission, not to unskilful workmanship on the part of the author of the short *Green Knight*. If we had his poem as he wrote it, we should undoubtedly find it consistent with itself, and we should recognize the plot as identical in almost every incident with that of the long English romance. Two theories are schematically possible: (1) that the author used as his source the long English romance, which he shortened and attempted to popularize; (2) that his source was the French *Gawain and the Green Knight*, now lost, which he reproduced in most particulars, though with a few changes and a certain amount of condensation. The first alternative may seem the easier hypothesis, but the second deserves consideration.

In the first place, we should not be much influenced by the lateness of the Percy Folio. That is not necessarily signifi-cant as to the age of any piece that the manuscript happens to contain, as is conclusively proved by the facts in the case of *Sir Lambwell*.[1]

[1] See p. 86.

Secondly, there is no antecedent general probability that any given Middle English poem goes back to an English rather than a French original. Indeed, the contrary is rather more likely *a priori*. Nor is it surprising to find two or more independent English versions of a single French work. The Old French *Octavian* is extant in two English versions, a Northern and a Southern, neither of them derived from the other. There are three English versions of Hue de Rotelande's *Ipomedon*. Both Gower and Chaucer utilized the legend of Constance in Nicholas Trivet's Anglo-Norman chronicle. Additional examples will occur to every student.

Thirdly, the mere lack, in the Percy *Green Knight*, of many details of the long romance, is not even presumptive evidence in favor of the derivation of the shorter version from the longer. The short *Green Knight* is probably a condensed version of something, but why may it not be condensed from the French as well as from the English ? Besides, in some instances the phenomena may not be due to omission at all.

The most cursory reading of *Gawain and the Green Knight* makes one thing plain to anybody who is at all familiar with the Old French episodical romances of Sir Gawain. The Middle English masterpiece is not a translation in any proper sense of the term. It must be utterly different in style and poetic manner from the lost French poem on which it is based, for in these particulars it bears no resemblance to anything in French literature. It marks the culmination of a development of style and poetic manner that is peculiar to England and to a certain part of England (the West Midland and Northern district), just as it marks the culmination of a kind of metrical development similarly limited in geographical scope. Furthermore, the English author has an individuality which distinguishes him from other English writers belonging to what we may vaguely call the same " school."

These observations are so patent that no one will dispute them; and if we bear them in mind, we cannot fail to understand the treatment which the French *Gawain and the Green Knight* must have received at the hands of the great anonymous West Midland poet of the fourteenth century. He followed the plot with substantial faithfulness, as we have already seen; but he elaborated every detail of description with a richness of fancy quite foreign to the sober narrative style of his original, he gave life to the personages and vividness to the action, and he inspired the whole with an ethical earnestness that ennobles the tale without making it less romantic. The Frenchman was a first-rate *raconteur* who combined two independent stories into a single plot with a high degree of constructive ability, and he was master of a flowing and limpid style exquisitely adapted to straightforward story-telling. The Englishman was an idealist and a true poet, who saw, in the capital story which his French predecessor had told so acceptably, the possibility of illustrating the finest traits of the mediæval gentleman, who controlled an elaborate and difficult poetical technique in such a way as to make it a natural vehicle not merely for the description in which he delighted but for dramatic action as well, and who built up, on the basis of the excellent French romance, which was on a par with numerous others quite as good and quite as well-told, a unique masterpiece in the grandiose manner.

Among the characteristic passages which were certainly added or greatly elaborated by the English author are: — the learned introductory stanza summarizing the fabulous settlements of Western Europe and mentioning the Siege of

Troy, Æneas, Romulus, "Ticius" of Tuscany, Langobard of Lombardy, and Felix Brutus of Britain; the description of the Christmas festivities (i, 3) and that of the Green Knight (i, 7–9); the challenge (i, 12–13) and the speech of Gawain (i, 16); the highly poetical stanzas on the changing seasons (ii, 1–2); the very elaborate description of the process of arming a knight (ii, 4–6), with the allegorical account of the pentangle of virtues (ii, 7); Gawain's itinerary, — Logres, North Wales, Anglesea, Holyhead, the wilderness of Wirral (ii, 9); the winter piece (ii, 10); the justly celebrated account of the three hunts (iii, 1 ff.).

The list is far from exhaustive, but it will suffice to illustrate the freedom with which the English poet treated his French source. All such elaborations are lacking in the Percy version. But this is no argument for the derivation of the Percy version from the English *Gawain*. Derive it from the French *Gawain*, and the conditions in this regard are well satisfied, since the details in question were certainly not found in the French.

Finally, there is one incident in the Percy version, but not in the long English romance, which was doubtless found in the French original: the Green Knight, after the fulfilment of the beheading compact, accompanies Gawain to Arthur's court, and inferentially becomes the king's vassal. Such a correspondence, it is true, is not enough to establish the derivation of the Percy version from the lost French *Gawain*, since the feature in question is a commonplace which could easily be added by the author of the short *Green Knight* out of his own general stock of romantic knowledge.

So far the case for a derivation of the short *Green Knight* from the French *Gawain* rather than from the long English romance, looks plausible or more than plausible. But we must weigh the alternative before we pass judgment.

First, there are a good many resemblances in phraseology between the two English poems, — quite enough of them not merely to outweigh the argument from recruiting (the only positive evidence we have noted for the derivation of the Percy version from the French), but also to leave a considerable margin in favor of immediate derivation from the longer English version. Many of these parallels are no doubt commonplaces; others might be explained as literal translations. But when all deductions have been made, the table of verbal similarities (pp. 282 ff., below) still gives valuable testimony for the thesis that the shorter *Green Knight* is condensed from the longer English version, not from the French original.

Secondly, the Percy text contains several pretty obvious remnants of passages that were not in the French at all but owe their existence to the elaborating hand of the great English romancer. Such remnants concern the arming of Gawain and Gringolet (No. 21 in the table), the account of wolves and wonders encountered by the hero *en route* (No. 22), particulars of the deer-hunt (No. 28), and the whetting of the Green Knight's weapon (No. 33).[1] These passages are almost enough to settle the question.

Thirdly, we must consider the presence at Bernlak's castle of an ancient and highly honored lady whose magic arts are the moving cause of the Green Knight's expedition and therefore of the entire plot.

There is no such character in either the Challenge or the Temptation. She is certainly an addition to the story. The question is: At what stage of its development did she first appear ? In the long English romance a full account of her is given when Bernlak unties all the knots for Gawain's benefit and the reader's. She is " Morgne la Fay,"

_____
[1] See pp. 57–58.

" Morgne the Goddess," King Arthur's half-sister and
Gawain's aunt, the daughter of the Duke and Duchess of
Tintagel; we are also informed that she was Merlin's mistress.[1] This genealogical excursus may be unhesitatingly
credited to the English author, who was a man of learning
and well acquainted with the ins and outs of the fully
developed Arthurian saga: it can hardly have stood in his
French original. Furthermore, Bernlak informs Gawain
that it was Morgan who set the machinery in motion. She
sent him to Arthur's court in strange guise to challenge the
knights to the beheading game. Her object was to cause
Guinevere to die of terror: —

> " For to have grieved Gaynor and made her to die
> With fear of that wight that spake in ghastly fashion,
> With his head in his hand, before the high table."

This, too, I think, must be ascribed to the Englishman alone.
He knew of the traditional hatred of Morgan the Fay for
Guinevere, and it occurred to him to turn it to account for
the moving cause of his whole romance. Perhaps he was
somewhat influenced by that form of the tale of the Magic
Horn which represents Morgan as sending the talisman to
court with the design of revealing Guinevere's unfaithful-
ness.[2] We note, besides, that the motive in question is not
well worked into the fabric of the story. Not only is the
Fay's trick a failure, but there is no indication, in our
author's own description of the scene at court, that Guinevere showed any particular alarm: certainly she was in no
danger of death from shock. Besides, one is rather surprised that Gawain should part with Bernlak on such
cordial terms after the blunt avowal of his evil errand.

[1] Vv. 2446 ff.

[2] So in the prose *Tristan*, Löseth, p. 39 (cf. Child, *Ballads*, I, 265; Miss
Paton, *Fairy Mythology*, pp. 104 ff.).

It is safe, I should suppose, to infer that we are here dealing with a substitution. In the French *Gawain* the moving
cause of the whole plot, as we have already seen, was Bernlak's desire to be disenchanted, a motive retained from the
Temptation story. In the Temptation, however (and
consequently in the French *Gawain*), the originator of the
spells was either nameless (as often), or at best was nobody
who had a status among the *dramatis personae* of the sys-
tematized Arthurian legend. Now our English author
shows at the beginning and at the close of his poem (in
passages that are surely his own) a distinct desire to attach
his narrative to the orthodox Arthur saga, referring to the
" Brutus Books " as his written source.[1] As a means to this
end, no doubt, he decided to make Morgan the Fay the
" only begetter " of the whole affair, at the same time
identifying her with that other famous enchantress, Niniane,
the mistress of Merlin. But if Morgan was to be the
wonder-worker in the mysterious background, — if it was
to be Morgan that sent Bernlak to court in strange guise
with his axe in his hand, — the object of the visit could no
longer be his disenchantment. That purpose had to disappear when she became herself the weaver of the spell.
Another reason had to be imagined, and our author found it
in Morgan's enmity toward the queen, which, indeed, was
in his mind an inseparable trait of her traditional character.

For using Morgan the Fay the English poet may have
found a suggestion in his French original. For it is far from
unlikely that Bernlak's household included an ancient dame
who held, perhaps, some more or less tutelary office with
regard to the lady of the castle, or may even have been
(though less probably) her mother. One remembers the
enchanted castle in Chrétien's *Perceval*, where Gawain

[1] V. 2523 (cf. vv. 1–36).

achieved the adventure of the Perilous Bed. Here live three queens, all under spells, from which they are released by Gawain. Later he learns that one of them, an old lady "with gray tresses," is Arthur's mother; that the second is her daughter, King Lot's widow, and consequently his own mother; and that the third is his sister Clarissant, of whom he has never heard.[1] Be that as it may, we must ascribe the presence of Morgan, as I have said, to the learned ingenuity of the English romancer, and likewise, of course, her rôle as the setter-in-motion of the entire plot.

Now Morgan appears also, in the same capacity of " close contriver of all harms," in the short *Green Knight*. She has lost both *nomen* and *numen*, — and has acquired instead the eccentric name Agostes (doubtless a corruption for something or other) and the character of a mere witch and procuress — the Green Knight's mother-in-law, who can transform men and has taught him the art of shape-shifting. But she still remains the motive-power of the whole transaction. It is she who despatches the Green Knight to court, and it is by virtue of her charms that he is enabled to pick up his head and put it back on his shoulders: " All this was done by enchantment that the old witch had wrought!"

So striking a correspondence between the two English poems in a feature that was certainly absent from the French *Gawain*, must, in all reason, decide for us the question as to the source of the short *Green Knight*. It is undoubtedly a condensed *rifacimento* of the long English romance.

True, it might conceivably be argued, since the French *Gawain* may have included in Bernlak's *ménage* an elderly lady-in-waiting, that the two English poets developed this character without collusion, each in his own way, equipping

---

[1] Vv. 10095 ff. (Potvin, III, 31–32).

her with magical powers and elevating her to the rank of mistress of the situation.

Such a theory, though pretty hazardous, would doubtless be admissible, at a pinch. We should be driven to accept it, perhaps, if there were strong reasons for believing that the short *Green Knight* was derived from the French original of the long English romance rather from the English romance itself. But there are no such strong reasons. Indeed, there are no reasons at all, except the agreement of the Percy text with the French *Gawain* (against the English) in the challenger's final submission to the king; and this trait, as everybody knows, is a mere commonplace of Arthurian story, and its testimony is much more than counterbalanced by the verbal resemblances between the two English poems. Even before we began to consider the ancient lady, we saw that the balance of probabilities was heavily on the side of deriving the shorter English romance from the longer, both on account of these resemblances and because of several points in which the Percy version appears to go back to something that stands in the English *Gawain* but was surely not in the French. All this being so, we cannot hesitate in coming to a decision. The *Green Knight* of the Percy Folio is merely a condensation of the English *Gawain and the Green Knight*, with a few changes introduced by the condenser and a crop of later errors chargeable to Adam Scrivener and defects of memory.

It has recently been argued [1] that the Percy *Green Knight* keeps an old feature of the legend — namely, the love of the knight's lady for Gawain, whom she has never seen, — that the lady is, in fact, the *fée* of the Fairy Mistress myth, and her husband merely the *fée's* agent and summoner. From this point of view, the short romance has been used as an

[1] Hulbert, *Modern Philology*, XIII, 49 ff.

important document in settling the history or mythology of the beheading game and of the temptation at Bernlak's castle.

It must now be clear that the poem in the Percy Folio has no evidential value for such purposes. The love of the lady for Gawain and her employment of her husband as a pandar are alterations in the plot — alterations made by the rhymer who condensed the English romance. They are not traits that came down to him *in the story* by a long line of tradition.

Under these circumstances, we are not bound to explain the rhymer's motive in thus changing the plot, beyond ascribing it to his *sic volo, sic iubeo*. But since a further explanation is easy, it may as well be given. Our rhymer disapproved of the object assigned in his source to Bernlak's visit to court. No wonder: every reader finds it unsatisfactory. It is the one weak spot in the superb English romance. Disapproving of it, he had to provide a substitute; and this he did, not by straining his imagination, but by adopting one of the most familiar of all Arthurian *données* — the lady who loves Gawain without having seen him. I have styled this convention one of the most familiar conventions in Arthurian story. I might have said one of the best known in all literature. "C'est là un trait que se rencontre dans nombre de fictions romanesques depuis la plus haute antiquité."

Be that as it may, it was a trait with which the rhymer was well acquainted, and it served his turn. The other changes almost made themselves. Morgan the Fay became the witch-lady (indeed, but for her name, she is hardly more in the longer poem) and annexed the rôle of procuress — a character quite as common as need be, both in the life and in the literature of the middle ages. *Voilà tout!*

CONCLUSION

The genial Frenchman who made the plot of *Gawain and the Green Knight* by combining two entirely independent stories, the Challenge and the Temptation, was of course a Pasha of Many Tales; for he was well acquainted with the machinery of Arthurian romance, and fairy stories of the nursery were part of his birthright. Equally of course, he was influenced as he worked, now by one feature of romance or *märchen*, now by another, precisely as a modern writer of fiction, whatever the main source or sources of his plot, is influenced by the conventional *données* of novel-writing, — the forged or stolen will, the supposititious child, the false accusation, the wandering heir, the scheming adventuress, the grand old gardener and his wife, the crash in speculation, the oppressive magnate, the unpractical inventor with his strange device to revolutionize some industry. And, in particular, our clever Frenchman had always present in his mind those old types of the folk-tale which we never fail to find whenever we open a book of such things. Thus, as his combined plot took shape under his hand, it was inevitable that it should conform to some type or other, partly because of the nature of the material, which was itself *märchenhaft*, partly because of the stock of ideas which stored his mind.

We are not astonished, therefore, to find that the finished product, taken as a whole, accords in its main outlines with a definite type of *märchen* to which neither of its chief components, the Challenge and the Temptation, belongs. This type is as follows: — The hero is challenged to play a game by a mysterious visitant, with life as the stake, or on the understanding that the winner shall fix a forfeit. The supernatural player wins. He then requires of the hero that within a fixed term (commonly a year and a day) he shall discover his abode and there present himself, and further, that he shall there perform certain tasks or labors. The hero is of course successful, but the details of his adventures are not to our purpose. His achievements may or may not include the winning of a wife from the Other World; sometimes, too, the story closes with the " kiss taboo " and the incident of the Forgotten Bride. There are many folk-tales that belong more or less to this class, and the varieties are kaleidoscopic.[1]

Two things, however, must be particulary noted with regard to this type of folk-tale. First, the game at the outset is a mere device to get the hero into the power of the supernatural being. This personage means him no good, and his object in exacting a pledge to visit strange lands is to destroy him. He cannot be interpreted as a messenger sent by a *fée* to lure her chosen hero to her arms, unless one is willing to adopt the long ago discredited methods of the sun-and-cloud mythologists and ignore the plain intent of the whole affair. And secondly, even if the supernatural gamester in the folk-tales *were* always a *fée's* messenger, that would mean nothing to us in our sober historical task of following the story of the Challenge, in almost the identical form in which it occurs in the *Fled Bricrend*, from Ireland to France and back again to England. For the challenger in the *Fled Bricrend* is not the emissary of a *fée*. There is no *fée* and no hint of a *fée* in *The Champion's Bargain*, and the visit of the big ugly black-clad carl is paid for the purpose of testing Cuchulinn's valor, not for the sake of embarking him for the Other World. The use of the Challenge as a means of getting Gawain to Bernlak's castle came into the tale under the hands of the French author, and was an act of literary craftsmanship synchronous with that by

[1] See pp. 196–197.

which he wove together the Challenge and another story, the Temptation, that never had been united with it before. This Frenchman, the immediate predecessor of the English poet, may have got the *impulse to combine* from his knowledge of the great class of quest-tales; or he may have brought his plot, as he framed and moulded it, into more or less conscious accord with some traditional type or inherited idea. So be it. Such considerations are interesting, but they concern only a comparatively late period in the history of *Gawain and the Green Knight*. They throw no light on the history of the Challenge between the time when it left Ireland in a highly elaborated literary form (well represented by the extant *Champion's Bargain*), and the moment when it came, substantially intact, into the possession of the French poet who combined it with the Temptation. Incidents which this Frenchman added to the Challenge in the thirteenth century cannot instruct as to what it was, or what it meant, before he wrote, — *a fortiori*, before he was born!

So, too, with regard to the lace or band which Gawain accepts from the lady at the castle. This likewise has been cited as an ancient feature.[1] No doubt it is ancient in one sense, for it is one of those protective or fortifying talismans in which the fancy of the folk has always delighted. Of course these things occur in Celtic tradition — Cuchulinn owned one, for instance,[2] and Brandubh mac Echach, king of Leinster had a girdle that " was of such a nature that neither sickness nor trouble would seize on the side on which it was." [3] But so had the dwarf-king Laurin in Germanic saga — a belt which gave him the strength of twelve men; [4]

[1] Miss Weston, *Legend of Sir Gawain*, pp. 101–102.

[2] Zimmer, Haupt's *Zeitschrift*, XXXII, 319.

[3] *Compert Mongain* (*Conception of Morgan*), chap. 27, ed. Meyer, *Voyage of Bran*, I, 69, 83).

[4] *Laurin*, vv. 185–194 (*Heldenbuch*, I, 204).

and the Australian aborigines know of a war-girdle that imparts force, security, and accuracy of aim.[1] That the Gawain of the romances should now and then acquire such an object [2] is inevitable, and indicates nothing whatever as to his original character as god or man. At all events, his possession of the lace in *Gawain and the Green Knight* is not an old feature of his legend, but the device of a Frenchman who did not find the talisman in his source. He was proceeding, to be sure, in accordance with the general practice of romancers and drawing upon his own stock of traditional story; but his procedure is not mythological evidence. And it is even possible that the lace did not enter the plot until the English author worked up the material. Anyhow, its acceptance and concealment are felicitous touches, for Gawain is thus removed from the unnatural category of schematic perfection and brought within the reach of human understanding.

Much has also been made by scholars, from time to time, of the greenness of the challenger,[3] for everybody is aware that green is a fairy color. But this feature likewise has a history that can be traced. The challenger is not green in the Irish tale of *The Champion's Bargain*: he is a gigantic uncouth carl, clad in a black garment and wearing a dingy hide over his shoulders.[4] In the next stage of the tale, the Anglo-Norman O, he remained an uncouth carl, black-clad (as in the Irish) or black of face (as in *La Mule*).[5] In the third stage, the French R, he was still of gigantic stature and strange aspect, but splendidly attired in green. This we know from the *Caradoc* and the English *Gawain*; [6] but we cannot be quite certain when he himself assumed the hue-

---

[1] Gillen, *Report of Horn Expedition*, Part IV, p. 182.
[2] Miss Weston, *Legend of Sir Gawain*, pp. 100 ff.
[3] See pp. 195 ff.
[4] See p. 11.
[5] P. 67.
[6] See p. 39.

of the leaves. Certainly, however, the green tint of horse and man cannot antedate the stage of our story that is represented by R, — that is, the third stage of its literary history, and the second of its literary history in the French language.

R, however, was apparently not much given to such *outré* variations, being chiefly concerned to render the narrative of O more courtly in its details. We are safest, therefore, if we conjecture that the greenness of the knight and his steed is due either to the author of the French *Gawain*, who did innovate appreciably, or to the English romancer, who always exercised the freedom of a man of genius. Between the two it is hard to choose.

Perhaps we had better let them share the honors. There is a Green Knight in Malory, with whom — as with his two brothers the Black and the Blue Knight, and with the Red Knight of the Red Launds — Gareth must do battle for the enfranchisement of Dame Lyones. The Black Knight is killed, but the others join the fellowship of the Round Table. When this Green Knight is first seen, he is " all in green, both his horse and his harness "; he blows a green horn, wears green armor, carries a green shield, and wields a green lance.[1] But it is abundantly evident that he is not green himself, — neither is his horse; and the same is true, *mutatis mutandis*, of his brothers. Where Malory got the episode of Gareth is unknown, but doubtless from a " French book," as he asserts. At all events, knights with trappings of a brilliant color are common enough in French romances.

We may reasonably conjecture, then, that the immediate French original of our English poem went somewhat farther than R in furnishing the challenger and his steed with verdant paraphernalia, but that, for the extension of

[1] *Mort Darthur*, vii, 8 (Sommer, I, 223).

this hue to face, hair, beard, and eyebrows, and to the horse's mane and hide, we are indebted to the English poet. To him also, with complete certainty, is to be credited the superb description of the Green Chapel and the surrounding landscape, with its rocks and crags, and the roaring torrent over which the Green Knight vaults when he comes out of the hollow mound. Nothing like this is found in any extant French romance, and it is in the highest degree improbable that such picturesque details were present in the French *Gawain*. The English poet was describing a scene that he knew, not copying from a manuscript. The Green Chapel is undoubtedly a fairy mound, but it is a fairy mound which the Englishman had often visited, — a haunted barrow in his own country. If it is Celtic, that is because the home of the English poet lay in a region still peopled with creatures of the Celtic imagination, still haunted — as it is to a less extent to-day — with Celtic thoughts and Celtic fancies.

We are not to reconstruct the Irish original on the strength of additions made by French or English writers, even if those additions have their roots in Celtic lore. Indeed, we are not to reconstruct the Irish original at all, for we have it, substantially intact, in *The Champion's Bargain*. The Green Knight in the English poem comes out of a fairy mound to welcome Gawain, and there are fairy mounds in Ireland and in Irish saga, — but there is no fairy mound in that particular Irish tale from which the Challenge in *Gawain and the Green Knight* descends in a direct and traceable line of strictly literary tradition.

Our starting point for this study lies not in the misty mid-region of Weir, not in the pan-Celtic Cloudcuckooland of myth and speculative folk-lore — pleasant countries, where I like to wander as well as anyone. It is just as fixed and definite as the point of our destination. We begin with *The*

Champion's Bargain, an Irish tale in a carefully elaborated literary form, preserved in a manuscript of about the year 1100. We end with *Gawain and the Green Knight*, an English romance in a carefully elaborated literary form, preserved in a manuscript of about 1400. Those points in which the latter document differs from the former are *changes* — additions, subtractions, or modifications. The questions are, with regard to each of them: *Who made the change — the Englishman or one of his predecessors? and, if one of his predecessors, which one?* These questions I have done my best to answer.

PART II

ILLUSTRATIVE MATERIAL

ILLUSTRATIVE MATERIAL

I. THE RETURNING OR SURVIVING HEAD

THE Challenge, or Beheading Game, in its simplest shape and even in some of its more developed forms, is a mere test of valor, like so many other encounters with uncanny beings in the mythology and heroic saga of every nation. Let us see if we can get some idea of the primitive character of the mysterious and gigantic challenger.

Originally he is a savage creature, quite outside the pale of humanity, inimical to mortals and destroying all men who cross his path. To every hero who comes into contact with him he allows the first stroke. This is delivered with an effect that is expected to slay the monster, but he is unharmed; his head returns to his shoulders (or he replaces it), and he then decapitates his opponent, who of course succumbs. Thus, *with respect to his actions*, the Green Knight is to be associated with the same general category as, for example, the Slavic noon-lady, who, if she catches a solitary human being in the fields at midday, accosts him with a long series of questions. If he can hold out to answer till the clock strikes two, her power terminates, and he escapes; otherwise, she beheads him with her sickle or strangles him.[1] We have already discovered a closer parallel in the demonic monster of the Australian aborigines, who always offers his victim the first blow, presenting him with his own weapon for that purpose, but who, unharmed, seizes the weapon again and kills his baffled opponent on the spot.[2]

[1] Laistner, *Das Rätsel der Sphinx*, I, 1 ff.   [2] P. 22.

Among such destructive monsters, our Green Knight belongs to a special class who have the curious property of recovering their heads after decapitation. Sometimes the head simply flies on again, sometimes the uncanny creature picks it up and replaces it. The belief in such beings encircles the globe. Let us begin with Celtic examples.

In J. F. Campbell's tale of *The Sea Maiden*, the hero whips off the crone's head with his sword. " But the sword flew out of his hand. And swift the crone gripped her head with both hands, and puts it on her neck as it was before." [1] In another version the hero has to fight a three-headed giant. He cuts off two heads (one each day). " The third head jumped on again as fast as it was cut off, but at last, by the advice of a hoodie, the cold steel of the sword was held on the neck till the marrow froze,[2] and then the giant was killed."[3] Again in *The Son of the Green Spring by Valour*, a variant of *The Knight of the Red Shield*, an old carlin is beheaded by the hero. Her head " leaps on again, he cuts it off again, and it flies up into the skies; he holds the sword on the neck, and looks up, and sees the head coming down and aiming at him; he leaps to one side, and the head goes four feet into the earth." [4] Again, in the long tale of *Conall Gulban*, the dreagan's [5] head keeps springing on again, by virtue of a magic balsam, till the marrow is frozen by holding the sword between the neck and the head.[6]

In MacInnes's tale of *Manus*, Manus keeps the hag's head and neck apart by the same device.[7] Exactly so Ceudach

---

[1] *Popular Tales of the West Highlands*, I, 83.

[2] This may possibly be a reminiscence of the widespread belief that iron dissolves a charm, as to which see Rhŷs, *Celtic Folklore*, Index, under " iron " and " fairies and iron."   [3] The same, I, 97.

[4] The same, II, 476.   [5] A big bird or griffin.   [6] The same, III, 238.

[7] *Folk and Hero Tales*, p. 367. The incident does not occur in J. F. Campbell's *Manus*, No. 84 (III, 350 ff.).

and the Beast in J. G. Campbell's *Lad with the Skin Coverings*.[1] So of a hag in Curtin's *Myths and Folk-Lore of Ireland*,[2] though here Gilla simply " stands between " head and body (when the former " jumped at " the latter and " tried to get its place again ") till the body was cold. A livelier case in the same collection is the adventure of Shaking Head. He had cut off the head of the giant, and " then began the greatest struggle that Shaking-head ever had, to keep the head from the body of the giant. The head fought to put itself on again, and never stopped till the body was dead; then it fell to the ground." [3] In *MacCool, Feolan, and the Mountain*, there is danger that the hag's head may rejoin her trunk; it has to be split and thrown into a well.[4] The head speaks (like the Green Knight's), enjoining a task.[5]

In a tale from Ulster, the hero kills three giants to win the hand of a princess. After he has decapitated the first, the head tries to get back on the body, but he leaps between the two, and the body expires.[6] This method of preventing resuscitation was really followed in ancient Ireland. It occurs in the Irish *Life of St. Berach*: nine miscreants slew one of the saint's monks, " and they went between his head and his body." [7] In a variant of the tale just cited, Ardh ó

[1] *The Fians*, p. 262. On this tale see MacRitchie, *Scots Lore*, I, 389; *Transactions of the Ossianic Society*, II, 131.   [2] P. 260.

[3] Pp. 199–200. This tale has something to do with the Oriental story of the princess who loved a monster (see Kittredge, [*Harvard*] *Studies and Notes in Philology and Literature*, VIII, 250, note). Shaking Head himself is an example of the Grateful Dead Man (see Gerould, *The Grateful Dead*, 1908).

[4] Cf. Curtin, *Myths and Folk-Lore of Ireland*, p. 201.

[5] Curtin, *Hero-Tales of Ireland*, pp. 496–497.

[6] *Maighdean an t-Soluis agus Sgéalta Eile*, Dundalk, 1913, pp. 20 ff.

[7] Chap. 29 (Brussels MS. 4190 × 4200 II f. 71) cited by Plummer, *Vitae Sanctorum Hiberniae*, I, cviii, note 1 (" ogus tangattar iter a chend ogus a cholann ").

Leabharcha beheads three giants in succession, and each time the head attempts to return to the trunk, declaring, " If I could get back on the body, neither you nor the men of Ireland would separate it [from me]." [1] The King of Dark Island belongs to the same category as these giants. His daughter betrays to Lorcan the secret of her father's nature: when his head is cut off, it will circle about in the air in the effort to descend upon the trunk, which will remain upright to receive it; but if Lorcan will strike down the trunk, the head cannot rejoin it. Lorcan follows instructions, and the king is permanently disposed of.[2]

In Curtin's *Cuculin*, the hero " went on his way till he came to Hung-up-Naked, who was hanging from a tree, his head on the ground near him. The Queen of the Wilderness had fastened him to the tree because he would n't marry her; and she said ' If any man comes who will put your head on you, you 'll be free.' And she laid the injunction on him to kill every man who tried to pass his way without putting the head on him." As Cuculin passed, Hung-up-Naked challenged him to fight. Cuculin, " picking up the head, clapped it on the body " and then said he was ready to fight. Hung-up-Naked then became friendly. He told Cuculin to take the head off and put it where he found it.[3] On his return from the adventure on which he was bound,

[1] Joseph Lloyd, *Sgéalaidhe Óirghiall*, Dublin, Gaelic League, 1905, pp. 3–6. Essentially the same story occurs in Quiggin's *Dialect of Donegal*, Cambridge, Eng., 1906, pp. 201 ff. Cf. Hyde and Dottin, *An Sgeuluidhe Gaodhalach*, No. 30, *Annales de Bretagne*, XVI, 96–97; Hyde, *An Sgeuluidhe Gaodhalach*, No. 13, pp. 100–102; *Céadtach mac Fhinn as Éirinn*, Gaelic League, Dublin, 1907, p. 20.

[2] *Madra na n-Ocht gCos agus Sgéalta Eile*, in the *Imtheachta an Oireachtais*, 1901, III, ii, 52 ff.

[3] *Myths and Folk-Lore of Ireland*, pp. 317–318. The episode of Hung-up-Naked is also found (apparently in better shape, and without the head-incident) in *Blaiman, Son of Apple* (Curtin, *Hero-Tales of Ireland*, pp. 387 ff.).

Cuculin took down the trunk, put on the head, struck Hung-up-Naked with a magic rod which he had obtained, " and made the finest looking man of him that could be found. The man went back to his own home happy and well." [1]

Sometimes the *motif* that we are studying is combined with the belief in Disenchantment by Decapitation, to which we shall return in a subsequent chapter.[2] This combination takes place in the first adventure in *Art and Balor Beimenach*. The princess of Greece will not marry Art unless he brings her the head of the Gruagach of the Bungling Leaps. Art fights the monster thrice. The first time he beheads him, but the body goes down through the earth, the head follows, and the next day the gruagach is whole and twice as strong as before. The second day, Art seizes the head before it has time to sink into the earth and starts off with it toward the king's castle. On the way he meets three men with a headless body. Art foolishly allows them to apply the gruagach's head to his trunk, and on the instant men, head, and body go down through the earth. The third day a raven carries off the head. Instructed and helped by a friendly old man, Art recovers the head, which he carries to the castle of the King of Greece. The princess consents to marry him, but he refuses her. Acting on the old man's instructions, Art carries the head back to *him*. " The old man threw the head on a body which was lying in the cabin; the head and the body became one, and just like the old man." The old man says: " The gruagach was my brother, and for the last three hundred years he was under the enchantment of . . . the only daughter of the King of Greece. The princess is old, though young in appearance;

[1] Curtin, *Myths and Folk-Lore of Ireland*, pp. 322–323.
[2] Pp. 200 ff.

my brother would have killed me as quickly as he would you; and he was to be enchanted till you should come and cut the head off him, and show it to the princess, and not marry her, and I should do as I have done. My brother and I will stay here, take care of our forests, and be friends to you." [1]

The extraordinary tale of *The Bare-Stripping Hangman* [2] presents interesting parallels. The Bare-Stripping Hangman, a giant, had carried off three of the four daughters of the king of Lochlan. Some of the king's champions went to the giant's castle and found him asleep. They struck off his head with their swords. Two of the kemps were immediately knocked down by a large golden eagle. The rest fled " But scarcely had they got outside through the gate of the Castle than they saw the Giant coming after them, and his head on him as it was before." [3] The Giant has sent word that he is coming for the fourth daughter in a year and a day. Alastir, son of the king of Ireland, undertakes to kill the giant, and after many adventures destroys the egg which contains his life. He then visits the castle, and finds the giant dead. [4] Alastir cuts off his head and feet and carries them to the king's court, where he casts them into a huge fire. " As soon as the hair of the head was singed and the skin of the feet burnt, the very handsomest young man they ever beheld sprang out of the fire." The king recognizes him as his brother who was stolen in childhood. [5]

In the last two *märchen* quoted, we cannot fail to observe a striking resemblance to the *Carl of Carlisle*. The bespelled person is a murderous monster until he is released from enchantment. [6] At the same time the two tales illustrate the peculiar accomplishment of the Green Knight. Thus we

[1] Curtin, *Hero-Tales of Ireland*, pp. 312 ff.
[2] Macdougall, *Folk and Hero Tales*, pp. 76 ff.
[3] P. 87.   [4] P. 110.   [5] P. 111.   [6] P. 88, above.

have concrete examples of a combination very similar to that which we have studied in the plot of the great English romance.[1]

In a tale from the Scottish Highlands, Ceudach's wife is sitting over his body on the shore, mourning. " She was not long there, when she saw two men of gigantic size coming towards her from the sea, and the one that was coming after throwing the head of the one who was before him, and the head going on him again as before. With the astonishment she felt, she lifted the sword that Ceudach had saying: ' Why should I not try the small play ? ' and threw off his head, when she found him alive and as well as when she parted from him." [2]   In another version of the same tale " she saw a small coracle coming with two men in it, one in the bow and one in the stern, each with a sword throwing the other's head off; and when they were near the shore one of them said to the other, ' Look at the dead man.' . . . She said to them, ' Will you not try the small game of old on the man lying here ? '   On this one of them threw the head off the body with his sword, and the dead man rose up alive and well as before." [3]   In still another variant " the man in the stern had a gold apple and a silver apple, and his work was throwing the apples at the man in the bow. When he threw one of the apples at the man in the bow he knocked his head off, and when he threw the other apple at him he put his head on again."   The wife borrowed the apples. " She threw one of the apples at her man and knocked his head off, and she threw the other at him, and put the head on him again; and he rose up alive and whole as he ever was." [4]

[1] Pp. 107 ff.

[2] J. G. Campbell, *The Fians*, pp. 228–229.

[3] The same, p. 267.

[4] Mac Innes, *Folk and Hero Tales*, pp. 380–383. In Larminie's *West Irish Folk-Tales*, p. 83, Kaytuch is brought to life by means of some leaves

In the tale of *Cael an Iairainn*, otherwise entitled *The Clown in the Gray Coat* (from Egerton MS. 154), the carl throws a handful of blackberries and meal at Cael and knocks off his head. " Then where the head was, thither he ran, and with it a second time let fly at the trunk in a way that he fastened it on as solid as ever it had been. The manner of him now, however, was with face to his back, his poll to his chest." [1] The apples in *Ceudach* suggest those which make horns grow and take them off again, as in Dekker's *Old Fortunatus* [2] and the folk-book of *Fortunatus' Sons*; [3] but there is no connection, apparently. Slaying by cast of apple (or venomous apple) occurs often enough in Irish, and may be compared with the sport with the huge tennis-ball in *The Turk and Gawain*.[4] The reversal of Cael's head is a mischance only less embarrassing than what happens in an Oriental story. A young woman, by the direction of a goddess, replaces the heads of her husband and her brother, and they come to life. Unfortunately, in her agitation she has exchanged the

which his wife sees a bird use for resuscitation. This is identical with the incident in Marie's *Lai d'Eliduc*, vv. 1032 ff. (see R. Köhler's note in Warnke's second edition, pp. clvi ff.). Cf. Bolte and Polívka, *Anmerkungen zu den Kinder- u. Hausmärchen der Brüder Grimm*, I, 128–129; Giraldus Cambrensis, *Topographia Hibernica*, bk. i, chap. 27 (Rolls edition, V, 60–61); D'Ancona, *Studj di Critica*, p. 352; Maspons y Labrós, *Cuentos populars Catalans*, 1885, p. 27 (note, p. 140); Hanusch, *Zeitschrift für deutsche Mythologie*, IV, 227; Knowles, *Folk-Tales of Kashmír*, pp. 12–13; Groome, *Gypsy Folk-Tales*, pp. 99, 111; Rivière, *Contes populaires de la Kabylie*, p. 199; Duff Macdonald, *Africana*, I, 291; Tremearne, *Hausa Superstitions and Customs*, pp. 19, 206–207; Treveylan, *Folk-Lore and Folk-Stories of Wales*, p. 175. See also Kelleher and Schoepperle, *Revue Celtique*, XXXII, 184 ff.

[1] O'Grady, *Silva Gadelica*, I, 295; II, 331. Cf. Hyde's note in Mac Innes, p. 490.

[2] Pearson's edition, I, 146 ff., 158.

[3] Zacher's article on Fortunatus in Ersch und Gruber's *Encyklopädie*, Section I, Part 16, pp. 178 ff.; notes to the Grimms' No. 122.

[4] See pp. 120, 221–222.

heads. The problem is offered: "Which of the two men was now her husband?"[1] The tale occurs in various collections. A well-known version from the *Cabinet des Fées* is included by Andrew Lang in his *Grey Fairy Book*.[2]

In *The Adventures of the Children of the King of Norway* (edited by Dr. Douglas Hyde from several eighteenth-century manuscripts and one of about 1600), among the marvels seen by Cod in the Forest of Wonders is a company of thirteen headless men. Their leader [who seems to have his head with him, though not upon his shoulders; perhaps he is carrying it; at all events, it is "the Head" that speaks] tells Cod how they came to be in that condition. They had met a little man with a harp, — " and the little man struck a fist on the mouth of the man of us who was nearest to him, and that man drew his sword to strike the man of the harp, as he thought, but it was not he whom he struck, but a man of us; so that it was ourselves who beheaded one another,[3] through the enchantment of the man of the harp." Cod afterwards beheaded this little " man of the harp." Thereupon the dwarf " rose up again and departed with his head in his hand, and his harp in the other hand." [4]

In a Breton tale, a prince who has to perform certain tasks at the behest of one Barbauvert, an enchanter, is helped by his taskmaster's daughter, after the manner of such stories. His final labor is to recover a big anchor from the bottom of the sea. He cuts off her head, which dives and brings up

[1] *Kathā-sarit-sāgara*, Book xii, Chap. 80 (*Vetāla*, 6), Tawney, II, 264. See Burton, *Vikram and the Vampire*, pp. 278 ff.

[2] Pp. 250 ff.

[3] Compare Cadmus and the Dragon's Teeth, and Odin's trick by which he causes the nine mowers to behead each other with their scythes in a scramble for the whetstone (*Bragaræður*, chap. 4).

[4] *The Lad of the Ferule*, etc. (Irish Texts Society, I), pp. 122–129. Dr. Hyde thinks "this story was a written one in perhaps the fourteenth century " (p. xiv).

the anchor. Then he replaces the head, and it grows on again.[1]

In *The Thirteenth Son of the King of Erin,* a tale of the Andromeda type, the hero cuts off the head of the sea-serpent (*urfeist*), but it rushes back and grows on again. Next day the hero cuts the monster in two, but the two halves rush together and are one as before. On the third day the beast is killed by means of a magic apple.[2] In a Færöe version, the hero cuts off the ten heads of a monster (*trødl*) and sets free the maiden whom he is on the point of devouring. The hero is assisted by three dogs, and it is arranged that one of these shall seize each head as soon as it is off and swim across the fjord with it. The dog is too slow the first time, and the head returns to its place on the monster's neck and has to be cut off again. Later in the story, the three dogs replace their master's head, which has been cut off by the typical " supplanter." They get it on hindside before and are obliged to cut it off and replace it properly. When this is done, he comes to life.[3] In a Magyar tale, the hero cuts off a dragon's twenty-four heads with his magic sword, but new heads grow instantly on which the sword has no effect.[4] In the Russian *skazka* of *Ivan Buiko-vich*[5] Ivan has to fight a twelve-headed monster called a *chudoyudo*, whose heads grow on as fast as they are cut off. A snake with many heads replaces the *chudoyudo* in a parallel adventure.[6] Both these stories might be derived from

[1] Luzel, *Contes populaires de Basse Bretagne,* II, 355 ff.

[2] Curtin, *Myths and Folk-Lore of Ireland,* pp. 165–166, 168–170. This story is studied, in connection with others of the type, by Hartland, *The Legend of Perseus,* III, 4 ff. Cf. J. F. Campbell, *The Celtic Dragon Myth.*

[3] Jakobsen, *Færøske Folkesagn og Æventyr,* No. 35, pp. 372–374.

[4] Curtin, *Myths and Folk-Lore of the Russians,* etc., p. 482 (from Merényi).

[5] Summarized by Ralston, *Russian Folk-Tales,* pp. 70 ff., from Afanasiev, *Narodnyja Russkija Skazki,* VII, 3.

[6] Afanasiev, II, No. 30; Ralston, pp. 66 ff.

Greek mythology, but this is improbable, and no such source will be suggested for the instances previously cited. And, at all events, the Lernæan hydra herself is a brilliant example of the class of monsters that we are studying. She had nine heads, one of which could not die. In place of each of the first eight, two others grew as fast as it was cut off. Iolaus helped Hercules by cauterizing each stump before the two new heads had time to sprout. The undying head was buried under a huge stone to prevent it from joining the neck.[1] The hydra myth has taken us away from Celtic territory, but it makes little difference what road we travel, for the world is full of creatures that resume their heads. Orrilo in the *Orlando Furioso* comes within our category. In his great fight with Oliver's sons, whenever his head is cut off, he gropes about till he finds it, — then he picks it up (" or pel crine ed or pel naso ") and replaces it on his shoulders. Once Grifone, to block this game, caught up the head and threw it into the Nile, but it was of no avail. Orrilo " swam to the bottom like a fish " and soon appeared on the bank with his head. Astolfo's book gives the necessary instructions: the monster's life resides in a certain hair.[2] Halewijn, the woman-slayer in the magnificent Dutch ballad that belongs with *Lady Isabel and the Elf-Knight* in English and *Kvindemorderen* in Danish, makes a good tragic pendant to the half-comic Orrilo. His head speaks after the heroic lady has cut it off with his own sword. It urges her to wind his [magic] horn to " warn his friends," and when she refuses, bids her go to the gallows-tree whereon he has hanged many maids, fetch a pot of salve from under it, and rub his red neck.

[1] See the references in Roscher's *Lexicon*, I, 2769–2770.
[2] Canto xv, sts. 65 ff. Madden cites this passage (*Syr Gawayne*, pp. 307–308).

" Gaet ginder onder de galge
En haelt daer een pot met zalve
En strykt dat aen myn rooden hals! "[1]

She again refuses, washes the head in a spring, and carries it away with her.   A similar incident is found in several versions of the corresponding German ballad.[2]   Halewijn is plainly a supernatural creature, and the ointment should not be necessary.   It betrays rationalization, and from that point of view we may compare the strange knight in the service of the damsel Lynet in Malory's *Morte Darthur*.[3]   A Tuscan folk-tale brings us back to the less sophisticated idea.   The hero, having beheaded a magician, loses no time in piercing the head with his sword: otherwise it would have united with the trunk.[4]

Monsters of the same kind are known in Eastern story. In the *Kathā-sarit-sāgara*, the hero Indivarasena fights with a rakshasa.   He " frequently cut off the rakshasa's head, but it grew again.   Seeing that magic power of his, and having had a sign made to him by the virgin at the rakshasa's side, who had fallen in love with him at first sight, the prince, after cutting off the head of the rakshasa, being quick of hand, again cut it in two with a stroke of his sword.   Then the rakshasa's magic was baffled by contrary magic, and his head did not grow again, and the rakshasa died of the wound." [5]

[1] Stanza 31, Hoffmann von Fallersleben, *Niederländische Volkslieder*, 2d ed., 1856, p. 41.

[2] See Child, I, 25, 26, 30, 49, 485-486, on this incident in various versions.

[3] Book vii, chaps. 22-23, ed. Sommer, I, 247 ff.   The heroine of a Portuguese tale enters the hall of the dead, finds certain pots containing the blood of two sisters marked with their names, puts heads and bodies together, and brings the girls to life with the help of their blood (Coelho, *Contos populares Portuguezes*, 1879, p. 64).

[4] Pitrè, *Novelle popolari Toscane*, pp. 33-39 (see references, pp. 39-40).

[5] Book vii, Chap. 42, Tawney, I, 385.   Cf. p. 49, above.

In a Papuan tale, a man pulled off his head, laid it on the beach, and waded into the sea. " And it came to pass that the man bowed himself, and a multitude of fishes rushed down the man's throat, which was open to the water." Returning to the shore, he replaced his head. A boy was on the watch and told what he had seen. Next day, when the man repeated his performance, one of the villagers removed the head from the beach and threw it into the bush. After crawling about in a vain search for his head, the man rushed into the sea, became a huge fish, and dived out of sight.[1]

An amusing anecdote illustrative of the ease with which savages believe in the possibility of replacing heads, is printed in *The Present State of New-England with Respect to The Indian War*, London, 1676.[2] " All being ready on both sides to fight, Captain *Moseley* plucked off his Periwig, and put it into his Breeches, because it should not hinder him in fighting. As soon as the *Indians* saw that, they fell a Howling and Yelling most hideously, and said, *Umh, Umh, me no stawmerre fight Engis mon, Engis mon get two hed, Engis mon got two hed; if me cut off un hed, he got noder, a put on beder as dis;* with such like words in broken *English*, and away they all fled and could not be overtaken, nor seen any more afterwards." After this one is not surprised to find material that is much to the purpose in the myths and legends of our aborigines.

In a North American Indian story a woman's husband and brother-in-law are detained by a chief and his daughter. After a meal, the chief lies down to sleep. " Wenn er schlief, fiel immer sein Kopf ab." The woman seized it and

---

[1] Annie Ker, *Papuan Fairy Tales*, pp. 94 ff. Professor Dixon gave me the reference.

[2] P. 12. This passage was given me by Mr. Albert Matthews. Most copies, Mr. Matthews notes, bear the date 1675.

anointed the neck with poison. Then the head and the
body could not unite, and the chief died.[1] Similarly, in
another story, in the case of an old woman who is a witch or
demon (her name means Mountain Lioness). She is beheaded while she sleeps, but head and trunk fly together
and join. The hero then decapitates her once more, and lays
magic herbs on the wound, thus preventing a junction.[2] In
a Hupa tale, the heads of the monster called Two-Neck,
when cut off by Coyote, jump on again.[3]

In a queer modern Aztec story, from Salvador,[4] a man's
wife steals away by night to her giant lover. The process is
rather occult. She puts a log in her husband's arms, then
flies up to the beams of the house, and falls headless to the
floor. Her head vanishes through the door. The husband,
who is wide awake, puts hot ashes on the severed neck, with
the result that the head on returning cannot unite with the
trunk. It settles on the husband's shoulder and sticks fast
until he gets rid of it by a trick. A device like that employed by the husband to keep his errant wife's head from
joining her body is used in a Philippine story with good
effect by some sailors to reduce certain vampire-like women
(called *asuangs*) to a *nonplus*. The *asuang* remains behind
with the part of the body that is below the waist — the rest
flies away on devilish errands. Ashes and a shift in the
positions of the trunks are the means used to prevent
reunion.[5]

[1] Boas, *Indianische Sagen von der Nord-Pacifischen Küste Amerikas*,
Berlin, 1895, p. 240 (a Heiltsuk tale).

[2] The same, p. 296 (a Tsimschian tale).

[3] Goddard, *Hupa Texts*, p. 167 (*University of California Publications,
American Archæology and Ethnology*, I).

[4] Hartman, *Journal of American Folk-Lore*, XX, 144–145.

[5] F. Gardner, *Philippine (Tagalog) Superstitions, Journal of American
Folk-Lore*, XIX, 198 (cf. 199).

From the Galela district of the island of Halmahera (Gilolo) in the Moluccas comes an anecdote of a man who took his head with him but left the trunk behind when he went off as a werewolf.[1]

What follows is from a myth of the Sioux: " In a great duel, the Monster struck off the head of Bladder [a hero], and it flew up and into the Divine Presence, where it asked, ' Shall I kill him?' . . . Receiving no reply, it fell upon the neck, where it belonged, and was reunited. Bladder then, in his turn, struck off the head of the Monster, and exactly the same thing occurred as to the head of Bladder. These blows were repeated in turn." . . . The fourth time Bladder received permission, " and while the head of the Monster was in the air, he pushed aside the body. Not falling upon the wonted place, the head of the Monster rebounded and continues to rebound to this day in the form of the sun! " [2]

In a Cheyenne story, a hero with magical powers, as an exploit (" that all the people might know what he could do"), pulled tight a bowstring round his neck while dancing and cut off his own head, which fell to the ground. The trunk continued to dance and the head rolled about and looked at the people. An old woman put head and body together, and he " rose with a smile on his face."[3] This reminds one of those Yakut shamans who " cut off their heads, laid them on the shelf, and danced about the *yurta* without them."[4] In a tale from the Philippines, the head

---

[1] Van Baarda. *Bijdragen tot de Taal-, Land- en Volkenkunde van Neder-landsch-Indië*, XLV, 435. I owe the reference to Professor Dixon.

[2] Meeker, *Siouan Mythological Tales, Journal of American Folk-Lore*, XIV, 162.

[3] Grinnell, *Some Early Cheyenne Tales, Journal of American Folk-Lore*, XXI, 271–272 (another version, XXI, 282–283).

[4] *Journal of the Anthropological Institute*, XXIV, 137.

and trunk of a decapitated girl are put together and she comes to life.[1]

A widespread tale of the North American and Northeast Asiatic aborigines, of which forty-two versions are known to me,[2] offers valuable evidence as to the kind of creature that

[1] Cole, *Traditions of the Tinguian, Field Museum of Natural History, Anthropological Series*, XIV, 157.

[2] (1) Morice, *Three Carrier Myths, Transactions of the Canadian Institute*, V, 4 ff.; (2) Kroeber, *Cheyenne Tales, Journal of American Folk-Lore*, XIII, 184 ff.; (3) Grinnell, *A Cheyenne Obstacle Myth, Journal*, XVI, 108 ff.; (4) Wissler, *Some Dakota Myths, Journal*, XX, 195–196; (5) Voth, *Arapaho Tales*, No. 12, *Journal*, XXV, 48–49; (6) Martha D. Harris, *History and Folklore of the Cowichan Indians*, Victoria, B. C., 1901, pp. 69 ff.; (7) Grinnell, *A Blackfoot Sun and Moon Myth, Journal of American Folk-Lore*, VI, 44 ff. (reproduced with slight changes by Spence, *Myths of the North American Indians*, pp. 205 ff.); (8) Petitot, *Traditions Indiennes du Canada Nord-Ouest*, pp. 407 ff. (Chippewayan); (9) Cree tale, Frank Russell, *Explorations in the Far North*, pp. 202–203; (10) Lowie, *The Assiniboine*, No. 22, *American Museum of Natural History, Anthropological Papers*, IV, 177–178; (11) Skinner, *Northern Saulteaux Tales*, in *Notes on the Eastern Crees and Northern Saulteaux, American Museum, Anthropological Papers*, IX, 168 ff.; (12) Schoolcraft, *The Myth of Hiawatha*, pp. 265 ff.; (13) Cree story, Maclean, *Canadian Savage Folk*, Toronto, 1896, pp. 71–72; (14) Dorsey, *Traditions of the Skidi Pawnee*, pp. 115 ff.; (15) Lowie, *Chipewayan Tales, American Museum of Natural History, Anthropological Papers*, X, 187–188; (16) Simms, *Traditions of the Sarcee Indians, Journal of American Folk-Lore*, XVII, 181–182; (17) Dorsey, *Traditions of the Arikara*, pp. 126–127; (18) Dorsey and Kroeber, *Arapaho Traditions*, No. 94, *Field Columbian Museum, Anthropological Series*, V, 227; (19) Boas, *Indianische Sagen von der Nord-Pacifischen Küste Amerikas*, p. 247; (20) Lowie, *The Assiniboine, American Museum of Natural History, Anthropological Papers*, IV, 178, note; (21) Dorsey, *Traditions of the Caddo*, pp. 66–67; (22) Petitot, *Traditions Indiennes du Canada Nord-Ouest*, pp. 24 ff.; (23) Leland, *Algonquin Legends*, pp. 278 ff.; (24) Teit, *Traditions of the Thompson River Indians of British Columbia*, pp. 83–84; (25) Teit, *The Shuswap*, No. 47, *Publications of the Jesup North Pacific Expedition*, II, 724–726; (26) Teit, *Traditions of the Lillooet Indians of British Columbia*, No. 29, *Journal of American Folk-Lore*, XXV, 334–335; (27) William Jones, *Fox Texts*, pp. 160 ff.; (28) Leland, *Algonquin Legends*, pp. 273–274; (29) Teit, *Traditions of the Lillooet Indians*, No. 30, *Journal of American Folk-Lore*, XXV, 335–336; (30) Bogoras, *Chukchee Mythology, Jesup Expedition*, VIII, 26–27, 28 ff.; (31) Rink, *Eskimoiske Eventyr og*

we are considering. A man suspects his wife of an intrigue and follows her to a lake,[1] where she is joined by a huge serpent (or water-monster) [2] that comes up from the depths. The injured husband cuts off his wife's head,[3] but it remains in full life and pursues her children (the husband in one version) with intent to devour.[4] They retard the

Sagn, 1866, No. 16, pp. 89–90 (No. 11 in the English translation, *Tales and Traditions of the Eskimo*, 1875, pp. 143–144); (32) Boas, *Indianische Sagen von der Nord-Pacifischen Küste Amerikas*, p. 162; (33) the same, pp. 234 ff.; (34) the same, pp. 257 ff.; (35) Farrand, *Traditions of the Chilcotin Indians*, No. 30, *Jesup Expedition*, III, 45 ff.; (36) Boas, *Indianische Sagen*, as above, pp. 281–282; (37) Teit, *The Shuswap*, No. 46, *Jesup Expedition*, II, 724–725; (38) Wissler and Duvall, *Mythology of the Blackfoot Indians, American Museum of Natural History, Anthropological Papers*, II, 154; (39) Will, *No-Tongue, a Mandan Tale, Journal of American Folk-Lore*, XXVI, 331 ff.; (40) Mechling, *Malecite Tales, Geological Survey of Canada, Memoirs*, XLIX, 50 ff.; (41) Stamp, *A Malecite Tale, Journal of American Folk-Lore*, XXVIII, 243 ff.; (42) Hoffman, *The Menomini, 14th Report Bureau of Ethnology*, pp. 174–175.

[1] It is a lake or some body of water in 2, 3, 5, 22–26, 28, 30, 31; a hollow tree or stump or the woods in 1, 4, 6, 7, 8, 9, 10, 11, 15, 16, 17, 20, 21, 27, 40, 41. In 12, 18, 19, 29, 32–36, the lover comes to the house or lodge by night. In 13, 14, 38, 39, there is no lover. 37 is eccentric.

[2] The quality of the paramour is of course different in different versions: — snake(s), 1, 2, 6, 7, 8, 9, 10, 20–23, 28; alligator, 5; water-monster, 3, 24, 25, 30; loon, 26; bear, 4, 16, 17, 18, 27, 40–42; ants, 15; "male being," 31; the man in the moon, 19; a man, 11, 12, 29, 32–37.

[3] In this point the versions differ much. The woman is beheaded in 1, 3, 5, 6, 7, 8, 9, 10, 11, 13, 14, 20, 32, 38; killed otherwise or in some undefined way in 2, 4, 12, 18, 25, 26, 27, 31, 33, 37, 39. She is not killed in 15 (is deserted), 16 (changes to bear), 17 (is beaten), 19, 21 (becomes a snake), 22 (goes into the marsh where the snakes live), 23 (is abandoned and marries the snake), 24 (leaves her husband for a time in shame), 28 (dies from snake venom), 29 (dies after eating of her lover), 30, 34 (is struck with lover's head and abandoned), 35 (like 34), 36, 40–41 (leaves her husband), 42.

[4] The children are thus pursued in 1–7, 9–14; the husband is the purposed quarry in 8 (cf. 38). In 12 the children and perhaps also the husband are pursued. In 38 (which is disordered by the intrusion of *märchen* elements that belong elsewhere) the head follows the husband, but only to serve him; later, however, it pursues and kills an inquisitive boy. There is some kind

chase by the familiar device of magic obstacles,[1] and the head finally falls into a stream and disappears forever.[2] In one version, the woman is repeatedly cut in two, but comes together again.[3] In another, she attacks her husband, on learning of the death of her paramour, but when he succeeds in beheading her after a fierce fight, the head pursues the children and the trunk continues to struggle with the man.[4] In others, the head pursues the children and the trunk the husband.[3] The varieties are almost infinite, as was to be expected. Many versions lack the pursuit by a head, and some have no pursuit at all.[6] Obviously, however, the wife is herself a creature of the Other World, a serpent-woman. There are other savage stories (of a very simple kind) which

of pursuit (though not by a head) or a surrogate in 15–19, 32–36, 40, 41. Every trace of this feature is wanting in 20–31, 37. 39, 42.

[1] So in 1–4, 6, 7, 9–11, 13, 14, 34, 35. In some of the other versions there is a trace of this feature.

[2] The woman eats of her lover unwittingly or drinks his blood in 6, 8, 9, 10, 11, 20, 21, 24, 29, 40, 41. She eats perforce in 4, 27 (cf. 31). The children eat of their mother without knowing it in 2, 3, 5, 14, 39. There is a trace of the wife's eating in 16, 22, 25, 32–35, 42; but nothing of the kind occurs in 1, 7, 12, 13, 15, 17–19, 23, 26, 28, 30, 36–38. In this trait of the husband's serving some portion of the lover to the wife for her eating, the tale coincides remarkably with one of the most celebrated of European stories — represented by Boccaccio's *Guiscardo and Ghismonda* (*Decameron*, iv, 1) and his *Rossiglione and Guardastagno* (iv, 9), by the romance of the *Châtelain de Couci*, by the biography of the troubadour Guillem de Cabestainh, by the luy of *Ignaure*, by the *Herzmäre*, and by many ballads. The same trait is found in North India in the adventures of Rājā Rasālu. The literature has been collected and discussed by Child in his remarks on the English ballad of *Lady Diamond* (No. 269, V, 29 ff., 303); cf. A. d'Ancona, *Studj di Critica e Storia Letteraria*, pp. 326–327. In some versions of the North American tale, the husband disguises himself in his wife's clothing (or imitates her signal) to entrap the lover. This, again, reminds one of a rather large class of European stories, discussed by Schofield, [*Harvard*] *Studies and Notes*, II, 185 ff.

[3] Version 1.

[4] Version 9 (cf. 7).

[5] Versions 6, 7; a trace remains in 15.

[6] See p. 163, note 4.

illustrate this tale, though they are not versions of it.[1] It is very common for denizens of the Other World to be regarded as ophidian, or for mortals under enchantment, their continual substitutes in *märchen* and romance, to appear in serpent form.[2]

The full strength of the occult quality that we are discussing, enables the head to fly back to the neck, or equips the giant with power to pick it up and replace it. In either case, the head grows on again spontaneously. Sometimes, however, assistance is necessary to replace the head,[3] and now and then the scientific spirit has added the requirement of anointing with magic balm, as in the ballad of *Halewijn* and in Malory's story of Lynet's knight with the axe.[4]

Miracle may of course take the place of magic or medicine, and it is not difficult to collect accounts of decapitated men or women who have thus been brought to life. A few instances will suffice, and these we may take from Celtic tradition — first from the lives of the Irish saints.

Three men had been beheaded by highwaymen on the road by which St. Aed was journeying. The robbers found

[1] Goddard, *Kato Texts, University of California, Publications in American Archæology and Ethnology*, V, 175-177, 234-235; Dixon, *Maidu Texts*, No. 13, pp. 196 ff.; Boas, *Kathlamet Texts*, pp. 225 ff.; Rink, *Eskimoiske Eventyr og Sagn*, No. 29, pp. 121-123; Jacottet, *Étude sur les Langues du Haut-Zambèze*, No. 22, *Publications de l'École des Lettres d'Alger, Bulletin de Correspondence Africaine*, Vol. XVI, Part ii, pp. 78-80. Cf. also Dorsey and Kroeber, *Arapaho Traditions*, No. 77, *Field Columbian Museum, Anthropological Series*, V, 147 ff.; Wissler and Duvall, *Mythology of the Blackfoot Indians, American Museum of Natural History, Anthropological Papers*, II, 150-151; Roth, *Animism and Folk-Lore of the Guiana Indians, 30th Report of the Bureau of American Ethnology*, pp. 204, 246 ff., 378.

[2] Mélusine, Rè Serpente, Kong Lindorm, the lady of Sinadoun in *Li Biaus*, and the damsel in the ballad of *Kemp Owyne* are celebrated instances. See Child, *Ballads*, I, 306 ff.; Schofield, *Studies on the Libeaus Desconus* 1895; Olrik, *Danske Studier*, I, 1 ff.

[3] Pp. 153 ff., 158, 161-162.   [4] Pp. 157-158.

themselves unable to move from the spot until the saint
came up, and his reproofs brought them to penitence. Then
he put heads and bodies together and called upon the murdered victims to rise in the name of the Lord Jesus Christ.
" Vnde ad verbum episcopi illi surrexerunt leti et sani,
benedicentes Christum et suum pontificem." [1]   In like
manner St. Buite recalled to life a young man who had been
decapitated by the order of an Irish chief.[2]   According to a
legend in the *Book of Hy-Many*, Cairbre Cromm, chief of the
Hy-Many in Connacht, was killed at Daire-Chonaidh
(Derryconny), and his head was left on a green flagstone in
the middle of the causeway of Cluain Boirenn. St. Ciaran,
on hearing of Cairbre's death, visited the place where the
head was, and took it away from a demon, whom he found
beside it. " Then the body and the head were carried to
Cluain [Clonmacnoise], and the head was placed on the
body. After this the pillow of Kieran was brought [and
placed] under the head, and the head adhered to the body
at the word of Kieran, and then Coirpre was resuscitated
from the dead, but there was a twist in his neck from that
forth, from which the surname of Crom clung to him ever
after." [3]

St. Cadoc of Wales is credited with a very impressive
miracle of this order. An Irish carpenter whom he has
employed in the erection of an oratory, is murdered by the
other workmen, who are envious of his marked superiority.
They cut off his head, tie a huge stone to his body, and sink
him in a pond. The Irishman's children weep for their
missing father and rouse St. Cadoc's compassion. He sus-

---

[1] *Vita Sancti Aedi*, cap. 12, Plummer, *Vitae Sanctorum Hiberniae*, I, 38.

[2] *Vita Sancti Boecii*, cap. 16, Plummer, I, 91–92.

[3] *Journal of the Kilkenny and South-East of Ireland Archæological Society*,
New Series, 1856–1857, I, 453, note 2 (text and translation).   I owe this
reference to Professor Cross.

pects the criminals and interrogates them sharply, but they protest that they do not know what has become of the carpenter. Then the saint calls together his clerics, and spends the night with them in prayer that the truth may be revealed. Next morning, when the orisons are finished, "ecce repente decollatus artifex caput in sinu suo gestans, magnumque lapidem super tergum ferens, madidusque cruentus truci horridaque specie, venerabili viro suisque discipulis apparuit." The head speaks: "Servant of God, put me back on my neck, and I will tell you everything you do not know about this matter." It is done, and the truth made known. Cadoc gives the carpenter his choice, to live on in this world or to die at once and inherit eternal life. He replies: "Let my soul return to everlasting rest" and breathes his last while yet speaking the words.[1]

St. Winifred was brought to life by St. Beuno. A savage young gentleman of Wales, who was persecuting her with his attentions, cut off her head at the chapel door. "Then Beuno returned to the corpse, and fitted the head which had been projected inside by the stroke of the sword, to the body which lay outside, and earnestly besought God to revive the body, lest the enemy should rejoice over it. And on the prayer, the body with its powers resumed the soul, without any scar appearing except a small scar on the neck; but the floor infected with her blood cracked, and a fountain sprang up in a torrent at the place, and the stones appear bloody at present as they did at first, and the moss smells as frankincense, and it cures divers diseases." [2] Another miracle of a similar nature is related of this same St. Beuno.[3]

---

[1] *Vita Sancti Cadoci*, cap. 17, Rees, *Lives of the Cambro British Saints*, Llandovery, 1853, pp. 46–47.

[2] *Life of St. Beuno*, Rees, as above, pp. 301, 518–519.

[3] The same, pp. 306–307.

A famous miracle of St. Éloi appears in an Irish folk-tale in a form that brings it within our scope. The daughter of the King of Leinster is afflicted with a malady that has twisted her head completely round. A young fellow cuts it off with due care and replaces it in a proper position. No blood flows and the princess becomes the most beautiful of women. A smith tries the same treatment on the King of Ulster's daughter but in vain, and he is in despair until the young fellow appears and finishes the cure.[1] The tale is an amusing variety of that known in English from the poem of *The Smyth whych that Forged him a New Dame*.[2]

In the materials thus far collected, we have seen super-natural beings in considerable variety (dragons, snake-women, giants, hags, rakshasas, wizards) whose heads come on again (or may be replaced) after they are cut off. The belief in this strange power is so widespread that it may put in a claim to universality. If we disregard miracles, the examples cited come from Ireland, Scotland, England, the Færöe Islands, Brittany, Holland, Germany, Hungary, Greece, Italy, Russia, India, the Philippines, Papua, the Moluccas, and many tribes of the North American aborig-ines, from the Far North to the Aztecs of Salvador.

Another conception is closely connected with this belief. It is that which allows the severed head of a man or monster to retain its life, or the trunk to go on acting though the head is off. Every conceivable variation on this theme is found in popular story, and only specimens are here presented. We may begin as before, with Celtic material, since the Green Knight has a well-established Irish pedigree.

[1] Marstrander, *Deux Contes Irlandais, Miscellany Presented to Kuno Meyer*, 1912, pp. 374 ff. (with a rich collection of European variants and a careful study of the cycle).

[2] Halliwell, *Contributions to Early English Literature* [No. 3]; Hazlitt,

A wild tale of attempted posthumous vengeance is contained in a very old Irish saga, *The Siege of Howth*,[1] which is mentioned in a poem [2] of the tenth century. Conall overcomes Mesgegra, King of Leinster, after a hard struggle. " ' I perceive that thou wilt not go, O Conall,' said Mesgegra, ' till thou takest my head with thee. Put thou my head above thy head and add my glory to thy glory.' " " Then Conall severed his head from him . . . and Conall took the head and put it on the flagstone on the ford's brink. A drop fell from the back of the head and went through the stone into the ground. Then he put Mesgegra's head on the stone, and it moved from the top of the stone to the ground, and moved on before him to the river." [3] Afterward the head shows its agitation by blushing and growing white.[4] The command " Put thou my head above thy head and add my glory to thy glory " is so oracular that there seems to be no reason why Conall should not have obeyed it. In other words, the story, as preserved in the *Book of Leinster*, is not quite intelligible. In a folk-tale, however, taken down within the last few years, the same incident is preserved in a thoroughly intelligible form — good evidence of the unwisdom of disregarding oral tradition. In *Balor on Tory Island*, Balor, whose grandson had overcome him, " called to the grandson and said, ' Come near now. Take the head off me and place it above your own head a few moments. *You will know everything in the world, and no one will be able to conquer you.*' Lui took the

Remains of the Early Popular Poetry of England, III, 200 ff.; Horstmann, *Altenglische Legenden*, Neue Folge, pp. 322 ff.

[1] *Book of Leinster*, 114*b*–117*a* of facsimile; edited and translated by Stokes, *Revue Celtique*, VIII, 47–64; revised translation in Hull, *Cuchullin Saga*, pp. 87–94; Thurneysen, *Sagen aus dem alten Irland*, p. 68.

[2] By Cinaed hua Artacain, who died in 975.

[3] Hull, p. 92.   [4] Hull, p. 94.

head off his grandfather, and instead of putting it on his own
head, he put it on a rock. The next moment a drop came
out of the head, made a thousand pieces of the rock, and
dug a hole in the earth three times deeper than Loch
Foyle." [1]

The rolling of Mesgegra's head reminds one of the act of
the head of a hag in a Tunisian story, which, when the hero
has cut it off, guides him to the well by means of which he
descends into the other world.[2] The head of Ghâzi Miyân,
who is " claimed as one of the first martyrs of Islâm in
India," and who was killed in battle, " kept rolling on the
ground long after it was severed from the trunk." [3]

An exceedingly curious instance of a head surviving its
body occurs in *Kil Arthur*, a somewhat conglomerate Irish
folk-tale.[4] Kil Arthur had cut off a certain giant's head with
the monster's own sword. He then carried the head " till he
came to a house. He went in and put the head on a table;
but that instant it disappeared, — went away of itself.
Food and drink of every kind came on the table. When Kil
Arthur had eaten and the table was cleared by some invisi-

[1] Curtin, *Hero-Tales of Ireland*, p. 294. The same story was taken down
from recitation by O'Donovan in 1835 and published in his *Four Masters*,
I, 18–21.

[2] Stumme, *Tunisische Märchen u. Gedichte*, II, 7. On the type to which
this story belongs, see Cosquin, *Contes populaires de Lorraine*, No. 1, I, 1 ff.,
and notes. The guiding head does not occur in any other version of the
märchen so far as I know. It may be compared with the ball that rolls to
guide the hero in many popular tales (see, for example, Curtin, *Myths and
Folk-Tales of the Russians*, etc., pp. 2, 77, 99, 190; Hyde, *Beside the Fire*,
p. 131; A. Seidel, *Geschichten u. Lieder der Afrikaner*, p. 32; *Folk-Lore
Record*, II, 186; Hull, *Cuchullin Saga*, p. 74; Spitta Bey, *Contes Arabes
modernes*, p. 17; S. O. Addy, *Household Tales*, p. 52; Curtin, *Myths and
Folk-Lore of Ireland*, pp. 35, 37; *Journal of American Folk-Lore*, XV, 216).

[3] Crooke, *Popular Religion and Folklore of Northern India*, Allahabad,
1894, pp. 131–132 (new ed., Westminster, 1896, I, 208).

[4] Curtin, *Myths and Folk-Lore of Ireland*, pp. 182–183.

ble power, the giant's head bounded on to the table, and with it a pack of cards." The head and Kil Arthur have a game; the head cheats. Kil Arthur showed the head how it had taken five points wrongfully. " Then the head sprang at him, struck and beat him till he seized and hurled it into the fire." [1] With this head which is so truculent we may compare that of Cathead in a story which is interesting in connection with the very old story of Arthur's Fight with the Cat. It is in Curtin's *Birth of Fin MacCumhail*.[2] Fin has already killed two of the hag's sons. She sent " her eldest son, who had not been out of the house for years (It was only in case of the greatest need that she sent him. He had a cat's head, and was called Pus au Chuine, ' Puss of the Corner'; he was the eldest and strongest of all the brothers)" to see why the two delayed. Fin was helped by his dog Bran; " but at length Cat-head fastened his teeth into Fin's breast, biting and gnawing till Fin cut the head off. The body fell to the ground, but the head lived, gnawing as terribly as before " and he " could neither kill nor pull it off." The hag's blood finally released Fin. He beheaded her, after a terrific fight, " caught some of her blood, and rubbed it around Cat-head, who fell off dead." [3]

[1] *Kil Arthur* is a version of the tale called by J. F. Campbell, *The Daughter of King Underwaves* (*Popular Tales of the West Highlands*, III, 403 ff.), much contaminated with other stories and somewhat confused and decayed. The hag-transformation (parallel to Chaucer's *Wife of Bath's Tale*) which forms the introduction in Campbell's version and serves merely as a device to bring together Diarmaid and his fairy-bride, is not in Curtin and is no original part of the story (see Maynadier, *The Wife of Bath's Tale*, pp. 33-34).

[2] *Myths and Folk-Lore of Ireland*, pp. 216 ff. For Carpre (Cairbre) Cathead see *Irische Texte*, 3d Ser., pp. 188, 206, 384-385, 422. Cf. *Revue Celtique*, XX, 335 ff.

[3] This loosening of the head by means of blood may be compared with the loosening from magic seats by blood: J. F. Campbell, *Popular Tales of the West Highlands*, II, 178-179; see also Joyce, *Old Celtic Romances*, pp.

The West Irish tale of *The Ghost and his Wives* [1] has some resemblance, in parts, to *Kil Arthur*. It is in essence the story of a man who is carried to the other world to learn how acceptable hospitality to the poor is to God. The " ghost " has three wives,[2] who are condignly treated in the other world in accordance with the kinds of meals which they gave to the poor in *this*. But the introduction to the story, which brings the man and the " ghost " into acquaintance, shows a singular confusion. A man, coming from a funeral, finds, as he is passing the churchyard, a man's head (it is not called a skull) in the road; he picks it up and deposits it in the churchyard. Farther along on the same road he meets " the appearance of a gentleman." The gentleman tells him it was *his* head, and adds " If you did anything out of the way to it, assuredly I would be even with you." " How did

195, 216; J. G. Campbell, *The Fians*, p. 74; Curtin, *Myths and Folk-Lore of Ireland*, pp. 230, 302, cf. 290; Macdougall, *Folk and Hero Tales*, p. 58. Compare the efficacy of the blood of the slain Eocho Glas in the shorter *Fled Bricrend* (*Yellow Book of Lecan*), *Irische Texte*, Series II, Heft I, pp. 184, 206.

[1] Larminie, *West Irish Folk-Tales*, pp. 31 ff.

[2] We have here a good example of how folk-lore behaves. The *Ghost and his Wives* shows at least five different *motifs* (found separately elsewhere) twisted together to form the introduction to an exemplary anecdote: (1) the man who invites a skull to dine with him; (2) the stealing of a skull or shroud or the like, which the dead owner comes to reclaim; (3) creatures that play fast and loose with their heads; (4) the thankful dead; (5) match with a supernatural being (" playing cards with the devil "). For (1) see, for example, J. W. Wolf, *Deutsche Märchen und Sagen*, p. 225; Müller, *Siebenbürgische Sagen*, No. 57, pp. 138 ff.; Reiser, *Sagen des Allgäus*, I, 414; *Annales de Bretagne*, XIV, 163–165; Le Braz, *La Légende de la Mort en Basse-Bretagne*, pp. 71 ff. (3d ed., I, 123 ff.); Dottin's note in Le Braz, 3d ed., I, 288–289, etc. For (2) see Wolf, as above, pp. 238–239; Luzel, *Légendes chrétiennes de la Basse Bretagne*, II, 155 ff.; Ralston, *Russian Folk-Tales*, pp. 307 ff., etc. For (4) see Gerould, *The Grateful Dead*, 1908. For (5) see pp. 196 ff., below. There is an extravagantly truculent death's head in a queer little tale in Cosquin, *Contes populaires de Lorraine*, No. 57, II, 174.

you lose your head ? " " I did not lose it at all, but I left it
in the place where you found it to see what you would do
with it." " I believe you are a good person (i.e., a fairy)."
The man invites him home to dinner, and after dinner the
stranger suggests a game of cards. But nothing comes of
the game.

In a Japanese saga, Yorimitsu beheads the monster
Shudenôji; but the monster's head flies up and bites at him.
He succeeds, however in killing Shudenôji at last.[1] In a Tinguian tale from the Philippines, a man beheads his wife's
lover. The head springs up and attaches itself to the
woman's breast, but later she is relieved of it.[2]

In an Indian story from Canada, the hero's enemies
torture him and cut off his head; but it survives and pursues them. They throw it into the fire, but fire will not
consume it. Finally they grind it to powder, and even then
it does not die, but changes into a cloud of mosquitoes.[3] In
a Modoc tale the head of Ndúkis is cut off by one of the
five Blaiwas brothers, who flies toward heaven with it; but
one of the two sisters of the slayer, breaking his prohibition,
looks up, and the head falls to the ground, flies at the other
four Blaiwas brothers, and kills them all. The head then
becomes the husband of the two sisters. Finally it is killed
by the surviving brother by the heat of the sweat-house.
When the house is opened, a fine young man is found there,
lifeless, instead of the head (disenchantment ?).[4] We have

[1] Mitford, *Tales of Old Japan*, 1871, I, 153 (1890, p. 153). For other
versions see Iwaya's *Fairy Tales of Old Japan, The Goblin Mountain*, Tokyo,
1903, pp. 37–38; Ozaki, *Warriors of Old Japan*, pp. 129–130; F. Hadland
Davis, *Myths and Legends of Japan*, p. 47. Cf. F. York Powell, *An English
Miscellany presented to Dr. Furnivall*, pp. 395–396.

[2] Cole, *Traditions of the Tinguian*, pp. 78–80 (*Field Museum of Natural
History*, Publication 180, *Anthropological Series*, Vol. XIV).

[3] Petitot, *Traditions Indiennes du Canada Nord-Ouest*, p. 405 (cf. p. 410).

[4] Curtin, *Myths of the Modocs*, pp. 189 ff.

already studied the North American story of the pursuit of
a man or his children by a severed head.[1]

Some Australian aborigines think it essential to destroy
the bones, and especially the skulls, of their enemies.
Otherwise the victims will come to life and follow those who
have killed and eaten them. One of their traditions tells of
two Lizard Men, brothers. The younger searched for the
elder, who had been slain, and found his head. He spoke to
it, and the man instantly came to life.[2]

In a story from Papua a husband mourns at his wife's
grave, with the result that her skull comes to the surface and
remarks, " You love me. I will follow you." [3] It is a skull
by day but a woman by night.[4] The tale seems to illustrate
the common belief that extravagant mourning disturbs the
repose of the dead.[5]

Horsemen that carry their heads on their saddle-bows and
ghosts that bear their heads in their hands are known the
world over. A great number of instances from Northern
India have been collected by Major Temple.[6] Everybody
will remember the Headless Horseman of Sleepy Hollow as
well as the ghost of young Hamilton Tighe in the *Ingoldsby
Legends*. Lund,[7] who has peculiar views about heathendom

[1] Pp. 162 ff.

[2] Spencer and Gillen, *Native Tribes of Central Australia*, pp. 475, 390.

[3] Van Hasselt, *Bijdragen tot Taal-, Land- en Volkenkunde van Neder-
landsch-Indië*. LXI, 492–493. I owe the reference to Professor Dixon.

[4] Cf. Maynadier, *The Wife of Bath's Tale*, pp. 201 ff.

[5] See Child, *Ballads*, II, 228, 234 ff., 512–513; III, 512–513; V, 62–63,
294–295.

[6] In a remarkable article entitled *Folklore of the Headless Horseman in
Northern India*, in the *Calcutta Review*, LXXVII, 158–183. See also Crooke,
Popular Religion and Folklore of Northern India, Allahabad, 1894, pp. 159–
160 (new ed., Westminster, 1896, I, 256–258). European examples might be
collected in endless numbers: see, for instance, J. W. Wolf, *Deutsche Märchen
u. Sagen*, pp. 315–316, 516–517.

[7] *Tolv Fragmenter om Hedenskabet*, I, 67.

and apparitions, is bold enough to recognize a man with his head in his hand on a Scottish sculptured stone reproduced by Stuart.[1]

Many East Indian worthies fought valiantly after their heads were off.[2] So did Starkaðr in the Elder Edda.[3] In a late Icelandic saga, an uncanny woman, Hólmgríðr, acts a familiar part in bringing certain giants to life, " og börðust höfuðlausir." [4] Klaufi, the terrific *revenant* in the *Svarfdœlasaga*, uses his own head as a club.[5] Fawdoun, in the *Wallace*, is almost as terrific as Klaufi, and quite as corporeal. Wallace has struck off his head " in ire " because he lagged behind. That night Wallace with a troop of thirteen takes lodging in Gask Hall. They hear a great din of hornblowing, and he sends his followers out, in relays, to see what it means, but none come back, and he is left alone. Then he goes to the door himself, and there stands Fawdoun, his head in his hand. He throws the head at Wallace, but he catches it by the hair and throws it back. Wallace runs up through the Hall " to a close stair," breaks the boards, and leaps " fifteen foot large out of that inn." As he flees, he looks back and sees that Fawdoun has set the Hall afire, or so it looks. The author thinks the apparition

[1] J. Stuart, *Sculptured Stones of Scotland*, I, plate 29.

[2] Temple, *Calcutta Review*, LXXVII, 158 ff.; Crooke, *Popular Religion and Folklore of Northern India*, 1894, p. 157 (1896, I, 217).

[3] *Helgakviða Hundingsbana* II, st. 27 (19), Bugge, *Norrœn Fornkvœði*, p. 196. Saxo Grammaticus says that the head of Starcatherus " corpori auulsum impactumque terre glebam morsu carpsisse fertur, ferocitatem animi moribundi oris atrocitate declarans " (book viii, p. 406, Müller and Velschow). A cannibal in Teit's *Traditions of the Thompson River Indians of British Columbia* goes on wrestling after he is decapitated (p. 81), and an old *diablesse* in Hungary continues to act her part in a similar condition (Klimo, *Contes et Légendes de Hongrie*, p. 292).

[4] *Saga af Fertram og Plato*, as quoted by Jiriczek, *Zeitschrift für deutsche Philologie*, XXVI, 23.

[5] *Svarfdœla Saga*, chap. 19 (*Íslendinga Sögur*, 1830, II, 164).

was the devil, but leaves that question to clerks.[1] O'Kearney remarks, "We have our stories about Colan gan cheann, and more than this it has come down to our own time." [2] The story of the man who lost his head for perjury and lived seven years without it is in the *Book of Leinster* [3] and elsewhere.[4]

The legends are innumerable of saints who rise immediately after their martyrdom and carry their heads in their hands, often to the spot where they wish to be buried. St. Denis is perhaps the most famous of this class. He bore his head two miles before he reached his burial place.[5] Other head-carrying saints in sacred legend or popular tradition are St. Savinian,[6] St. Proculus of Bologna,[7] St. Januarius,[8] St. Osith,[9] St. Sidwell (Sativola),[10] the Welsh St. Decuman,[11]

---

[1] *Wallace*, Book v, vv. 103 ff.

[2] *The Festivities at the House of Conan*, Ossianic Society, II, 147, note. Cf. J. F. Campbell, *Popular Tales of the West Highlands*, II, 89–91; J. G. Campbell, *Witchcraft and Second Sight in the Highlands and Islands of Scotland*, pp. 191–194; Douglas Hyde, *The Lad of the Ferule*, pp. 106–107.

[3] O'Grady, *Silva Gadelica*, I, 416 (translation, II, 453).

[4] See O'Grady, *Silva Gadelica*, I, 74 (II, 78); II, xix, 548; *Mirabilia* in the Appendix to Todd's edition of the Irish Nennius, pp. 206–207 (and note); Wright and Halliwell, *Reliquiae Antiquae*, II, 105; Four Masters, ad ann. 539 (ed. O'Conor, p. 151).

[5] Hilduin, *Vita Sancti Dionysii*, cap. 32 (Migne, CVI, 47). Cf. *Acta Sanctorum*, October, IV, 794; *Vie et Histoire de Saint Denys*, ed. Omont, p. 10, plate XVI; *Légende de Saint Denis*, ed. Henry Martin, pp. 59–60, plates LXVII–LXIX. D'Arbois de Jubainville (*Revue Celtique*, XII, 167–168) compares St. Denis with Uath in *Fled Bricrend* (see pp. 17 ff., above); see also his *Cours de la Littérature Celtique*, V, 147.

[6] *Acta Sanctorum*, January, II, 943; A. Socard, *Livres Populaires imprimés à Troyes de 1600 à 1800* (Paris, 1864), p. 39.

[7] Keysler's *Travels*, English translation, 1757, III, 119; Kornmann, *De Miraculis Mortuorum*, Pt. iv, chap. 11 (*Opera Curiosa*, 1694, p. 104).

[8] See the plate in B. Croce, *Pulcinella*, pp. 54–56.

[9] Stanton, *Menology of England and Wales*, 1887, pp. 477–478; Bond, *Dedications and Patron Saints of English Churches*, 1914, pp. 126–127, 326.

[10] Bond, as above, pp. 126, 127, 328.   [11] *Acta Sanctorúm*, August, VI, 24.

St. Aude and St. Noyale in Brittany.¹ Father Cahier has collected about eighty examples.² It is a good conjecture that many of these legends arose from images of saints holding their heads as a sign of the manner of their martyrdom.

Whether or not a severed head can speak is briefly discussed by Aristotle in the *De Partibus Animalium*. He tells a good Carian story of a priest's head that was said to have denounced his murderer. But he rationally objects that speech is impossible when the windpipe is cut and there can be no notion communicated to the vocal organs from the lungs. He admits, however, that there is nothing unreasonable in the idea that the trunk may move forward a little, even after the head is off.³

However, heads that speak have been a well-attested phenomena in Ireland for more than a thousand years. In one of the oldest saga-texts ⁴ that we have, *The Destruction of Da Derga's Hostel*,⁵ Conaire Mór is besieged in his palace by a troop of Irish and British pirates led by the one-eyed Ingcel, son of the British king. MacCecht forces his way through the besiegers and brings water to Conaire. On his return, he finds two foemen in the act of striking off the dead king's head. He kills them both, and pours the water into Conaire's neck, whereupon the severed head speaks a little poem in praise of MacCecht.⁶

¹ Baring-Gould and Fisher, *Lives of the British Saints*, I, 186; IV, 10–11.
² *Caractéristiques des Saintes dans l'Art Populaire*, II, 761 ff.; cf. *Acta Sanctorum*, October, VII, 819.
³ iii, 10, 9–12.   ⁴ Zimmer, Haupt's *Zeitschrift*, XXXV, 13.
⁵ Edited and translated by Stokes, *Revue Celtique*, XXII, 9 ff., 165 ff., 282 ff., 390 ff. For analysis and discussion, see Zimmer, Kuhn's *Zeitschrift*, XXVIII, 554 ff.; see also Nettlau, *On the Irish Text* Togail Bruidne Da Derga *and Connected Stories*, *Revue Celtique*, XII, 229 ff., 444 ff.; XIII, 252 ff.; XIV, 137 ff.
⁶ *Revue Celtique*, XXII, 321–323; Kuhn's *Zeitschrift*, XXVIII, 562.

Another very old Irish story of a speaking head is preserved in Cormac's *Glossary*. Cormac fell in 903, and the best authorities regard the passage in question as belonging to the oldest portion of the text.[1] Finn's fool Lomna Drūth reveals an intrigue between Coirpre and one of Finn's concubines. Coirpre, at the woman's instance, slays the fool and carries off his head. " Finn goes upon the track of the soldiers [Coirpre and his men] and found Coirpre in an empty house cooking fish, . . . and Lomna's head was on a spike by the fire." The head speaks twice. " ' Put out the head,' says Coirpre." Then it speaks a third time "from outside." What prompted these speeches, it seems, was Coirpre's neglect to give the head even a morsel of the fish.[2] With the anecdote of Lomna should be compared an Irish fragment on the Death of Finn in Egerton MS. 92,[3] in which Finn's head speaks when his beheaders are eating by the fire.

A splendid epic story is that of the warning of Sualtaim, Cuchulinn's father. He has ridden to Emain Macha to summon the Ulstermen to protect their land against the raid of Ailill and Medb. He receives no good answer, and as he rides away in fury, his horse caracoling brings the sharp edge of the shield against Sualtaim's neck and takes off his head, which falls into the hollow of the shield. The horse returns to Emain on the gallop, with the head on the shield and the shield upon his back, and the head again shouts the words of warning: " Men are slain, women are carried captive, kine are driven away." This time his summons is heeded.[4]

---

[1] Zimmer, Haupt's *Zeitschrift*, XXXV, 37–38; Stokes, in Nutt's note to MacInnes, *Folk and Hero Tales*, p. 407.

[2] Stokes, *Three Irish Glossaries*, pp. 34–35; *Cormac's Glossary*, translated by O'Donovan, edited by Stokes, 1868, pp. 130–131.

[3] Edited by Kuno Meyer, *Zeitschrift für celtische Philologie*, I, 462–465.

[4] *Tāin Bō Cuailgne, Book of Leinster*, pp. 93a–94a; translated by Zimmer,

The severed head of Fothad sang a song — which is preserved — to the woman with whom he had a tryst. She had recovered the head and brought it to the grave. " Hush woman, do not speak to me! " [1] Donnbo, a famous harper and story-teller, had promised Fergal, the night before a battle, to entertain the company next day. He is killed in the fight, but his head redeems the promise. There is much conversation between the head and a young warrior. The head is placed upon a pillar and sings a most piteous lay. Later the same young warrior took the head to the body and " fixed it on the neck." [2] With this incident Kuno Meyer [3] compares one of the " wonders of Ireland," — the skull of a merry man, which, being dug up many years after his death and laid on a high stone in the churchyard, makes everybody laugh who sees the place where the mouth and tongue used to be. This particular " wonder " (which reminds one whimsically of Yorick) is not mentioned among the Irish *mirabilia* in Todd's edition of Nennius,[4] nor does it occur in the list given by Giraldus Cambrensis,[5] but it is No. 20 in the Old Norse *Speculum Regale*.[6]

Stokes [7] sees some resemblance between Donnbo's head and that of Bendigeit Vran in the mabinogi of *Branwen*

Kuhn's Zeitschrift, XXVIII, 470; by O'Grady, in Hull, *Cuchullin Saga*, pp. 204–205; ed. Windisch, chap. 24, pp. 666–667.

[1] *Reicne Fothaid Canainne*, ed. by Kuno Meyer, *Fianaigecht*, p. 8 (Todd Lecture Series, XVI). A skull sings in one of Boas's *Kwakiutl Tales*. It is the head of a woman, and its song is very pretty and pathetic (*Columbia University, Contributions to Anthropology*, II, 106–107).

[2] O'Donovan, *Annals of Ireland, Three Fragments*, pp. 33 ff. (Irish Archæological and Celtic Society).

[3] *Folk-Lore*, V, 314.   [4] Pp. 192–219.

[5] *Topographia Hibernica*, book ii.

[6] Christiania, 1848, cap. 11, p. 28; ed. Brenner, 1881, p. 45; Kuno Meyer, *Folk-Lore*, V, 313–314, and *Ériu*, III, 13–14. Cf. Thurneysen, *Zeitschrift für celtische Philologie*, I, 168.

[7] *Revue Celtique*, V, 232.

Daughter of Llyr. There is not much similarity, but the Welsh tale deserves a place in our register. Bran bids his followers cut off his head, carry it to the White Hill at London (*Llundein*), and bury it there with the face toward France. They will be a long time *en route*, he predicts. At Harlech they will remain at table seven years, and his head will be as agreeable company for them as it ever was when it was on his shoulders. At Gwales they will spend eighty years. All these predictions come to pass. While the charm is on them, they are happy, oblivious of fatigue and of the lapse of time. At last they reached London and buried the head. So long as it remained buried, no invading host could enter the island. Its subsequent disinterment was a great stroke of misfortune.[1]

Instances of speaking heads in modern Irish folk-lore have already been cited.[2] One, like the Green Knight's, enjoins upon the hero a perilous expedition.[3]

There is a talking death's head in the lost Gawain story tantalizingly outlined by Pierre Bersuire.[4] " Quid dicam de

[1] Loth, *Les Mabinogion*, I, 90 ff. (2d ed., I, 145 ff.; cf. pp. 120, note, 239 ff.); Lady Guest, *Mabinogion*, III, 124 ff. For the Welsh text see Rhŷs and Evans, *Red Book of Hergest*, I, 40 ff. See also Rhŷs, *Hibbert Lectures*, pp. 96 ff., *Arthurian Legend*, pp. 253–261, 394; Anwyl, *Zeitschrift für Celtische Philologie*, I, 286–287; A. Reinach, *Revue Celtique*, XXXIV, 50 ff. Nutt, in *Folk-Lore Record*, V, 14, cites two excellent Irish cases of the burial of a body with its face to the foe as a defensive charm (O'Donovan, *Four Masters*, I, 145, 180). The burial of Bran's head reminds one of Guortemir's wish to be interred on the shore of the port from which the barbarians had sailed away (Nennius, cap. 47, *Monumenta Hist. Brit.*, p. 69). Liebrecht compares with Bran's head that of Tolus (*Zur Volkskunde*, pp. 289–290). A magic wooden head protects a fortress in Grey, *Polynesian Mythology*, pp. 279 ff. Cf. Dorsey, *The Pawnee, Mythology*, p. 494.

[2] Pp. 149–150.

[3] Curtin, *Hero-Tales of Ireland*, p. 497.

[4] *Reductorium Morale*, Prol. to book xiv, *Opera Omnia*, ed. 1631, II, 901. The passage is quoted, in English, by Madden, *Syr Gawayne*, p. xxxii. There is some resemblance between this and Curtin's *Kil Arthur* (see p. 171,

mirabilibus quae in historijs Galuagni, & Arcturi ponuntur, quorum vnum de omnibus recito, scilicet de palatio quod Galuagnus sub aquam casu raptus reperit, vbi mēsam refertam epulis, & sedem positam inuenit, ostium vero per quod exire valeret, non vidit, qui cum famesceret & comedere vellet, statim caput hominis mortui positum in lance affuit,[1] & gigas in feretro iuxta ignem iacuit, giganteque surgente, & palatium capite concutiente, capite vero clamante, & cibos interdicente, nunquam de cibis comedere ausus fuit, qui post multa miracula exijt, sed nesciuit qualiter exiuit."

With the talking heads in Irish story may be compared the oracular head of Mímir in the *Ynglingasaga*,[2] the oracular human heads of the Harrânians[3] and of various East Indian savage tribes,[4] and the mediæval conception of the Hebrew teraphim.[5] There is a wild tale of one Joseph, an

---

above). It also reminds one slightly of *The Turk and Gawain* and more strikingly of *Finn and the Phantoms*, *Revue Celtique*, XIII, 14. Bersuire's fifteenth book, *De Fabulis Poetarum*, where (if anywhere) one would expect him to give the whole story, is preserved, but has never been printed. It is in the main an allegorical commentary on Ovid's *Metamorphoses*. See Hauréau, *Mem. de l'Institut, Acad. des Inscriptions et Belles-Lettres*, XXX, ii, 48 ff. Dr. A. C. L. Brown has examined the manuscript, and tells me that it contains nothing that in any way resembles the lost tale of Gawain and no mention of Gawain or any other knight of the Round Table.

[1] On the death's head in the plate, cf. J. Prätorius, *Anthropodemus Plutonicus*, Pt. I, ch. 8, p. 360 (1666).

[2] Chaps. 4, 7; *Völuspá*, st. 46 (Bugge, *Norrœn Fornkvæði*, p. 8). Cf. Chantepie de la Saussaye, *Religion of the Teutons*, translated by Vos, p. 232; Kahle, *Zeitschrift des Vereins für Volkskunde*, XVI, 415–417.

[3] Chwolson, *Die Ssabier und der Ssabismus*, II, 19 ff., 148 ff.

[4] Alfred C. Haddon, *Head-Hunters, Black, White, and Brown*, pp. 91–92, 182–183; Dall, *Third Report of the Bureau of Ethnology*, pp. 94 ff.

[5] Kircher, *Oedipus Aegyptiacus*, I, 260 ff. (1652); Chwolson, II, 148 ff.; Liebrecht, *Zur Volkskunde*, p. 290; *Am Ur-Quell*, Neue Folge, V, 92–93, 117 ff.; Bodin, *De la Demonomanie des Sorciers*, ii, 3 (Paris, 1580, fol. 72 r°; 1587, fol. 78 v°); Wier, *De Lamiis*, ii, 15, Basel, 1582, col. 211; John Weemse,

English Hospitaller at Acre during the Crusades, who desired to know what was happening at home. A young man who had learned magic of the Saracens went down to the seashore, dug up a death's head, " et facta aliquamdiu incantatione sua iussit idem loqui." The skull was a Saracen's who had died a hundred years before, but it was a demon that gave the response.[1]

Jean Bodin, the eminent political philosopher, in his celebrated treatise *De la Demonomanie des Sorciers*, puts on record a story that he heard from two highly respectable acquaintances of his, the Sieur de Noailles, French ambassador at Constantinople, and a Polish gentleman named Pruinski, who had been ambassador at Paris. " One of the great kings of Christendom" consulted a Jacobin necromancer about the future. The friar said mass and consecrated the host; then he had a first-born boy of ten years beheaded and caused his head to be placed upon the host. " Puis disant certaines paroles, & vsant de characteres, qu'il n'est besoin de sçauoir, demanda ce qu'il vouloit." The experiment was a dismal and tragic failure. The head uttered only two words: " Vim patior." And immediately the king entered, raging and crying out, " Take away that head! " and died "ainsi enragé." The thing, adds Bodin, is held for certain and indubitable in the whole realm where it occurred, though but five persons were present when it happened.[2] This anecdote reminded Bodin of the madness and death of

Works, 1636, IV, 88 (*A Treatise of the Foure Degenerate Sonnes, the Atheist, The Magitian, the Idolater, and the Iew*); Increase Mather, *An Essay for the Recording of Illustrious Providences*, Boston, 1684, p. 183 (reprint, ed. Offor, p. 130).

[1] *Speculum Laicorum* (Additional MS. 11284, fol. 22, British Museum), Herbert, *Catalogue of Romances*, III, 382, §152; Thoms, *Altdeutsche Blätter*, II, 77.

[2] ii, 3, Paris, 1580, fol. 71 v°; 1587, fol. 78.

the great Theodoric, who thought the head of a fish was
that of the murdered Symmachus.[1] " Humanity," writes
Gibbon, " will be disposed to encourage any report which
testifies to the jurisdiction of conscience and the remorse of
kings." [2]

Bodin adds that " ceux qui tiennent des testes de mort,"
unless they are physicians or surgeons, are usually ne-
cromancers. He cites — mistakenly, I think, — the ocular
evidence of Joachim Camerarius [3] and appends a Parisian
example.[4]

John Cotta, the early seventeenth-century English physician, who has the reputation of being on the right side in the
witchcraft debate,[5] repeats from Pico della Mirandola the
statement that " a famous magician of *Italy* in his time, did
keepe the skull of a dead man, out of which the Diuell did
deliuer answeres vnto men enquiring, when the wizard had
first vttered certaine words, and had torned the skull toward
the Sunne." [6]

Both Kornmann and Garmann, in their ghoulish treatises
De Miraculis Mortuorum, accumulate examples of speaking
heads.[7] Antiquity lent weight to such fancies. There was

[1] Procopius, *Bell. Goth.*, i, 1 (Byzantine Corpus, [XVIII,] 11).

[2] Chap. 39 (Bury's 3d ed., 1908, IV, 203).

[3] Camerarius, discussing the question, " Quae est Gorgon seu Gorgo ? "
admits the possibility of " suspecting " that such a head, fatal to all be-
holders, may have been prepared by charms and magic: " quemadmodum
& nobis aliquando legere contigit quaedam, quibus obseruatis operando, &
incantando peractis, caput hominis mortui responsa esset daturum " (*Pro-
blemata*, Decuria iii, No. 1, ed. Heidelberg, 1594, pp. 216–217).

[4] *Demonomanie*, bk. ii, ch. 3 (ed. 1587, fols. 80 v°–81 r°). On cephalo-
mantia in general cf. Del Rio, *Disquisitiones Magicae*, lib. iv, cap. 2, quaest.
6, sect. 4, § 11 (ed. Venice, 1616, pp. 544–545).

[5] *Studies in the History of Religions presented to C. H. Toy*, 1912, pp. 21–22.

[6] *The Infallible True and Assured Witch*, London, 1624, p. 106. I have
not found the place in Pico.

[7] Kornmann, *De Miraculis Mortuorum*, Part iv, chaps. 1, 5, 18, 19, 33,

the singing head of Orpheus, which became a Lesbian oracle and uttered a riddling prophecy for the benefit of the elder Cyrus.[1] Phlegon of Tralles, in the second century of our era, wrote of Polycritus, the Ætolarch, who died soon after his marriage. His wife brought forth an hermaphrodite. The monster was taken to the market place and the people were deliberating on the advisability of destroying it, when the dead Polycritus appeared, dressed in black, and begged them to give him his offspring. They showed unwillingness, and he straightway tore the child to pieces, devoured it, all but the head, and vanished. The head, which lay on the pavement, spoke and pronounced a long oracle in verse, which our author preserves.[2]

These superstitions are not dead yet in Italy, or if so, have very recently expired. In a Sicilian folk-tale we hear of a certain robber who kept by him a witch's head (*testa di mavara*) that always gave him information when he was about to undertake anything.[3]

Artificial heads that speak play a distinguished part in history and romance.[4] One thinks of the brazen head variously ascribed to the art of Friar Bacon,[5] Pope Silvester

---

pp. 98–99, 101, 109–110, 117–118 (*Opera Curiosa*, 1694); Garmann, *De Miraculis Mortuorum*, 1709, Book ii, tit. 5, § 17, p. 463.

[1] Philostratus, *Heroicus*, v, 3 (p. 704 Olearius); Roscher, *Ausführliches Lexicon*, III, i, 1168.

[2] Phlegon, *Mirabilia*, cap. 2 (ed. Franz, 1785, pp. 22–37, Westermann, Παραδοξογράφοι, pp. 121 ff.). In cap. 3 (Franz, pp. 57 ff.), one Publius, a Roman general, allows himself to be eaten by a wolf; his head, which remains lying on the ground, speaks prophetically.

[3] Gonzenbach, *Sicilianische Märchen*, 1870, No. 22, I, 135 ff.; Crane, *Italian Popular Tales*, p. 67.

[4] See Warton, *History of English Poetry*, I (1774), 401 (ed. Hazlitt, II, 339).

[5] Selden, *De Dis Syris*, i, 2; Thoms, *Early Prose Romances*, 2d ed., I, 181 ff.; A. W. Ward, *Old English Drama*, pp. xcvii ff.; Greene's *Friar Bacon and Friar Bungay*, iv, 1 (*Plays and Poems*, ed., Collins, II, 61 ff.). Greene

II,[1] Grosteste,[2] or Albertus Magnus,[3] and utilized in *Valentine and Orson* [4] as well as in an Irish story.[5] Here belongs also the head which the Templars were accused of worshipping, for this appears to have been regarded not only as an idol but as an oracle too.[6] In one of their confessions it is brought into vague relations with an extraordinary piece of gossip from the Orient. There was a certain nobleman (so this distracted witness had heard) who possessed a woman's head that served him as a kind of Medusa against his enemies.[7] The details are quite terrific. The unhappy Templar had picked up, and credited, a local legend of the Gulf of Satalia, told with additional circumstances of horror by Benedict of Peterborough [8] and copied from him by Roger of Hoveden.[9] It is reproduced with variations in

makes Mahound speak out of a brazen head in *Alphonsus King of Arragon*, iv, 1 (Collins, I, 112–115). A satirical poem by William Terilo, *A Piece of Friar Bacons Brazen-heads Prophesie*, 1604, illustrates the popularity of the theme (ed. Halliwell, Percy Society, 1844; Hazlitt, *Early Popular Poetry*, IV, 263 ff.).

[1] William of Malmesbury, *Gesta Regum Anglorum*, ii, 172 (Migne, *Patrol. Lat.*, CLXXIX, 1145; ed. Hardy, p. 283).

[2] Robert of Bardney, metrical *Life of Grosteste*, cap. 20, Wharton, *Anglia Sacra*, II, 333; Gower, *Confessio Amantis*, iv, 234–243 (Macaulay's edition, II, 307, and note, p. 502).

[3] Del Rio, *Disquistiones Magicae*, lib. i, cap. 4 (ed., Venice, 1616, p. 31); cf. Sighart, *Albertus Magnus*, pp. 71–72.

[4] A brazen head reveals to Valentine and Orson their parentage, *L'Histoire de Valentin et Orson*, 17th century, chap. 23, pp. 65 ff.; English, *Valentine and Orson*, 1694, chaps. 28, 30, pp. 97 ff., 101 ff.; *The New History of Valentine and Orson*, 1724, chaps. 18, 20, pp. 78–79, 84–85; *Historia de i due Nobilissimi et Valorosi Fratelli Valentino et Orsone*, Venice, 1558, chap. 23, pp. 154 ff. Cf. Seelman, *Valentin und Namelos*, p. lv.

[5] Curtin, *Hero-Tales of Ireland*, p. 271.

[6] Wilcke, *Geschichte des Ordens der Tempelherren*, 2d ed., II, 266–274; Lavocat, *Procès des Frères et de l'Ordre du Temple*, pp. 352 ff.

[7] Michelet, *Procès des Templiers*, II, 223–224.

[8] *Gesta Regis Ricardi*, ed. Stubbs, Rolls Series, II, 195–196.

[9] *Chronica*, ed. Stubbs, Rolls Series, III, 158.

Maundevile's *Travels*.[1] A resemblance is discernible to the
eccentric version of the Perseus myth registered in the
Chronographia of Joannes Malalas.[2]

There is a speaking and otherwise miraculous skull in one
of the legends in the *Popol Vuh*.[3] In a tale, or myth, in
Schoolcraft, a more or less divine personage gives orders
that his own head shall be cut off and carefully treasured; it
has strange powers, including that of speech, and is afterwards united with his body.[4] The profoundest magic, as
well as a very savage philosophy, may be discerned in a
Gascon story, in which the severed head of an enchanter
speaks, bidding the hero eat its ears, etc., in order that he
may attain superhuman knowledge.[5] It seems odd that a
baffled magician should act with such officious benevolence
toward his slayer. Possibly the narrative has suffered by
oral tradition. In that case the original object of the speaking head may have been some kind of posthumous vengeance, as in the famous and admirable tale of *The King
and the Physician* in the *Arabian Nights*.[6] In a Cashmirian
variant of the widely distributed folk-tale of *The Faithless
Mother* [7] the head of the monster speaks when the woman
opens the forbidden chamber.[8] There are speaking heads of

[1] *Voiage and Travaile*, ed. 1725, pp. 32–33; ed. Halliwell, pp. 26–27;
The Buke of John Maundeuill, ch. 5, ed. Warner, Roxburghe Club, 1889,
p. 14 (the Cotton MS. reads *a neddere* for *an hede* [Egerton; *teste* in the
French]). Bojardo, *Orlando Innamorato*, book i, canto 8, sts. 47 ff., has
something of the same kind.

[2] Book ii, p. 41 (Oxford), pp. 35–36 (Dindorf, 1831), Byzantine *Corpus*,
[XIV].

[3] Ed. Brasseur de Bourbourg, p. 93; Pohorilles, *Popol Wuh*, p. 30; cf.
Hartman, *Journal of American Folk-Lore*, XX, 148–150.

[4] *Algic Researches*, I, 96 ff.

[5] Bladé, *Contes populaires de la Gascogne*, I, 191–192.

[6] Sixteenth Night (Galland, 1832, I, 129 ff.).

[7] See pp. 228 ff.

[8] Knowles, *Folk-Tales of Kashmír*, p. 3.

much simple impressiveness in an Indian story from the North Pacific coast.[1] Everything that heart can wish about the preservation of heads for oracular or other purposes may be found in Pinza's stupendous monograph.[2]

Heads may speak by miracle as well as magic. When St. Edmund, the holy king of the East Angles, was killed by the Danes in 870, " his heed lay i-hidde among busshes, and spak to hem that souȝt hym in the contray longage, and seide, ' Heere, heere, heere.' "[3] About 1200 a skull was found at Vienna with lips and tongue intact. It spoke, declared itself to be the head of a pagan judge who had never passed an unjust sentence, and called for baptism.[4]

Among the miracles of St. Udalric, Bishop of Augsburg in the tenth century, is the following. A certain count invited the bishop to pay him a visit. At dinner the count's wife appeared, wearing a dead man's head attached to a chain round her neck. She ate with the dogs in a corner of the hall. The bishop asked for an explanation, and was informed by the count that this was the skull of one of his knights whom he had suspected of being his wife's lover. After prayer by the bishop, the head spoke, exonerating the lady. Then the holy man caused the body to be dug up and laid on the table, and the head was placed at its feet. Instantly the trunk turned about and united with the head,

[1] Boas, *Indianische Sagen*, p. 285.

[2] *La Conservazione delle Teste Humane*, *Società Geografica Italiana*, *Memorie*, VII, 305–492. Cf. also A. Reinach, *Les Têtes Coupées et les Trophées en Gaule*, *Revue Celtique*, XXXIV, 38 ff., 253 ff. (especially, p. 274, note 1).

[3] Higden, *Polychronicon*, book v, chap. 32 (Trevisa's English), Rolls edition, VI, 343. The miracle is recorded by William of Malmesbury, *Gesta Pontificum Anglorum*, book ii (ed. Stubbs, Rolls Series, p. 153), and *Gesta Regum Anglorum*, book ii, § 213 (ed. Hardy, I, 366).

[4] Werner Rolewinck, *De Westphalorum . . . Situ, Moribus*, etc., book i, ch. 3, ed., 1602, p. 16.

and the knight came to life and protested his innocence.
The count restored his wife to favor, and the knight entered
the bishop's service, in which he continued for twenty-seven
years, when he died a natural death.[1]

Various tribes of our Indians and of the Northeast Asiatics
have traditions of cannibalistic demons consisting merely of
a skull or a head, which rolls or bounds along the ground,
pursuing to devour.[2] Sometimes, like other goblins, these
creatures woo or abduct women, commonly with the intention of eating them.[3] But they are not always malevolent.
A buffalo skull speaks helpfully in one story.[4] In another, a
girl marries a skull. It speaks and bids her throw it into the
fire; she obeys, and a man stands before her, — her husband
freed from spells.[5] When, as is usually the case, the pursuing
skull or head is cannibalistic, its intended victims may
thwart it by means of magic obstacles or the like.[6] Now and

[1] *Acta Sanctorum*, July, II, 86 (July 4). The anecdote occurs in a collec-
tion of " miracula et quaedam notabilia " in Additional MS. 18364 (British
Museum), fol. 39b (14th century). See Herbert, *Catalogue of Romances*,
III, 612, who refers to the *Acta*. For the head of a lover served up to a wife,
see *Arthur and Gorlagon*, cap. 23, [*Harvard*] *Studies and Notes in Philology and
Literature*, VIII, 162, with the parallels (VIII, 245 ff.).

[2] Sapir, *Takelma Texts, University of Pennsylvania, Anthropological Publications*, II, 174. Cf. the artificial skull in Boas, *The Eskimo of Baffin Bay
and Hudson Bay, American Museum of Natural History, Bulletin*, XV, 254–
255.

[3] Dorsey, *The Pawnee, Mythology*, pp. 31 ff., 119 ff., 447–448; Dorsey and
Kroeber, *Arapaho Traditions*, Nos. 5, 6, 124, *Field Columbian Museum,
Anthropological Series*, V, 8 ff., 13–14, 278 ff. In the tale first cited (Dorsey,
pp. 31 ff.) the head, when split, reunites.

[4] Lowie, *The Assiniboine*, No. 4, *American Museum of Natural History,
Anthropological Papers*, IV, 143.

[5] Bogoras, *Chukchee Mythology, Publications of the Jesup North Pacific
Expedition*, VIII, 28 ff. Cf. Curtin, *Myths of the Modocs*, pp. 189 ff., for
what looks like a similar case of disenchantment.

[6] Dorsey and Kroeber, *Arapaho Traditions*, Nos. 5, 6, 35, 124, *Field
Columbian Museum, Anthropological Series*, V, 8 ff., 13–14, 70–71, 278 ff.

then the existence of such a creature is accounted for in a singular way: a man, we are told, eats himself up piecemeal until nothing is left but his head, which then pursues people in mad eagerness for human flesh.[1] It is not always easy to see any essential difference between these cannibalistic skulls and the " rolling rock " so familiar in North American folk-lore.[2]

Some of our aborigines have traditions of the Flying Heads, so called, hideous demonic beings that fly through

---

[1] Curtin, *Creation Myths of America*, p. 327; Sapir, *Yana Texts, University of California, Publications in American Archæology and Ethnology*, IX, 115 ff.; Dixon, in Sapir, as above, pp. 200 ff.; Dixon, *Maidu Texts*, No. 11, pp. 188 ff.; Dixon, *Maidu Myths, American Museum of Natural History, Bulletin*, XVII, 97–98. For such " disintegration " see Boas, *Mythology of the Bella Coola Indians, Jesup North Pacific Expedition*, I, 99; Jochelson, *The Koryak, Jesup Expedition*, VI, 296, 309; Boas, *Kwakiutl Tales, Columbia University, Contributions to Anthropology*, II, 166–167; cf. Waterman, *Journal of·American Folk-Lore*, XXVII, 44, 45. In Dorsey's *Traditions of the Osage*, a man takes a second wife, whereupon his first becomes reduced to a head; this is put between the couple as they lie in bed; it swallows them and others, and afterwards pursues a little girl (*Field Columbian Museum, Anthropological Series*, VII, 21 ff.).

[2] Dorsey, *Traditions of the Arikara*, pp. 143–147; the same, *Traditions of the Skidi Pawnee*, Nos. 29, 62, pp. 105–106, 260–262 (see references, p. 346); Dorsey and Kroeber, *Traditions of the Arapaho*, Nos. 32–34, 81, *Field Columbian Museum, Series in American Anthropology and Ethnology*, V, 65–70, 159 ff.; Grinnell, *Blackfoot Lodge Tales*, pp. 165–166; Kroeber, *Ute Tales, Journal of American Folk-Lore*, XIV, 261 ff.; McDermott, *Folk-Lore of the Flathead Indians of Idaho, Journal*, XIV, 245–247; Rand, *Legends of the Micmacs*, pp. 316–317; Turner, *Ethnology of the Ungava District, Hudson Bay Territory, Eleventh Report of the Bureau of Ethnology*, pp. 336–337; Matthews, *Navaho Legends*, pp. 125–126; Frank Russell, *Explorations in the Far North*, pp. 210–211; J. A. Mason, *Myths of the Uintah Utes, Journal of American Folk-Lore*, XXIII, 306, 307 ff.; Wissler and Duvall, *Mythology of the Blackfoot Indians, American Museum of Natural History, Anthropological Papers*, II, 24–25; Lowie, *The Northern Shoshone*, same series, II, 262–263; Goddard, *Jicarilla Apache Texts*, same series, VIII, 105, 234; Dorsey, *The Pawnee, Mythology*, pp. 446–447; Mooney, *American Anthropologist*, XI (1898), 208.

the air and devour mortals.[1] They are supposed to consist
of a head only, but David Cusick's grotesque drawing pro-
vides one of them with a pair of diminutive legs![2] A
Wyandot legend accounts for these demons. There were
certain giants, we are told, who lived in caverns under the
bed of a river and who dragged canoes and passengers down
into the depths. At last these giants were captured by the
warriors of the Little Turtle and decapitated. Their heads
were thrown into the river. Next morning, however, the
heads rose from the river, and thereafter these Flying Heads
constantly plagued the Wyandots; they were cannibals and
vampires, they caused sickness, they blighted the crops.[3]
Another myth declares that the bodies of the giants wriggled
to the edge of the precipitous river bank and fell into the
water, when they were transformed into monstrous serpents.[4] Ophidians again!

A frightful creature called Children's Death — sometimes
male and sometimes female — who is a mere mouth smeared
all round with dried blood, figures in the mythology of the
Chukchee of the North Pacific coast of Asia.[5] There is also
a being who is all head in the *Popol Vuh*, but there seems to
be no harm in him.[6]

A lame Philippine story concerns a couple who prayed for
a child, even if it should be only a head. They had their

[1] Converse, *Myths and Legends of the New York State Iroquois*, pp. 79–81
(*New York Education Department Bulletin*, No. 437); Canfield, *Legends of the
Iroquois*, pp. 125–126; Erminie A. Smith, *Myths of the Iroquois, Second
Report of the Bureau of Ethnology*, pp. 59–62; Dorman, *Origin of Primitive
Superstitions*, p. 281; Hartland, *Folk-Lore*, XI, 191.

[2] Cusick, *Sketches of Ancient History of the Six Nations*, 2d ed. (Tuscarora
Village, Lewiston, N. Y., 1828). Cusick's story is reprinted by Beauchamp,
The Iroquois Trail, 1892, p. 14.

[3] Connelley, *Wyandot Folk-Lore* (Topeka, 1899), pp. 83–86.

[4] The same p. 86.

[5] Bogoras, *Chukchee Mythology, Jesup Expedition*, VIII, 18 ff.

[6] Ed. Brasseur de Bourbourg, p. 79; Pohorilles, *Popol Wuh*, p. 25.

prayer, and the ambitious head wished to marry the chief's daughter.[1] A far better tale of the sort is reported from Madagascar.[2] A similar birth is soberly chronicled and solemnly discussed by Garmann.[3] A mediæval *exemplum* in a thirteenth-century manuscript tells of a youth who " prays for release from temptation; he is haunted for three years by a gigantic head threatening to devour him; at length the head joins its body, which the youth sees lying beside a pit, and the monster plunges into the pit and disappears." [4]

We have roamed among many tribes in our head-hunting, and have gathered good store of trophies. Some of them are more curious than valuable, but such as they are, they illustrate the varied possibilities of naïve thinking on a simple theme. We shall hardly be called upon to trace all these vagrant fancies to any single source in primitive philosophy. Magic, miracle, and medicine are alike represented. Rudimentary scientific observation has played its part, and hasty inferences from actual phenomena have helped to establish the tradition. Bad dreams have no doubt had their share. Indeed, our collectanea would make first-rate pabulum for the thoroughgoing Freudian psychologist. — Before dropping the subject, however, we ought to return to our proper topic — those mythical creatures whose severed heads return *by nature* to their bodies.

From the evidence at hand, it seems pretty clear that the category to which the Green Knight originally belonged, before his story was wrought out, or, indeed, before he had any story properly so called, is the widespread category of

[1] Maxfield and Millington, *Visayan Tales, Journal of American Folk-Lore*, XIX, 106–107.

[2] Renel, *Contes de Madagascar*, I, 180.

[3] *De Miraculis Mortuorum*, lib. iii, tit. 1, § 135 (1709, p. 912).

[4] Herbert, *Catalogue of Romances*, III, 472, § 14 (Egerton MS. 1117, fol. 181b).

dragons, water-monsters, or serpent-men. It is not to be supposed that all creatures who play fast and loose with their heads in story, are, or ever were, ophidian; for a peculiar faculty like this is easily transferred from one mysterious or supernatural being to another of a different order. But the evidence certainly suggests that this faculty belongs primarily to this particular class.

It is often difficult to enter into the thoughts of savage man so as to feel any sympathy with his psychological theories or his views about the natural world. In this matter of the heads, however, we are in a better position than usual. It is a fact of common observation that a snake does not die when it is beheaded. We find little difficulty in believing the anecdote of the Italian apothecary's apprentice who died from the bite of a viper's severed head that lay neglected among the rubbish in a corner of the shop.[1] Wild inferences come easy to primeval science. A serpent's head, according to the belief of some Scottish Highlanders, " should be completely smashed, and removed to a distance from the rest of the body. Unless this is done, the serpent will again come alive. The tail, unless deprived of animation, will join the body, and the head becomes a *beithis*, the largest and most deadly kind of serpent." [2]

Again, it is a matter of common observation among savages and civilized men alike, that a bird does not die as soon as its head is cut off. We know, too, that the severed end of a finger will grow on again if quickly replaced and kept in a proper position. It is natural to infer, from all this, that a clean cut that severs the head from the body without mangling either, does not cause instant death, —

[1] Garmann, *De Miraculis Mortuorum*, 1709, lib. ii, tit. 5, § 19, pp. 464–465.

[2] J. G. Campbell, *Superstitions of the Highlands and Islands*, Glasgow, 1900, p. 224.

that the head still retains consciousness and is capable of speech or of motion of the eyelids, and even that, if quickly returned to the shoulders, it may reunite with the neck. When the executioner buffeted the head of Charlotte Corday, bystanders saw (or thought they saw) a deep blush spread over the cheek at the indignity. In the Irish *Siege of Howth* (mentioned by a poet who died in 975) the head of Mesgegra " at one moment flushed, and at another whitened again " when it appeared that Conall, his slayer, was to carry off the dead man's wife.[1] King Charles's head opened its eyes and looked reproachfully at the executioner.

These stories, whether true or not, seem half credible even to men of the twentieth century. When the vikings of Jóm were about to be executed, one of them requested to be cut down rapidly in order that an experiment might be tried. He had often discussed with his comrades, he said, the question whether a man, if quickly beheaded, knows anything, and he wished to take advantage of this opportunity to settle the problem for himself.[2] The saga-man regards the anecdote as a mere specimen of intrepidity; but to us, who have known of physicians who inoculate themselves with dreadful diseases to put their antidotes to the test, the Norse pirate seems like a martyr to science — so close are savage men to ourselves in the essential belief that lies at the heart of *Gawain and the Green Knight*.

In these speculations, however, we are dealing, not with the history of *Gawain and the Green Knight,* nor even with the history of its Irish source, — but with their *pre*-history. Long before *The Champion's Bargain* was written, many

---

[1] See Stokes's translation, *Revue Celtique*, VIII, 62–63; revised, Hull's *Cuchullin,* p. 94.

[2] *Jómsvíkinga Saga*, chap. 53 (ed. Carl af Petersens, 1879, pp. 92–93); *Saga Ólafs Tryggvasonar,* chap. 46 (*Konunga Sögur,* ed. Copenhagen, 1816, I, 246–247); *Heimskringla,* ed. Unger, p. 159.

creatures originally serpentine had ceased to be so regarded, and the ability to resume a lost head had extended itself, as an article of the popular creed, to hags and giants not serpentine at all. The challenger in *The Champion's Bargain*, and his lineal descendant the Green Knight, are not themselves ophidian, whatever their ancestors may have been in the backward and abysm of time.

II. THE DEMON OF VEGETATION

WE have seen reason to believe that the general class of monsters who play fast and loose with their heads were, in the original conception, though not in the actual tale that we are investigating, Snakes or Serpent-Men. It is not impossible, however, that the particular guise in which our Green Knight shows himself, owes something to another creature of the primitive imagination or primitive philosophy. He may have taken on, in part, the qualities of a Wood-Deity or Demon of Vegetation.[1]

His greenness, we remember, is not merely a matter of clothing, but extends to his skin, to hair, beard, and eyebrows; his horse is also green; and he carries in his hand a bob of holly, " that is greatest in green when groves are bare ";[2] green too is the magic lace that the lady gives to Gawain.[3] Wood-demons are commonly either dwarfs or giants. They are sometimes green or dressed in green, and they often carry a tree (frequently one torn up by the roots) as a staff. To their ranks may belong the Centaurs, as well as Silvanus and other beings of some traditional dignity.[4] They sometimes have power to change their shape.[5]

Green men are not uncommon in folk-lore. " A ragged green man " of immense strength is an important character in Larminie's *Bioultach*; he turns out to be under spells.[6]

---

[1] Cf. Henderson, *Arthurian Motifs in Gadhelic Literature, Miscellany Presented to Kuno Meyer*, 1912, pp. 26–27.

[2] Vv. 147–150, 175 ff., 233–236, 305, 2227–2228.   [3] Vv. 1832, 2517.

[4] See, in general, Mannhardt, *Wald- und Feldkulte*; in particular, for green color or clothing, I, 88, 117–119, 124, 138, 147 and note 2; for tree as staff, I, 96, 97, 105; for the Centaurs and Silvanus, II, 46, 123. On giants as wood-spirits or tree-spirits, cf. Weinhold, Vienna Academy, *Sitzungsberichte*, XXVI, 290.

[5] See, for example, Mannhardt, I, 138, 140, 144, 145, 146.

[6] *West-Irish Folk-Tales*, pp. 50 ff.

The " thankful dead man " in Douglas Hyde's version appears as a green dwarf.[1] There is an elemental green man in the *Siddhi-Kür*.[2] One of Curtin's Magyar tales is *The Green Daughter of the Green King*.[3] There are green dogs in a modern Celtic tale.[4] Vetāla, the king of the Bhūts, is green and rides a green horse.[5]

The Green Man of Noman's Land is especially interesting. It is a Welsh Gypsy tale [6] which begins thus: " There was a young miller, who was a great gambler. Nobody could beat him. One day a man comes and challenges him. They play. Jack wins and demands a castle. There it is. They play again, and Jack loses. The man tells Jack his name is the Green Man of Noman's Land, and that unless Jack finds his castle in a year and a day he will be beheaded. The time goes by. Jack remembers his task, and sets out in cold and snow." Jack finds the castle, and tasks follow, the Green Man's daughter performing them for him. " The Green Man gives in, and Jack weds his daughter." The story is of a familiar type; [7] but the precise form in which it appears in Wales is interesting. Our Green Knight's head-play may

---

[1] *Beside the Fire*, pp. 18–47.   [2] Jülg, No. 3.

[3] *Myths and Folk-Tales of the Russians*, etc., pp. 477 ff.

[4] *Celtic Magazine*, XIII, 279.

[5] Crooke, *Introduction to the Popular Religion and Folklore of Northern India*, p. 150 (cf. p. 152).   [6] Groome, *Gypsy Folk Tales*, pp. 254–255.

[7] As Groome remarks, it is identical with J. F. Campbell's *Battle of the Birds* (No. 2), fully treated by Köhler, *Orient und Occident*, II, 103 ff. (*Kleinere Schriften*, I, 161 ff.), where variants are given from India to Ireland. Others are added by Groome. Losing a game to a supernatural opponent is a common device to start the hero on a course of adventures. The following examples will suffice: *Celtic Magazine*, XII, 12 ff., 57 ff.; Campbell, *Popular Tales of the West Highlands*, I, 1 ff.; Mac Innes, *Folk and Hero Tales*, pp. 94 ff.; Larminie, *West Irish Folk-Tales*, pp. 10 ff.; Curtin, *Myths and Folk-Lore of Ireland*, pp. 32 ff.; J. F. Campbell, *The Celtic Dragon Myth*, pp. 103 ff., 121; Dottin, *Contes Irlandais* (translated from Hyde), pp. 68 ff., 161 ff., 190 ff.; Kennedy, *Legendary Fictions of the Irish Celts*,

be regarded as a kind of game in which Gawain loses; and, like Jack, Gawain must set out, in the winter, to search for the Green Man of Noman's Land; both have to submit to tests, nor is there any doubt that Gawain, like Jack, would have lost his head if he had failed in any essential point in their performance. I am far from maintaining genetic connection between the Welsh-Gypsy tale and the English romance. What concerns us here, is the folklore figure of a Green Man who seeks to entrap the hero. But a comparison is nevertheless instructive. It shows how easily the developed Irish literary form of the Challenge might have been modified under the influence of some current folk-tale of a quest with which it had originally only a slight and accidental resemblance.[1] Another and better version of the same folk-tale — this time from Connaught — bears the title of *Curadh Glas an Eolaig*, or " The Green Knight of Knowledge." The knight challenges the hero to play cards. The hero loses the third game and the Green Knight bids him neither eat nor rest till he shall find his dwelling, and if he shall not find it within a year and a day, his life is to be the forfeit.[2] Unfortunately the Irish adjective *glas*, which is applied to the challenging knight, is rather ambiguous, and may mean " gray " as well as " green."

Macdougall prints a Highland tale called the *Son of the Knight of the Green Vesture*.[3] The son in question marries

pp. 255 ff.; Curtin, *Hero-Tales of Ireland*, pp. 325 ff., 408 ff., 465 ff., 484 ff.; Cosquin, *Contes populaires de Lorraine*, II, 254–255; Jiriczek, *Zeitschrift für deutsche Philologie*, XXVI, 6; cf. *Kathā-sarit-sāgara*, Tawney, II, 575 ff. We may note the chess-play between Midir and King Eochaid Airem in the *Tochmarc Etaine* (d'Arbois, *Cours*, II, 315 ff.; Nettlau, *Revue Celtique*, XII, 232). Cf. [*Harvard*] *Studies and Notes*, VIII, 214 ff.

[1] See p. 137.

[2] *Curadh Glas an Eolaig*, edited by the Rev. J. M. O'Reilly, Irish Book Company, 1905.

[3] *Folk and Hero Tales*, pp. 222 ff.

the daughter of the King of the Green Mound.[1] There is fairy-lore enough in this story to satisfy anybody, but I do not see that it helps us here. In short, it is idle to accumulate references to things and persons that are called green. Everybody knows that this is a fairy color and that folktales are fond of *fées*. We are just where we were before. The Green Knight of the English romance is somehow supernatural, and his color suggests the wood-deity or the demon of vegetation. All this we knew at the outset.

Another point of comparison might be the decapitation. The Slavic noon-lady will cut off your head with her sickle if you cannot answer her questions.[2] She is manifestly a demon of vegetation, as well as of the noonday. But truculence is a trait common to many kinds of supernatural beings, so that this comparison does not advance us a particle either.

There is, however, a "wild man" in certain popular mummings who promises rather better, for he is sometimes green, and sometimes a "vegetation demon," and sometimes he is killed and afterwards revives. Mannhardt has much to say about this personage,[3] and Mr. E. K. Chambers, in his learned discussion of such dramatic festivals, is bold enough to equate him with our hero. His statement is downright and categorical: "The green man of the peasantry, who dies and lives again, reappears as the Green Knight in one of the most famous divisions of Arthurian romance."[4] Mr. Cook, if a little more cautious in manner, is still more daring in opinion. He appears to feel quite

---

[1] P. 232.   [2] See p. 147.

[3] Mannhardt, *Wald-und Feldkulte*, I, 420, cf. 333 ff., 357, 359. See also the references in E. K. Chambers, *The Mediæval Stage*, chaps. vi–x. It is hardly necessary to mention Frazer's *Golden Bough*, distinguished alike for its erudition and its fantastic theories.

[4] *The Mediæval Stage*, I, 186, and note 1.

assured that our Green Knight is the Italic tree-god Virbius.[1] One is equally at liberty, so far as I can see, to identify him with Esus, since he carries an axe and knows how to use it.[2]

All such conjectures have only a mythological interest — and they are not very good mythology either. For the challenger in the Irish story is neither green nor in any way associated with trees or vegetation, except that the hair of his head is bushy![3] He appears as green in no extant version of the Challenge until we reach the English romance. Whoever gave him that color first, whether the English poet or some French predecessor,[4] was influenced, of course, by current folk-lore, and that folk-lore may have descended to the innovator in question from primeval ideas about the forces of nature. So much we must grant, but that is all. Neither the Irish author of *The Champion's Bargain* nor any of his successors in the line had any notion of associating the challenger with Celtic " probably arboreal " deities, Arician groves, spirits of vegetation, or the annual death and rebirth of the embodied vital principle. To them he was merely an enchanter, a shape-shifter, or else a human being under spells, and they wasted neither ink nor oil in mythologizing. And so we may drop this question into limbo, with the parting observation that thought is free.

[1] *Folk-Lore*, XVII, 340–341.

[2] See the references in d'Arbois de Jubainville, *Cours*, VI, 173, 178. Cf. Rhŷs, *Hibbut Lectures*, pp. 61 ff., 646; Reinach, *Revue Celtique*, XVIII, 137 ff.; d'Arbois, *Revue Celtique*, XIX, 246 ff.; XX, 89 ff. For trees cut down with one blow by a supernatural creature see, e.g., J. S. Gardiner, *Journal of the Anthropological Institute*, XXVII, 511; Kroeber, *Cheyenne Tales, Journal of American Folk-Lore*, XIII, 173. Compare the West Finnish axeman in Abercromby, *The Pre- and Proto-historic Finns*, I, 326–327.

[3] P. 11.   [4] Pp. 140, 141.

III. DISENCHANTMENT BY DECAPITATION.[1]

DECAPITATION as a means of disenchantment occurs in both *The Carl of Carlisle*[2] and *The Turk and Gawain*.[3] In the *Carl*, the bespelled person is a cruel monster until he is released from enchantment; in the *Turk*, he takes the rôle of Helpful Attendant, performing superhuman tasks as a substitute for the hero. In both, he urges the reluctant Gawain to cut off his head,[4] and this is the final act in a somewhat complicated process of disenchantment. The efficacy of decapitation in undoing a spell is a widespread popular belief, and many of the tales in which it occurs are otherwise parallel either to *The Carl of Carlisle* or to *The Turk and Gawain*. In what follows, there is, of course, no attempt at exhaustiveness. My purpose has been to illustrate the belief by means of typical examples, and to bring out its significance as an article of the popular creed.

We may begin with the Decapitation of Helpful Animals.

In a Gaelic tale a serviceable steed bids the hero " take a sword and . . . take the head off me." The hero objecting, the horse replies: " In me there is a young girl under spells, and the spells will not be off me till the head is taken off me." In the same story a serviceable raven makes a similar request: " A young lad under spells am I, and they will not be off me till the head comes off me." The pair are transformed and make a fine couple.[5] This is an instructive

---

[1] Reprinted, with a few changes, from *The Journal of American Folk-Lore*, January–March, 1905, XVIII, 1–14.

[2] See pp. 87 ff.

[3] See pp. 119 ff.

[4] There is no beheading in the Porkington version of the *Carl* (edited by Madden), but this text has omitted the *motif* of disenchantment altogether, to the manifest injury of the romance.

[5] *The Rider of Grianaig*, J. F. Campbell, *Popular Tales of the West High-*

example because it is outspoken. Usually, however, and more properly, the animal does not tell the hero or heroine why the beheading is to be performed. So, for instance, in a Swedish tale, *Den underbare Hästen*, the horse simply asks the hero to strike off his head, and when this is done he recovers his proper shape, that of a prince, the brother of the heroine.[1]

In the Lettish epic *Needrischu Widwuds*,[2] the hero Widewut is much helped by a werewolf (*wilkata*), who, among other services, replaces the heads of the hero's two companions and brings the dead men to life by means of a magic elixir. The wolf then insists on being beheaded in his turn, and, when his request is granted, is transformed into a handsome youth.

lands, No. 58, III, 16–18; cf. Curtin, *Hero-Tales of Ireland*, pp. 354–355. See also *The Black Horse*, from Campbell's manuscript collections, Jacobs, *More Celtic Fairy Tales*, pp. 57 ff., and, on the supposed Indian provenience, Hartland, *Folk-Lore*, V, 331–332. Cf. Leskien u. Brugman, *Litauische Volkslieder u. Märchen*, p. 386, and Wollner's notes, pp. 537–542.

[1] Eva Wigström, *Sagor ock Äfventyr upptecknade i Skåne*, p. 74, in *Nyare Bidrag till Kännedom*, etc., vol. V. In the Norwegian ballad of *A'smund Fregdegœvar*, the hero, who has rescued the king's daughter from the land of the trolls by the aid of a magic horse, strikes off the horse's head: " deð vart ein kristen mann," namely, the queen's youngest brother, Adalbert, son of the English king (Landstad, *Norske Folkeviser*, No. 1, sts. 62–63, p. 21). Cf. Curtin, *Myths and Folk-Tales of the Russians*, etc., pp. 293, 405, in both of which the horse makes the reason known; Rittershaus, *Die neuisländischen Volksmärchen*, p. 98. Bayard, the helpful horse in *Le Prince et son Cheval* (Cosquin, *Contes pop. de Lorraine*, I, 133 ff.), does not ask to be disenchanted, but simply requests his dismissal. He is certainly bespelled, however: " Je suis prince aussi bien que vous: je devais rendre cinque services à un prince " (I, 137). A Christianized incident of this sort is in Vernaleken, *Österreichische Kinder- u. Hausmärchen*, No. 46, p. 252: a horse says, " Hew off my head," and when this is done, a white dove flies forth and up to heaven.

[2] Put together by Lautenbach-Jusmina, song 17, Jelgawå, 1891, pp. 211 ff.; see summary by H. Wissendorff de Wissukuok, *Revue des Traditions Populaires*, XII, 160–161.

The serviceable cat becomes a princess on being decapitated in Mme. d'Aulnoy's *La Chatte Blanche*, and in the
Norwegian *Herrepeer* (Sir Peter).[1] In Perrault's *Le Chat
Botté* there is no beheading and no disenchantment, but,
instead, a delicious specimen of French wit: " Le Chat
devint grand Seigneur, et ne courut plus aprés les souris, que
pour se divertir." [2] In a Tyrolese story the hero, at the
cat's request, takes the animal by the hind legs and dashes
her against the hearth till he sees her no more. Immediately
she reappears as a beautiful maiden, whom he marries.[3]

In the Welsh Gypsy tale of *The Black Dog of the Wild
Forest*, two helpful little dogs, Hear-all and Spring-all, who
have saved the hero's life, require him to cut off their heads,
threatening to devour him if he refuses. As Jack travelled
on, grieving, " he turned his head round at the back of his
horse, looking behind him, and he saw two of the handsomest young ladies coming as ever he saw in his life." They
are Hear-all and Spring-all.[4] Similarly, three black dogs in
a German tale, who have served the king well, are beheaded
at their own request: " Siehe, da standen nun einmal drei
Königssöhne." [5]

---

[1] Asbjørnsen og Moe, *Norske Folkeeventyr*, 2d ed., 1852, p. 162 (translated
by Dasent, *Popular Tales from the Norse*, 2d ed., 1859, p. 347); so in *Kong
Knud fra Knølande* (variant), p. 431, and in another version (in which the
cat becomes a prince), p. 433. See Lang, *Perrault's Popular Tales*, 1888,
Introd., p. lxxii. Asbjørnsen and Moe cite a number of parallels. Cf. the
German *märchen* of *Der Federkönig* (Haltrich, *Deutsche Volksmärchen aus dem
Sachsenlande in Sieben-bürgen*, 3d ed., 1882, p. 50). In *Das weisse Kätzchen*
(Kuhn u. Schwartz, *Norddeutsche Sagen*, p. 334), the kitten's paws and
head are cut off, and the transformation begins on the amputation of the
first paw.

[2] Lang's ed., as above, p. 35.

[3] Zingerle, *Kinder-und Hausmärchen*, 1852, No. 9, p. 52; ed. 1870, p. 42.

[4] Groome, *Gypsy Folk-Tales*, pp. 267–271. There are unspelled green
dogs (which remind us of the fancy *brachets* in French romance) in a tale in
the *Celtic Magazine*, XIII, 279.   [5] Haltrich, as above, pp. 107–108.

In the West Highland tale of *Mac Iain Direach*, the fox, who has assisted the hero materially, remarks as they come to a spring by the side of the road: " Now, Brian, unless thou dost strike off my head with one blow of the White Glave of Light into this spring,[1] I will strike off thine." Brian complies, and " in the wink of an eye, what should rise up out of the well, but the son of the King that was father of the Sun Goddess." [2]

When we pass from Helpful Animals who are unspelled by decapitation to Helpful Servants who are released from enchantment by the same means, we approach sensibly nearer to the situation in *The Turk and Gawain*. Frequently (as in that poem) the helpful attendant wears a monstrous or dwarfish likeness until he is disenchanted.[3]

In the Welsh Gypsy story of *An Old King and his Three Sons in England*, Prince Jack has been entertained and helped at various stages of his journey by three brothers, whose heads, at their request, he cuts off and throws into a

---

[1] The spring is significant. Immersion in water or some other liquid is often a means of dissolving a charm, and sometimes operates as one of several measures conducing to that end. See Child, *Ballads*, I, 338, 507; II, 505; III, 505, and add Laistner, *Rätsel der Sphinx*, § 31, I, 252 ff.

[2] J. F. Campbell, No. 46, II, 358–359. Campbell's story was derived from John Macdonald the tinker, whom Mr. Hindes Groome makes out to have been a Gypsy (*Gypsy Folk-Tales*, pp. lviii–lxi; cf. Nutt, *Folk-Lore*, X, 241–242). It is reprinted, with valuable notes, in Groome's *Gypsy Folk-Tales*, pp. 283–289.

[3] Cormac's *Glossary*, s. v. *prúll*, Stokes, *Three Irish Glossaries*, pp. 36–38, and O'Donovan's translation, ed. Stokes, pp. 135–137; O'Curry, *Manners and Customs*, II, 89; Nutt, *Revue Celtique*, XII, 194–195; the same, *Holy Grail*, pp. 139–141, 205–206; Zimmer, Kuhn's *Ztschr.*, XXVIII, 438; *Imtheacht na Tromdhaimhe*, ed. Connellan, Ossianic Society, *Transactions*, V, 114 ff.; *Life of S. Féchin of Fore*, §§ 37–38, ed. Stokes, *Revue Celtique*, XII, 342–345; MacInnes, *Folk and Hero Tales*, pp. 91–93 (with Nutt's note, pp. 454, 467–468); Maynadier, *Wife of Bath's Tale*, pp. 65 ff., 195 ff.; J. F. Campbell, III, 299–300; Curtin, *Myths and Folk-Lore of Ireland*, pp. 235 ff.; Macdougall, *Folk and Hero Tales*, pp. 35 ff.; Hyde, *Beside the Fire*, pp. 18 ff.

well. What happens may be seen from the case of the eldest of the three: " No sooner he does it, and flings his head in the well, than up springs one of the finest young gentlemen you would wish to see; and instead of the old house and the frightful-looking place, it was changed into a beautiful hall and grounds." There is complete disenchantment, it will be observed, of place as well as of person. The oldest brother is described as a frightful creature: " He could scarcely walk from his toenails curling up like rams' horns that had not been cut for many hundred years, and big long hair," and so on.[1]

In the Irish *Mac Cool, Faolan, and the Mountain*, an old forester, who has assisted Dyeermud and Faolan in some very perilous adventures, asks Dyeermud to cut off his head. Dyeermud consents after the old man has told him that he is under enchantment and cannot be otherwise released. " He cut off his head with one blow, and there rose up before him a young man of twenty-one years." He had been enchanted by his stepmother.[2]

Sometimes the person disenchanted by beheading is not a helpful animal or attendant, but the heroine of the story. There is a good instance in the Saxon tale of *Sausewind*.[3] Here a woman who lives with the ogre Sausewind tells him of three enchanted princesses and gets from him the answer: " Wenn einer ein Schwert nimmt und schlägt dir den Kopf ab, so bist du die eine; dort unten am Wasser steht ein Erlenbusch, wenn davon der rechte Ast . . . abgehauen

---

[1] Groome, *In Gypsy Tents*, 1880, pp. 299–317; the same, *Gypsy Folk-Tales*, No. 55, pp. 220–232; see also *Journal of the Gypsy Lore Society*, 1891, III, 110–120. From the first of these publications the tale was reproduced, with changes and comments of which Mr. Hindes Groome complains (*Gypsy Folk-Tales*, p. 232), by Jacobs, *More English Fairy-Tales*, pp. 132–145, 232–233.   [2] Curtin, *Hero-Tales*, pp. 510–511.

[3] Schambach u. Müller, *Niedersächsische Sagen u. Märchen*, pp. 260 ff.

wird, so ist das die zweite; und oben am Wasser steht noch
ein Busch, wird davon ebenfalls ein Ast abgehauen, so ist
das die dritte; dann sind alle drei wieder beisammen." A
visitor — a young man — then effects the disenchantment
in the way prescribed. Again, in the Saxon tale of *Der
dumme Hans* (a variant of a well-known *märchen*),[1] Hans
serves a mouse, the mistress of an enchanted castle, for three
years. At the end of the third year, the mouse bids him beat
her till she is covered with blood (*blutrünsiig*). He does so.
Immediately the castle is disenchanted and full of life; the
mouse becomes a crown-princess and marries Hans. In a
variant,[2] a cat takes the place of the mouse, and Hans has to
cut wood during his three years of service, make a huge fire,
and finally throw the cat into the flames.

Sometimes the disenchanted person is a prince, and the
maiden who releases him wins him as a husband. Thus in a
West Highland tale [3] which is a variant of the well-known
Frog Prince, the frog, for whom the girl has made a bed
beside her own, finally says: " ' There is an old rusted glave
behind thy bed, with which thou hadst better take off my
head, than be holding me longer in torture.' She took the
glave and cut the head off him. When the steel touched
him, he grew a handsome youth; and he gave many thanks
to the young wife, who had been the means of putting off
him the spells, under which he had endured for a long time."

---

[1] Schambach u. Müller, *Niedersächsische Sagen u. Märchen*, pp. 268 ff.

[2] The same, p. 368. This story has great similarities to the Swedish
märchen of *Den Förtrollade Grodan* (Hyltén-Cavallius and Stephens, *Svenska
Folk-Sagor och Äfventyr*, No. 15, I, 251 ff.), translated by Thorpe, *Yule-Tide
Stories*, pp. 226 ff. (*The Enchanted Toad*). In Afanasief, vol. V, No. 28
(Ralson, *Russian Folk-Tales*, p. 134), a helpful bull-calf tells the hero to
kill him and burn his carcass; from the ashes there spring a horse, a dog,
and an apple tree, all three of which play an important part in the next act
of the drama.

[3] J. F. Campbell, No. 33, II, 130 ff.

In an Annandale version of *The Frog Prince*, the frog asks the girl to cut off his head with an axe.[1] In Grimm's version and some others, the frog is dashed against the wall by the girl in anger at its request to be taken into her bed, and the transformation follows.[2]

The *Frog Prince* is particularly interesting, since it combines, in some of its versions, disenchantment by personal contact with disenchantment by decapitation or by some other method of killing the magical body. In some forms of the great class of " animal-spouse " tales, the mysterious husband is a man by night and an animal (frog, serpent, wolf, etc.) by day, and lays aside his beast-skin when he assumes human shape.[3] This gives us a clear insight into

---

[1] R. Chambers, *Popular Rhymes of Scotland*, 1842, p. 52 (ed. of [1870], pp. 88–89), from C. K. Sharpe, who learned it from a nurse about 1784.

[2] See R. Köhler, *Orient u. Occident*, II, 330; Landau, *Ztschr. f. vergl. Litteraturgeschichte*, I, 17. There is an English version from Holderness in Jones and Kropf, *Folk-Tales of the Magyars*, Folk-Lore Society, pp. 404–405, in which, as in a version of *The Frog Prince* given by F. Pfaff in his *Märchen aus Lobenfeld* (*Alemannia*, XXVI, 87, 88), the frog is taken into bed, but there is neither smashing nor decapitation. In Haltrich, *Deutsche Volksmärchen aus dem Sachsenlande in Siebenbürgen*, 3d ed., 1882, p. 37, a little creature, apparently a dwarf or elf, who has been changed into a toad by enchantment, resumes his proper shape when the toad is smashed to pieces. Cf. Laistner, *Rätsel der Sphinx*, I, 59.

[3] On the Frog Prince or Princess, and on the burning of the frog (or other) skin or of the whole frog to effect the transformation or to ensure its permanence, see Benfey, *Pantschatantra*, I, *Einl.* § 92, pp. 266–269 (where there are many references). There is some good material in De Gubernatis, *Zoölogical Mythology*, II, 376 ff. See also *Der Prinz mit der Schweinshaut*, Köhler, *Kleinere Schriften*, I, 315 ff. A Zulu story of a prince in serpent form (Callaway, *Nursery Tales of the Zulus*, I, 321 ff.) is a fine example of confusion between a person who really has the shape of a serpent and one who is disguised by being clad or inclosed in a serpent's skin. The narrator cannot keep the distinction in mind at all. For one shape by day, another by night, see Child, *Ballads*, I, 290; IV, 454; V, 289; Maynadier, *The Wife of Bath's Tale*, 1901, pp. 201 ff.; Kroeber, *Cheyenne Tales*, No. 18, *Journal of American Folk-Lore*, XIII, 181. Many references for the transformation of animal spouses are collected by S. Prato, *Bulletin de Folklore*, I, 316–335.

the real meaning of disenchantment by beheading. We shall return to the point later.

Especially important for the illustration of *The Carl of Carlisle* are the instances in which the bespelled person who is released by decapitation is a cruel and murderous demon or monster until he is relieved from enchantment. This comes out clearly in the first adventure of *Art and Balor Beimenach*.[1]

The Highland tale of *The Widow and her Daughters*[2] is another case in point. It is a Bluebeard story, curiously modified by the *motif* of unspelling decapitation. A great gray horse (who is also called a king, and who apparently is a man by night)[3] abducts a widow's three daughters one after another. He decapitates the first two for entering a forbidden chamber. The third escapes by a ruse and reaches her mother's house. Her lover pursues " in a wild rage." " When he reached the door he drove it in before him. She was standing behind the door, and she took his head off with the bar. Then he grew a king's son, as precious as ever came," and they were married.[4]

[1] Curtin, *Hero-Tales*, pp. 312 ff. See p. 151, above.

[2] J. F. Campbell, *Popular Tales of the West Highlands*, No. 41, II., 265 ff. See Campbell's references, II, 275. Köhler, *Orient and Occident*, II, 679 (*Kleinere Schriften*, I, 256–257), and *Jahrb. f. rom. Litt.*, VII, 151 ff. (*Kleinere Schriften*, I, 312 ff.), adds little that helps us here. See also Laistner, *Rätsel der Sphinx*, II, 101. In *Die singende Rose* (Zingerle, *Kinder-u. Hausmärchen*, 2d ed., 1870, No. 30, p. 154), an old graybeard makes the princess strike off his head; a key comes out of it, which opens all the doors and chests in the castle.

[3] This may be said to be implied, though it is nowhere stated.

[4] In a variant reported by Campbell (II, 274–275), the transformation is missing. Here the girl beheads the giant (who is previously called a horse) with a sword and holds it on the spinal marrow till this cools, in order that the head may not go on again. This is clearly the proper ending. It is instructive for our present purpose to observe how the idea that beheading releases from enchantment has affected the catastrophe in the other version.

The very formidable giant called the Bare-Stripping
Hangman, in the Gaelic tale of that name,[1] turns out to be
under spells, from which he is released when the egg which
contains his life has been crushed, and when his hands and
feet have been cut off and cast into a fire. " As soon as the
hair of the head was singed and the skin of the feet burnt,
the very handsomest young man they ever beheld sprang
out of the fire." He is the king's younger brother, " who
was stolen in his childhood." This is also an instructive
example. The Bare-Stripping Hangman belongs to the
class of giants who have no soul in their body, — Koshchei
the Deathless, *corps-sans-âme*, Punchkin, and the rest,[2] —
and should be destroyed, not disenchanted. By the addition
of the disenchantment *motif*, the monster is made into a
bespelled mortal.[3]

The idea that fierce or destructive creatures need only to
be subdued or disenchanted to make them kindly, or even to
win them in marriage, is familiar enough from the story of
Brynhildr. An instructive instance from North America is
the Dakota legend of two cannibalistic wives who wish to
kill their husbands, but become harmless when freed from
the spell. The phrase is, " He made them good." [4] There

---

[1] Macdougall, *Folk and Hero Tales*, pp. 76 ff.

[2] See Cosquin, *Contes pop. de Lorraine*, I, 173 ff.; Hartland, *Legend of
Perseus*, index, under *external soul*; Ralston, *Russian Folk-Tales*, pp. 84 ff.;
Curtin, *Russian Myths and Folk-Tales*, pp. 165 ff.; J. W. Wolf, *Deutsche
Märchen u. Sagen*, pp. 87–93; Rand, *Legends of the Micmacs*, p. 245; Köhler,
Orient u. Occident, II, 100–103 (*Kleinere Schriften*, I, 158–161); Frazer
Golden Bough, 1890, II, 296 ff., 2d ed., 1900; III, 351 ff.; Seklemian, *The
Golden Maiden and other Folk Tales and Fairy Stories told in Armenia*, Cleve-
land and New York, 1898, p. 133; Friis, *Lappiske Eventyr og Folkesagn*, pp.
46, 51; Toy, *Introduction to the History of Religions*, p. 17.

[3] Cf. a similar confusion in Maspons y Labrós, *Lo Rondallayre, Quentos
populars catalans*, No. 27, II, 104–110.

[4] S. R. Riggs, *Dakota Myths*, in *Contributions to North American Ethnology*, IX, 141–142.

is a very interesting parallel in the wild Armenian tale of *Zoolvisia*, which also shows the confusion between an immortal won as a bride and a mortal released from spells.[1]

A few other examples of disenchantment by decapitation may be cited to show how readily this feature attaches itself to almost any kind of tale of supernatural creature.

In a German tale a girl hears night after night a voice calling on her to rise. At last she gets out of bed and sees a woman, who asks her to come and free her. The girl follows through a long subterranean passage, entering at length a brilliantly lighted hall. Here sit three black men at a table, writing, and on the table lie two bright swords. " Take one of these swords," says the woman, " and cut off my head: *so bin ich erlöst.*" The girl is about to obey, when her brother, who has followed her, interferes. The woman seizes the girl angrily and throws her violently to the floor, so violently that she becomes a heap of ashes. Then there is a loud noise, and palace and all disappear.[2]

A cowherd is besought by a White Lady to strike off her head, since he alone, she says, can release her. He alleges,

[1] A king's son and his companions follow an antelope into a forest, where they find a tent by a fountain. Within is a table spread with delicious viands. The prince does not eat or drink, like his companions, but explores the neighborhood and is shocked to find, not far from the tent, a heap of human skeletons. The food and water are poisoned, and all his companions die. Soon horsemen approach and pillage the dead men, the prince looking on from a place of concealment. The robber leader turns out to be a beautiful virago, Zoolvisia, with whom he falls in love. She it was who had enticed hunters to the spot in the form of an antelope. The youth visits Zoolvisia's castle and manages to deprive her of the talisman on which her power depends. " You have overcome me," says Zoolvisia; " you are brave and a real hero worthy of me. No one except you has ever heard my voice and lived. Now my talisman is broken, and I have become a mere woman." Thereupon she accepts the prince as her husband. Seklemian, *The Golden Maiden and other Folk Tales and Fairy Stories told in Armenia*, 1898, pp. 59 ff.

[2] Kuhn, *Märkische Sagen u. Märchen*, No. 94, pp. 99–100.

in excuse, that he has no axe. She fetches one with a silver handle, but he runs away. In another form of the same story, the White Lady brings with her a block, a broad-axe, and a bunch of keys. She tells the herd that she is under a ban (*verwünscht*), and begs him to cut her head off before noon, in order to release her. She promises him great treasures. He delays too long, and she vanishes, declaring that not for another hundred years will one be born who can set her free.[1] This is an ordinary legend of a White Lady, the only peculiarity consisting in the manner of disenchantment: kissing is far more common.[2] In another version the White Lady conducts the peasant into a hill and gives him treasure, which, however, disappears when twelve o'clock strikes and the blow has not been dealt.[3]

Disenchantment by beheading is, by a singular confusion, introduced into a Swabian version of the widespread story of the *Thankful Dead Man*. A bird flies to Karl's window with a dagger in its beak and tells him to cut off its head. The bird has assisted him and Karl is unwilling but at last he obeys. The head of the bird falls into the room; the trunk flies away, and there stands before Karl the spirit of the merchant whose corpse he had ransomed.[4]

So far, we have confined our attention, in the main, to *decapitation* as a means of unspelling, but we have compared a few stories in which some other forms of violent death

[1] Schambach u. Müller, *Niedersächsische Sagen u. Märchen*, No. 106, pp. 77–78.

[2] See examples in Child, *Ballads*, I, 307 ff., 338, note; II, 502, 504; III, 504; IV, 454; V, 214, 290; Schofield, *Studies on the Libeaus Desconus*, in *Studies and Notes*, IV, 199 ff.

[3] Schambach u. Müller, No. 107, p. 79.

[4] E. Meier, *Deutsche Volksmärchen aus Schwaben*, No. 42, p. 151. Cf. Simrock, *Der gute Gerhard u. die dankbaren Todten*, Bonn, 1856, p. 57. On the Thankful Dead, see Hippe, Herrig's *Archiv*, LXXXI, 141 ff., and Gerould, *The Grateful Dead*, 1908.

have the same effect. Beheading, then, is only a special means of putting to death: the main point is to kill the enchanted body. Thus in the Irish *Mac Cool, Faolan, and the Mountain*, Faolan pierces a man with his sword in the darkness. " The man fell dead; and then, instead of the old man that he seemed at first, he rose up a fresh young man of twenty-two years." He was Faolan's uncle, and could not be freed from enchantment till pierced with a particular sword, which Faolan carried.[1]

Transformation from a dwarf to a man, as in *The Turk and Gawain*, occurs in an Austrian tale, *Der erlöste Zwerg*. A laborer gives a dwarf such a stroke in the head that he falls dead; but he immediately becomes a beautiful youth and thanks the laborer for his " Erlösung." [2]

The *Kathā-sarit-sāgara* tells of a Vidyādhara who has been compelled by a curse to take the form of a camel. He is to be restored only when he is killed in that form by a certain king, — which happens.[3] So, in the same collection, a Yaksha is doomed by a curse to be a lion till he is killed by a certain king with an arrow. This happens, and he regains his human form.[4]

The following is perhaps merely an anecdote of condign punishment after death, not an instance of disenchantment. A *Senn* in the Watthenthal saw a red bullock, which advanced in a threatening way. He caught him by the horns and forced him over the brink of a ravine. The bullock fell and was dashed to pieces. Up came the spirit of another *Senn*, and thanked him for his release. He had masquer-

---

[1] Curtin, *Hero-Tales*, pp. 495–496. The incident is really out of place in this tale, which, at this point, is a case of the attempt to resuscitate dead warriors (the " Hilda-saga ").

[2] Vernaleken, *Österreichische Kinder- u. Hausmärchen*, p. 171.

[3] Bk. xii, ch. 69, Tawney, II, 141–142.

[4] Bk. i, ch. 6, Tawney, I, 37.

aded in this shape as a punishment for once having thrown a peasant's bullock into this chasm.[1]

Often a wound that is not sufficient to cause death is enough to effect a disenchantment, so as to make the person who suffers it return to his proper shape. Indeed, the mere drawing of blood may be all that is required. So in a story from Annam, a farmer, while cutting grass, accidentally amputates the tail of a serpent. The snake immediately becomes a fine young man.[2] Again, in a story from Brittany, a beautiful woman has been changed into a turtle. Two men are fighting for her hand. Throwing herself between them to end the combat, she is wounded, and, as soon as her blood flows, her metamorphosis is at an end.[3] In a legend of Auvergne a wicked baron is condemned for his crimes to wander as a *loup-garou* till a Christian shall make his blood flow. Wounded by a woodcutter, he resumes his human form and dies instantly.[4] In a Lapland tale a lad draws blood from the hand of one of two fairy maidens who are dancing about him. Instantly the boatload of persons among whom the women have come vanishes, boat and all. Only the maiden remains. "Now you must take me to wife," says she, "since you have drawn blood upon me."[5]

In a Gypsy story from Transylvania, two wild geese, on being shot, fall to the ground as two beautiful maidens.[6] In

---

[1] Von Alpenberg, *Deutsche Alpensagen*, No. 98, pp. 96–97.

[2] Landes, *Contes et Légendes Annamites*, pp. 12–13. In a Tyrolese story, a bride accidentally steps on her snake-husband's tail and crushes it, whereupon he becomes a handsome prince: Schneller, *Märchen u. Sagen aus Wälschtirol*, No. 25, p. 65 (see Crane, *Italian Popular Tales*, pp. 324–325, with the references).

[3] Sébillot, *Contes populaires de la Haute-Bretagne*, [I], 13–14.

[4] Antoinette Bon, *Revue des Trad. Pop.*, V, 217–218 (reproduced by Sébillot, *Litt. Orale de l'Auvergne*, p. 231).

[5] Friis, *Lappiske Eventyr og Folkesagn*, No. 7, pp. 24–25, cf. p. 39.

[6] Von Wlislocki, *Märchen u. Sagen der transylvanischen Zigeuner*, No. 14,

a Maori legend, the god Maui, in pigeon-form, is hit with a
stone, and he immediately turns into a man.[1] A precisely
similar incident is found in the Irish *Wooing of Emer:*
Derbforgaill, daughter of the King of Lochlann, wishing for
the love of Cuchulinn, takes the form of a bird and flies to
Ulster, along with one of her maids, who is also in bird-
likeness. Cuchulinn wounds her with a stone from a sling.
Immediately both resume their mortal shape. The rest of
the saga does not now concern us.[2] In the Latin *De Rebus
Hiberniae Admirandis,* as well as in the *Mirabilia* in Todd's
Irish Nennius,[3] there is an account of a man who threw a
stone and brought down a swan. Running to pick up the

p. 33. In a Lithuanian tale, St. George (*Iurgis*), tired with hunting, sits
down on a stone; out comes a black serpent and creeps towards him; he
shoots her down and she immediately becomes a beautiful maid, whom he
marries: Veckenstedt, *Mythen, Sagen und Legenden der Zamaiten,* I, 289–290.
Veckenstedt's collection is discredited (see Karlowicz, *Mélusine,* V, 121 ff.),
but this incident must be substantially correct.

[1] Buller, *Forty Years in New Zealand,* London, 1878, p. 185.

[2] *Tochmarc Emire,* translated by Kuno Meyer, *Archæological Review,* I,
304 (same, revised, in Hull, *Cuchullin,* p. 82); see *Ériu,* V, 214. Cf. Zimmer,
Haupt's *Ztschr.,* XXXII, 217–218; Kuno Meyer, *Revue Celtique,* XI, 437–
438; Nutt's note in Mac Innes, *Folk and Hero Tales,* p. 477; Hartland,
Legend of Perseus, III, 50; the Modena *Perceval,* Weston, *Legend of Sir
Perceval,* II, 51–55.

[3] An hexameter list of the Wonders of Ireland, printed by Thomas
Wright, *Reliquiae Antiquae,* II, 103–107. This is No. 18 in the list (p. 105),
and No. 21 in that given in Todd's *Irish Nennius,* pp. 210–211. It does not
occur in Giraldus Cambrensis, *Topographia Hibernica,* ii, 4 ff. (*Opera,*
Rolls Series, V, 80 ff.), nor in the Norse *Speculum Regale* (see Kuno Meyer,
Folk-Lore, V, 299 ff.). Clearly by "demons" we are to understand "fairies."
The idea that persons thought to be dead have really been abducted by the
fairies is common in Ireland and elsewhere. It underlies the beautiful Middle
English romance of *Sir Orfeo,* which, as the present writer has conjectured,
may be based on a combination of the Irish tale of the *Wooing of Etain* with
the story of Orpheus and Eurydice (*American Journal of Philology,* VII,
176 ff.; *Studies and Notes,* VIII, 196, note; cf. Brandl, Paul's *Grundriss,*
II, 630; Bugge, *Arkiv för Nordisk Filologi,* VII, 108; Herz, *Spielmannsbuch,*
2d ed., pp. 361–362).

bird, he found it was a woman. She told him that she was
thought to have died, but that really she was carried off in
the flesh by demons. He restored her to her astonished
relatives. In a German story, Hans cuts and slashes among
a lot of animals with a sword, whereupon they are disenchanted and become mortals.[1]

We have already seen that decapitation, etc., must have
been regarded as a slaying of the enchanted body (the
beast or bird form) and therefore as the release of the human
shape, so that the article of the primitive creed which we
are studying has its close association with the belief in swan-
maidens and werewolves and their feather-garment or
beast-skin. The real (human) body was thought of as clad
in the enchanted body or covered by it. This comes out
with perfect clearness in those stories in which the enchanted animal is to be opened or skinned, and in which,
when this is done, the real person emerges from the skin or
belly.

Thus the Breton Péronic kills and skins the enchanted
horse at its own request. He is much surprised " de voir
sortir de sa peau un beau prince." [2] In the same collection,
a black cat, born of a woman, asks to be placed on its back
on a table and to have its belly ripped up with a sword.
This done, " il en sortait aussitôt un beau prince." [3]

A Catalan story has this feature in a singularly complicated form. A wolf who has guided the cast-off daughter of

<hr>

[1] Vernaleken, *Österreichische Kinder- u. Hausmärchen*, No. 54, p. 316.

[2] Luzel, *Contes populaires de Basse-Bretagne*, II, 66–67; cf. the modern
Irish *Story of Conn-eda*, translated by N. O'Kearney, *Cambrian Journal*, II,
101 ff., 1855 (reprinted in *Folk-Lore Record*, II, 188–190, and by Yeats,
Irish Fairy and Folk Tales, pp. 306 ff.).

[3] Luzel, III, 166. So also in *Le Chat et les deux Sorcières* (III, 131),
which is in effect another version of *Le Chat Noir*. Something similar may
once have stood in *The Red Pony* (Larminie, *West Irish Folk-Tales*, p. 215),
where the disenchantment (p. 218) is confused and distorted.

a king to his palace, gives her elaborate directions for his own disenchantment. Accordingly the girl builds a fire; kills the wolf; rips him up; catches the dove that emerges; puts the dead wolf in the fire; extracts an egg from inside the dove; breaks it, — and there emerges a beautiful prince, who marries the girl.[1]

A queer variation of the skinning process occurs in a Swedish tale, *Kidet ock Kungen*. A kid has become the trusted counsellor of a king. One day he bids the king behead him, turn his skin inside out, and force it on the flayed body again. It was a hard job; but when it was finished, there stood a handsome prince whom the king greeted as his son.[2] Still more elaborate are the directions given by a helpful ass (a prince under enchantment) in a Færöe story: " You must chop off my head and tail, skin me, cut off my legs, put the head where the tail was and the tail in the neck, turn my hoofs up toward my legs, and sew my hide together about me with the hair inside." [3] Here the symbolism of reversing a spell is carried out in a grotesquely thoroughgoing fashion. Compare, for a part of the process, the well-known trick of turning one's coat inside out for luck in gaming, or to prevent being led astray by Robin Goodfellow or other errant sprites.[4] Turning a

---

[1] Maspons y Labrós, *Lo Rondallayre*, II, 104, 110. This will be at once recognized as a variant of the folk-tale best known as *Beauty and the Beast*. There is also a forbidden chamber, or cupboard, as in *Blue Beard*. The elaborate directions for liberating the prince are properly directions for putting an effectual end to a monster with a " separable soul " like Koshchei. Here, then, as in *The Bare-Stripping Hangman*, we have a composite (see p. 208, above).

[2] Eva Wigström, *Sagor ock Äfventyr upptecknade i Skåne*, p. 10 (*Nyare Bidrag*, vol. V).

[3] Jakobsen, *Færøske Folkesagn og Æventyr*, p. 399 (cf. pp. 401, 406, 407).

[4] There is a good instance in Bishop Corbet's *Iter Boreale* (Dryden, *Miscellany Poems*, 1716, VI, 376; Corbet's *Poems*, 4th ed., edited by Gilchrist, 1807, p. 191). Cf. Tyndale, *Exposition of the First Epistle of St. John*,

somersault is a regular preliminary to transformation in Gypsy stories.[1] In a legend of Derbyshire, a certain treasure chest in an underground passage " can only be fetched away by a white horse, who must have his feet shod the wrong way about, and who must approach the box with his tail foremost.[2]

In the remarkable Zulu tale of *Umamba*, a prince born in the form of a snake asks his young wife to anoint him and to pull off his snake-skin, when he appears in his true shape.[3] The teller of the tale seems partly to have rationalized it, as if the prince wore his snake-skin as a disguise. At all events, there is very instructive confusion between a prince in snake-form and a prince concealing his true form by wearing a snake-skin, and the close psychological connection between the idea underlying the belief we are discussing and that which underlies the belief in werewolves and swan-maidens comes out very clearly. It does not appear that Umamba would ever have abandoned or been released from his snake-form if he had not found a woman willing to marry

Prologue: " They wander as in a mist, or (as we say) led by Robin Good-fellow, that they cannot come to the right way, no though they turn their caps " (*Works of Tyndale and Frith*, ed. Russell, 1831, II, 388).

[1] See Groome, *Gypsy Folk-Tales*, pp. 16, 24, 40, 58, 59; M. Klimo, *Contes et Légendes de Hongrie*, 1898, p. 243; J. F. Campbell, *The Celtic Dragon Myth*, pp. 93 ff.

[2] S. O. Addy, *Household Tales*, London, 1895, p. 58.

[3] Callaway, *Nursery Tales, Traditions and History of the Zulus*, I, 327. This is the tale mentioned, without a reference, by H. Husson, *La Chaîne Traditionelle*, Paris, 1874, p. 130 (cited by Prato, *Bulletin de Folklore*, I, 334). Cf. the Roumanian-Gypsy tale of *The Snake who became the King's Son-in-law*, translated from Constantinescu, *Probe de Limba si Literatura Tiganilor din România*, Bucharest, 1878, No. 3, pp. 61 ff., by Groome, *Gypsy Folk-Tales*, pp. 21–24. See also Giambattista Basile's *Lo Serpe*, *Pentamerone*, ii, 5, ed. Croce, I, 209 ff. (Liebrecht's translation, *Der Pentamerone*, 1846, I, 191 ff.; J. E. Taylor's, *The Pentamerone*, 2d ed., 1850, pp. 153 ff.; Keightley, *Tales and Popular Fictions*, 1834, pp. 185 ff.; Olrik, *Danske Studier*, I, 1 ff.).

him. Thus *Umamba* connects itself with *The Frog Prince*[1] and similar instances of disenchantment. That the animal skin is conceived of as a *covering* to be stripped off comes out clearly in stories in which the bridegroom is enveloped in several such skins and the bride tells him to take them off.[2]

In an Armenian tale, *Dragon-Child and Sun-Child*,[3] we have a clear case of an enchanted prince born in monstrous shape, half man and half dragon, who, released from the spell, issues from the dragon-skin, which bursts. While in dragon form the prince had been a destructive being, devouring a maiden every week (like St. George's dragon). His habitation is a dry well, and this associates him with the familiar class of water-stopping monsters.

It would be useless, as well as wearisome, to multiply examples further. Enough has been said to make it clear that both *The Carl of Carlisle* and *The Turk and Gawain*, whatever their dates may be, preserve, in the matter of disenchantment, a naïve and ancient superstition, which may fairly claim universal currency.

[1] See pp. 205, 206, above.

[2] Köhler, *Kleinere Schriften*, I, 318, note 2.

[3] Seklemian, *The Golden Maiden and other Folk Tales and Fairy Stories told in Armenia*, Cleveland and New York, 1898, pp. 73, 74.

IV. DUELLING BY ALTERNATION [1]

SAXO's comment on the ancient method of alternate blows in single combat is worth quoting: " Non enim antiquitus in edendis agonibus crebre ictuum uicissitudines petebantur, sed erat cum interuallo temporis eciam feriendi distincta successio, rarisque sed atrocibus plagis certamina gerebantur ut gloria pocius percussionum magnitudini, quam numero deferretur." [2] Elton, in his translation (1894), remarks that this style of fighting " is still in use among native Australians." [3]

In the *holmgang* of Gunnlaugr and Hrafn, the latter gives the first blow since he is the challenged party,[4] and this order is mentioned as regular in the *Kormaks Saga*.[5]

Wolfdietrich [6] visits the heathen with the express purpose of trying conclusions with him in the game of knife-throwing. To engage with all guests in this game is the custom of the castle. Strangers receive hospitality on no other terms. The heathen calls it his " right " (*reht*), and Wolfdietrich wishes to submit to " guest's law." Each of the two combatants, stripped to the shirt, stands on a stool, and has three knives and a little buckler a span wide. The host is con-

---

[1] See pp. 21–22.

[2] *Historia Danica*, bk. ii (ed. Stephanius, p. 30; ed. Müller and Velschow, p. 87; ed. Holder, p. 56). See also the poem (Stephanius, p. 36; Müller and Velschow, p. 103; Holder, p. 64).

[3] *The First Nine Books of the Danish History*, translated by Oliver Elton, p. 68, note 2.

[4] *Gunnlaugssaga Ormstungu*, cap. 11, ed. Mogk, p. 23: " Hrafn átti fyrr at höggva, er á hann var skorat."

[5] " Sá skal fyrr höggva er skorat er á " (cap. 9). See Thorlacius, *Ueber Zweykämpfe im heidnischen Norden* (*Populäre Aufsätze*, translated by L. C. Sander, Copenhagen, 1812, pp. 317, 318, 335, 354, 355).

[6] *Wolfdietrich B*, sts. 534 ff. (*Deutsches Heldenbuch*, III, 247 ff.); cf. *D*, vi, 1 ff. (IV, 73 ff.), and *A* (Dresden MS.), sts. 252 ff. (III, 154 ff.).

fident of victory.   Five hundred heads of previous adventurers crown the pinnacles of his tower;   there is one
pinnacle empty, and that is waiting for his present opponent's head.

> " Sihstu dort an den zinnen   fünf hundert houbet stân,
> Diu ich mit mînen henden   alle verderbet hân ?
> Noch stât ein zinne lære   an mînem türnlîn:
> Dâ muoz dîn werdez houbet ze einem phande sîn." [1]

The host claims the first three throws, for such is his custom.
But he tells Wolfdietrich where he means to hit him: — first
throw at his head, next at his feet, third at his heart.   Wolfdietrich dodges all three knives.   He then informs the
heathen that his first throw shall be at his right eye or his
left foot, and the heathen is in doubt which to guard.   Then
Wolfdietrich appears to aim at his eye, but really aims at
his foot, pinning him to the stool.   For the second throw,
he bids him guard the top of his head.   The heathen holds
up his buckler, but the knife cleaves both that and his
skull.   At the third throw, the heathen falls dead from the
stool, the knife in his heart.

An adventure of Lancelot's at the very outset of his
career, is a close parallel to the experiences of Wolfdietrich
with the heathen.   It is recounted by Ulrich von Zatzik-
hoven in his *Lanzelet*,[2] which was composed at the end of the
twelfth century or the beginning of the thirteenth.[3]   The
host appears at the chamber door with two bucklers and two
double-edged knives: " Take this shield in your hand and
stand by this wall.   I will take my place on the other side of

---

[1] *Wolfdietrich B*, st. 595.

[2] Vv. 708 ff., ed. Hahn, pp. 17 ff.   Cf. Heinzel, *Ueber die Ostgothische
Heldensage*, p. 79 (Vienna Academy, *Sitzungsberichte*, CIX); Hermannn
Schneider, *Die Gedichte und die Sage von Wolfdietrich*, 1913, pp. 261-263,
287 ff.

[3] See *Romania*, X, 465 ff.; XII, 459 ff.

the room. You may have your choice — to begin the game
or to let me throw first." Lancelot thinks it right that his
host should begin. The knife goes through Lancelot's
sleeve, wounding him slightly, and sticks into the wall.
Lancelot springs across the chamber and stabs his opponent.
This ends the game. " The host fell upon the floor and
never spoke another word." [1]

It is instructive to put by the side of these two adventures
— Wolfdietrich's and Lancelot's — a Tinguian legend
recently reported from the Philippines. The hero, arriving
at the town of " the old man," challenges him to single combat. The old man sends for his head-axe and spear, but
grants the adventurer the first throw: " Go on, and throw
your spear, if you are brave." But the hero disdains to take
advantage of his opponent. " If I am the first to throw my
spear," he retorts, " you will never have a chance to throw
yours, for I will kill you at once. You [had] better throw
yours first." Then the old man grows angry, and hurls his
spear, but it glances off the hero's body. He tries to cut off
the hero's head with his axe, but in vain, for he is invulner-
able. The old man is a good sport: " Throw your spear at
me; for if you can hit me, it is all right, for I have killed
many people." Then the hero pierces the old man with his
spear and cuts off his head. [2]

The duel between Wrennok and Gandeleyn is in the ballad
of *Robyn and Gandeleyn*, preserved in a manuscript of about
1450.[3] "Who shall have the first shot?" asked Gandeleyn.
" I," answered Wrennok. But he missed Gandeleyn, whose
arrow then " clef his herte on too." For the duel with darts

[1] Vv. 1113–1183, pp. 27–28.

[2] Cole, *Traditions of the Tinguian*, pp. 76–77 (*Field Museum of Natural
History, Anthropological Series*, XIV); cf. Cole, pp. 103–104, 125–126, for
similar duels.

[3] Child, *Ballads*, No. 115, III, 12–14 (from Sloane MS. 2593, fol. 14*b*).

in the Madagascar tale, see Charles Renel, *Contes de Madagascar*, pp. 116–117.

The game of exchanging buffets is admirably illustrated by a passage in the Middle English romance of *Richard Coer de Lion*.[1] The incident is thus summarized by Child: — " Richard is betrayed to the king of Almayne by a minstrel to whom he had given a cold reception. The king's son, held the strongest man of the land, visits the prisoner, and proposes to him an exchange of this sort. The prince gives Richard a clout which makes fire spring from his eyes, and goes off laughing, ordering Richard to be well fed, so that he may have no excuse for returning a feeble blow when he takes his turn. The next day, when the prince comes for his payment, Richard, who has waxed his hand by way of preparation, delivers a blow which breaks the young champion's cheekbone and fells him dead." [2] A similar game is called " plucke-buffet " in *A Gest of Robyn Hode* (sts. 424–426). The king and Robin " shoot at pluck buffet " as they ride together, the one who wins a shot having the right to give the other a blow. Robin is of course the better archer.

> And many a buffet our kynge wan
> Of Robyn Hode that day,
> And nothynge spared good Robyn
> Our kynge in his pay.[3]

In *The Turk and Gawain*, a challenge to an exchange of buffets occupies the same place that the challenge to the beheading game holds in *Gawain and the Green Knight*.[4]

---

[1] Vv. 746–798 (Weber, *Metrical Romances*, II, 32–34); vv. 738–798 (ed. Brunner, pp. 118–120, *Wiener Beiträge zur englischen Philologie*, XLII).

[2] *Ballads*, III, 55.

[3] Child, III, 77.

[4] Madden, *Syr Gawayne*, pp. 243–255; *Bishop Percy's Folio Manuscript*, ed. by Hales and Furnivall, I, 88–102.

For the very curious scene in Chapman's *Alphonsus Emperor of Germany*, see the Pearson edition of the *Comedies and Tragedies*, 1873, III, 229–230.

The contest with the venomous apple in the heroic saga of Finn proceeds in accordance with the alternate method. In the Irish *Finn and Lorcan*, Finn visits the land of the King of the Dark Island in quest of the Sword of Light. Lorcan is his helpful companion, and undertakes to provide the usual comforts, — shelter, bed, food, etc. For food he applies to the king's butcher, who proposes a game (*cleas*). He says he has a poison-apple and claims the first cast with it; then Lorcan may have the second shot. Lorcan bids him make haste. The butcher hits Lorcan in the forehead and such is the force of the blow that the apple is driven out to daylight at the back of his head. Lorcan pulls out the apple with his finger and heals the wound with his thumb. Then he throws the apple in his turn, and it goes clean through the butcher's head, pierces an iron door, and sinks seven fathoms deep in the earth. This finishes the butcher and Lorcan helps himself to provisions.[1] In another version the game is played with the king's baker instead of the butcher.[2]

In a Highland version of the favorite Irish saga known as *The Fairy Palace of the Quicken Trees*,[3] a gigantic cave-dweller asks the King of Eirin, who has entered his retreat in pursuit of a hare, " Whether do you like best to play at the venomous apple or at the hot gridiron ? "[4] The king chooses the apple. And "every time he threw the venomous apple across," says the king in reporting the incident, " he

[1] *Finn agus Lorcán, Imtheachta an Oireachtais*, II, i, 7 ff. (Dublin, 1903).

[2] *Imtheachta an Oireachtais*, III, ii, 41 ff. (1901).

[3] Nineteen versions are enumerated in [*Harvard*] *Studies and Notes*, VIII, 209–210 (one in a MS. of 1600, another in a MS. of 1603).

[4] Compare the brazier in *The Turk and Gawain*, vv. 199–223.

killed one of [my] gentlemen; and when I threw it back he
intercepted it with the point of a penknife."[1] There is a
contest with a "golden apple" in one of J. F. Campbell's
versions of the same saga, and likewise a huge cauldron (as
in *The Turk and Gawain*).[2] The contest with the apple
becomes, in *The Turk and Gawain* a game of hand-tennis
(*jeu de paume* or "palm-play") between the Turk and the
King of Man's Giants. The " tennis ball " was of brass: no
knight in Arthur's hall was strong enough to " give it a
lout," no man in all England strong enough to " carry it."[3]

[1] Mac Innes, *Folk and Hero Tales*, p. 87.
[2] *Fionn's Enchantment, Revue Celtique*, I, 196 ff.
[3] Vv. 187–189, 140–142.

V. THE BOOK OF CARADOC

THE relation of the Challenge to the remainder of the *Livre de Caradoc* deserves consideration. In that poem it occurs as one of a little cycle of adventures told of Caradoc. We have studied it, however, by itself, without reference to the rest of the *Livre*.[1] There is ample justification for such procedure. The Challenge in Celtic belongs properly to Cuchulinn and not to Caradoc, and it has an existence in French quite independent of the latter hero. It forms, then, no essential part of Caradoc's legend.

Further, the only document (the *Livre*) which actually attaches the Challenge to Caradoc, is so closely related to *Gawain and the Green Knight* as to force the inference of a common original (R) from which these two poems have derived the incident in question. Now the English poem has nothing but the Challenge in common with the *Livre de Caradoc*. The natural conclusion is that R was an episodical French romance of Gawain containing simply this incident and nothing more.[2] This becomes a certainty when we compare the Challenge in *La Mule sanz Frain* with the other versions; for we find ourselves forced to infer that R was itself derived from an earlier French poem (O), which was the common source of both R and the Challenge in *La Mule*. As it is extremely improbable that R contained any of the adventures that stand in the *Livre de Caradoc* except the Challenge, so is it (*a fortiori*) almost inconceivable that O contained any of them except that story. In brief, the shape in which the Challenge occurs in all the extant versions is simply and easily explained by a construction which makes that story pass into French from Irish, by whatever path, but once,[3] and that *once* must have been before the incident

---

[1] Pp. 26 ff.   [2] P. 38.   [3] P. 47.

was attached to the other adventures with which it is now associated in the *Livre de Caradoc*. If, on the other hand, we maintain (with Gaston Paris) [1] that the Challenge had attached itself to Caradoc on Celtic soil (whether in Wales or in Brittany), we shall be obliged to assume a double source for the French *Livre* in this particular adventure, — holding that some French poet who found the incident in his Celtic source, revised it on the basis of a French poem (R) which was itself derived from Celtic. Otherwise, the peculiar resemblances between the *Livre de Caradoc* (as we have it) and *Gawain and the Green Knight* cannot be explained. The hypothesis is excessively complicated and altogether improbable, especially since there is absolutely no necessity for resorting to it to explain the phenomena.

A scrutiny of the rôle of the Challenge in the *Livre de Caradoc* confirms our opinion that this is no proper part of the Caradoc cycle but was inserted from some French poem that was unrelated to him. The plot of the *Livre* is as follows: —

Isaune,[2] Arthur's niece, marries Caradoc, King of Nantes in Brittany. Her lover, the magician Eliavrès, deprives Caradoc of his wife for the first three nights after the wedding, but furnishes magic substitutes so that the outrage is not discovered. Thus our hero, Caradoc the younger, is really the son of Eliavrès, not of his putative father. At the proper age he crosses the Channel and visits the court of his great-uncle, King Arthur, who gives him the accolade at a Pentecostal feast. On this occasion an unknown knight appears and challenges the Round Table to the game of decapitation. Caradoc accepts, and the events follow that we have already studied. When the stranger has tested Caradoc's valor sufficiently, he spares his life, and, taking him aside, reveals himself to him as his father, the magician; he even explains the details of the trick of substitution that he had played on the elder Caradoc years before. The young man, not pleased, calls Eliavrès a liar, but he feels that he has spoken the truth. The enchanter rides off at the top of his speed. The court breaks up, and

---

[1] *Romania*, XXVIII, 229.　　　　　[2] Or *Isave*.

Caradoc hastens home to Brittany and repeats to his supposed father everything that Eliavrès has said. Isaune does not attempt to deny her guilt, and her husband shuts her up in a tower of stone.

Caradoc the younger returns to King Arthur, meaning to devote himself to arms, as befits a chevalier. After reaching England, and while on his way to Carlion, he falls in with a knight named Aalardin du Lac who is carrying off Guimer, the sister of Cador of Cornwall. Caradoc protests but is bluntly advised to " mind his own business." In the fight that ensues, Aalardin is worsted and yields himself prisoner to the lady, by Caradoc's instructions. All three now hunt up Cador, who is lying on the ground almost lifeless — the result of a recent combat with Aalardin, for the abduction had taken place while Cador and Guimer were riding to court.

Aalardin conducts them all to his pavilion, which is pitched in a fair meadow. Here they see many wonderful things, the work of enchantment, and make the acquaintance of Aalardin's sister, who cures Cador without delay. [It is certain that he and his sister are supernatural beings.] The three knights swear everlasting brotherhood and accompany the two ladies to Carlion. By this time Caradoc and Guimer, Cador's sister, are in love with each other. After an account of the festivities at court, including an insufferably tedious tournament,[1] the story passes over to Brittany.

Isaune, we remember, has been shut up in a tower of stone. But her lover Eliavrès, being a magician, has no difficulty in visiting her continually, and they lead a merry life. By his magic he makes musicians appear, who play for them, and women who dance and tumble to amuse them. The neighbors are amazed at the sounds of revelry. Caradoc the elder sets a watch, but the magician always eludes his vigilance. At length a summons is sent to young Caradoc, who is still at Arthur's court. He returns to Nantes, takes up the affair, and succeeds in surprising Isaune and Eliavrès together. The enchanter is seized, and the injured husband subjects him to a barbarous punishment, which is meant, however to be condign, for it repeats with savage variations the tricks that Eliavrès played upon him at the outset.

Isaune appeals to her lover for vengeance on their son. He produces by his arts a serpent horrible and black, puts it in her *aumaire*, and bids her send Caradoc thither, when next she sees him, on the pretext of fetching her mirror. She obeys, and when Caradoc puts in his hand, the serpent fixes on his arm and begins to suck his blood.

---

[1] The tournament is lacking in some manuscripts and is manifestly not by the same author as most of the *Livre*.

He has not two years to live. Half-mad with his sufferings, Caradoc wanders about in the woods, often confessing himself at some hermitage, and bitterly repentant for his treatment of his father and mother. He is found by his friend Cador, the brother of his *amie*, after a long search. Cador wishes to cut away the reptile, but Caradoc assures him that if it were injured, he should die in a moment.

So Cador visits Isaune in her tower and reproaches her for what she has done to Caradoc. He finds her remorseful, and she ascertains from Eliavrès the sole means of removing the serpent. This involves an act of devotion on the part of Guimer, Caradoc's *amie*, but she does not hesitate. The serpent is killed and Caradoc saved, but Guimer loses the nipple of her right breast. Caradoc's supposed father, the king of Nantes, dies soon after, and he succeeds to the throne, having taken Guimer to wife.

One day Caradoc falls in with his friend Aalardin in the forest, follows him to his [other-world] mansion, and receives from him the boss of a magic golden shield, with instructions as to its efficacy. This he applies to his wife's breast,

> Et li ors s'i joint maintenant
> Et fu tout d'autretel samblant
> Come l'autre mamele estoit.

Then the *Livre* closes with the famous adventure of the horn from which no husband of an unfaithful woman can drink without spilling the wine. Caradoc does not spill a drop, and compliments Guimer with charming simplicity and grace: " Lady, I give you my thanks! No wife ever did her husband greater honor at court."

All this makes a straightforward and consistent narrative with the exception of the Challenge. This disorders the plot. The intrigue between Eliavrès and Caradoc's mother is a secret, and it is for the enchanter's interest to keep it quiet. Yet by his conduct in connection with the Challenge he reveals everything and causes Isaune to be imprisoned, thus wantonly getting himself and her into difficulties. Omit the Challenge and all is clear and logical with only the slightest possible bit of adjustment. The revelation of the intrigue and the imprisonment of Isaune will result, not from the absurd acts of her lover, but from young Caradoc's discovering the pair together. Then will follow the vengeance of the guilty couple, Caradoc's terrible affliction, his relief by the devotion of Guimer, and their happy marriage. The tale might end with the death of the king of Nantes, the coronation of Caradoc and Guimer, and the cure by the magic shield. The episode of the wondrous horn, makes, however, a good epilogue.

Nobody seems to have noticed, or at all events to have thought it worth while to promulgate, the obvious fact that the story of Caradoc and the Serpent is an adaptation of the widespread folk-tale known as *The Faithless Mother* (or *Sister*).[1] About a hundred versions are in print.[2] They fall into several groups and exhibit considerable variety, but the type is not to be mistaken. In one group the hero is the son of a princess who has been shut up in a tower to seclude her from wooers (Danaë type) but has conceived in a miraculous manner (from a grain, a leaf, a flower, a glance of the eye). She has been driven from home and is alone in the wilderness with her boy. He discovers the habitation of certain uncanny creatures (dragons, cyclopes, ogres, blacks), kills them all but one, and shuts that one up, half dead. The mother releases the captive and gives him her love. They fear discovery and plot the hero's destruction. It is usually the woman who makes the suggestion but the paramour who tells her what to do. She feigns sickness and sends her son on dangerous errands to fetch something that will cure her. He always succeeds in these quests by the aid of a supernatural being who is commonly feminine (*fée, lamia*, etc.). Sometimes this person is an enchanted princess whom he has freed. The plots thus failing, the mother binds him

---

[1] P. 27.
[2] Bolte and Polívka, *Anmerkungen zu den Kinder- u. Hausmärchen der Brüder Grimm*, I, 551 ff. (No. 60).

by a trick, and the lover kills him, cuts him into bits, and
puts the fragments on the back of the hero's magic horse.
The horse carries the mangled body to the abode of the
supernatural helper, who restores the hero to life. Sometimes he marries her.

In another group there is usually little or no trace of
mysterious parentage. The hero is sent on errands as before.
On one of these quests he rescues a princess who has been
carried off by giants. Instead of being killed, his eyes are
put out and he is turned adrift in the woods. He is guided
to the princess by helpful animals or otherwise. She marries
him and restores his sight, and he succeeds to the kingdom.

In an erratic story from Tripoli, which is related to this
cycle but refuses to conform, there is a most striking parallel
to the method adopted by Eliavrès in his revenge on Caradoc. A woman has married a person who has the power to
turn himself into a snake, a dog, or a monster. Her brother
lives with them, and she wishes to get rid of him (for no
assigned reason) and urges her husband to kill him. " Very
well, I will turn into a snake and hide in the date-cask, and
when he sticks in his hand, I 'll bite him." The plot fails,
for reasons that need not here be particularized.[1]

The saga of Caradoc and the Serpent as told in the *Livre*
follows the type as closely as could be expected in a case of
adaptation to chivalric romance. The essential features are
well preserved — amorous intrigue with an uncanny being,
hatred of the mother for her son, her appeal to her paramour
to kill him and his suggestion of a method, errand on which
the son is sent by his mother with intent to destroy, death
or dreadful affliction of the son, his resuscitation or cure by
a woman (sometimes his *amie*). The peculiarity of the
Caradoc version consists in the fact that the mother's para-

[1] Stumme, *Märchen und Gedichte aus der Stadt Tripolis*, 1898, pp. 104 ff.

mour is the father of the hero, and this is due, as we have
seen, to the influence of what may be called the Nectanabus
theme.[1] In so styling it, however, I do not mean to suggest
any borrowing from the Alexander legend. If we had a
good old Welsh account of Caradoc, we might or might not
discover that he was the son of a Celtic divinity, but that
would have no bearing on the episode of the Challenge in
the *Livre* or elsewhere.

This is not the place to examine the Celtic antecedents of
the *Livre de Caradoc* in those adventures which properly
belong to Caradoc's cycle (the serpent story and the test
with the magic horn). The subject has been restudied, on
the basis of the interesting discoveries of Miss Harper,[2] by
Gaston Paris and F. Lot.[3] I will merely suggest that the
removal of the Challenge from the Caradoc cycle in no way
affects the main results at which those distinguished scholars
have arrived.

[1] See Weinreich, *Der Trug des Nektanebos*, Berlin, 1911. Henderson's
conjecture that in an older version of the *Fled Bricrend* than any that we
have, Cuchulinn's father Sualtam was the challenger in the beheading game,
is improbable in itself, and cannot appeal to the *Caradoc* for support (see
Henderson's *Fled Bricrend*, pp. xlv, and note, 199).

[2] *Modern Language Notes*, November, 1898, XIII, 209 ff.

[3] *Romania*, XXVIII, 214 ff., 568 ff. Cf. Rhŷs, *Celtic Folklore*, II, 689–
690.

VI. LA MULE SANZ FRAIN

In *La Mule sanz Frain*, as in *Le Livre de Caradoc*, the episode of the Challenge is an intrusion, — that is, in both cases it has been put into a plot to which it did not originally belong. Accordingly, in our investigation in Part One we have not found it necessary to analyze the plot of *La Mule*, but have treated the Challenge as a story by itself.[1] Yet perhaps the subject ought not to be dismissed without further scrutiny, and the plot of *La Mule* offers many interesting features which will repay the trouble of examination.

One has but to read Paien's poem attentively to perceive that it bears some relation to certain well-ascertained types of folk-tales, — in particular, to *The Fairy Mistress* or *The Visit to the Other World* (so familiar in Irish literature and legend) and to *The Enchanted Princess* or *The Release of a Captive Maiden*. Before attempting to analyze the romance, we must define these types with care.

I. *The Fairy Mistress.* — An immortal woman, a *fée*, resident in the land of joy and perpetual youth (which is conceived as an island or an underground realm or as somehow separated from this world by a river or the sea), is enamored of a mortal here and summons him to her presence.[2] The messenger may be an attendant nymph [3] or an animal. In the latter case, the animal is not an ordinary

---

[1] Pp. 42 ff.

[2] On this type see A. C. L. Brown, [*Harvard*] *Studies and Notes*, 1903, VIII, 19 ff., where references to previous treatment may be found. The type may be said to have two antitypes: (1) stories in which a god wooes a mortal woman, and (2) those in which a *fée* or other supernatural woman (swan-maiden, mermaid) becomes for a time an inhabitant of this earth as the wife or mistress of a mortal hero. For the latter see Cross, *Modern Philology*, XII, 585 ff. (on *Lanval* and *Graelent*); for the former see Cross, *Revue Celtique*, XXXI, 413 ff. (on *Yonec*).

[3] As in *Lanval* and the *Serglige Conchulaind*.

beast but a magical creature in the service of the *fée*, and may even be a transformed fairy maiden. Thus, in a familiar variety of the type, the hero is hunting and pursues a white doe or a great boar, which conducts him to the presence of his expectant mistress.[1] Sometimes the *fée* goes in person to summon her favorite to the other world,[2] or the animal is the *fée* herself in a temporary disguise. It may suffice for the hero to go to the *fée's* land; or he may be forced to prove his worthiness by performing tasks or overcoming obstacles before he wins her. These terms may appear to be quite wantonly imposed by the *fée* herself, but they are really conditions to which she is bound by the very quality of her divine nature.[3] The hero may remain with the *fée* forever, but sometimes he returns to this world, homesick for the kindly race of men.[4]

II. *The Giant's Daughter.* — A hero makes his way into the Other World and desires to marry the daughter of its ruler. The god is angry or reluctant, and wishes to destroy or eject the intruder. At best, he is under the necessity of testing the suitor's worthiness to become an immortal. In any case, he either tries to kill the aspirant (sometimes in single combat, often by trickery) or sets him dangerous or apparently impossible tasks. In these the hero is frequently

[1] As in *Guingamor* and the story of the *Biche Blanche*.

[2] As in the story of *Connla Ruad*.

[3] Just as sometimes a *liaison* between mortal and immortal must be broken off when it becomes known — not because the parties wish to separate, but because they cannot help themselves (cf. *American Journal of Philology*, VII, 191, note).

[4] So swan-maidens and other supernatural brides are almost certain to leave their mortal husbands and return to their mysterious realm. On "the fairy mistress in the world of mortals" see Cross, *Modern Philology*, XII, 594 ff., in a fundamentally important paper on the *Celtic Elements in the Lays of Lanval and Graelent*. Some of the tests applied to mortal lovers by fairy mistresses are certainly borrowed from other types of *märchen*.

helped by the daughter or by animals. In the end, the bride is won, for the god is either baffled and subdued or else he is satisfied to accept the hero as son-in-law.[1] In a variety of this type, the hero runs away with the daughter and is pursued but makes good his escape, frequently by the aid of magic obstacles.

Many tales of this type are frankly mythological. In many, however, the Other World is replaced (or represented) by the abode of a giant (ogre, ghoul, rakshasa), who is savage and malignant by nature but has a beautiful wife or daughter.[2] There are tasks, as before, and helpful animals; or the lady assists the quester, since she has no fondness for her monstrous husband (or father) — none, at all events, that does not quickly evaporate under the charm of the hero's presence. When the giant has been killed and the lady won, the hero may continue to inhabit the giant's castle, or he may return to his native country, enriched with the spoils of victory. The original object of his quest may not have been to get a wife, but to steal some precious object like the Golden Fleece. In this case the lady is an additional prize which crowns the adventurer's felicity.

Types I and II are superficially alike, since both involve the winning of a wife of the Other World; but the distinction between them is elementary and abysmal. In the first type the lady is a powerful goddess, who acts of her own volition and controls the destinies of her chosen hero. In the second, the government of the Other World is masculine, and the lady is subject to the will of her father (or husband). At best, he is a fierce and despotic divinity (or tyrant king) against whom her only weapon is craft. Often he is a cruel

---

[1] See Lowie, *The Test Theme, Journal of American Folk-Lore,* XXI, 134 ff.

[2] In rude forms of this variety, the lady may be the giant's wife or mistress. Finer feeling makes her a captive maiden whom he wishes to marry but who has resisted his importunities.

giant or a man-eating demon. In some varieties, indeed, the lady languishes in captivity, from which she can be freed by the hero only. Neither of these types can by any conceivable chance have developed out of the other. In their controlling ideas they differ utterly and *ab initio*. Nor is it useful or even reasonable to try to distinguish their comparative "primitiveness." Both were already ancient and widespread and solidly established long before the earliest date that concerns us here.

Yet, despite their essential difference, there are certain points in the two types that are or may become coincident. In both, for example, the hero must go to the Other World — and since the journey seems likely in any case to be difficult and dangerous in itself, there is ample opportunity for any tale-teller to attach (at will or by confusion) adventures *en route* to a story belonging to either type. So too of perils, tasks, and proofs undergone by the hero after he has crossed the Great Divide. The animus behind the tests or tasks will, of course, be different, but the *res gestae* may be identical. Finally, there is a fine chance for confusion in the helpful or guiding animal. Such beasts are kittle cattle even for the professed anthropologist: they are mere *lutins espiègles* to any student of literature who undertakes to annex the vast domain of folk-lore in a fortnight.

Originally and properly the helpful animal is quite unconnected with either of the typical *märchen* that now occupy us. He may be literally of the hero's kin, — his brother, even his twin brother (as in the "congenital" examples). He may be constructively or mystically of his kin, — his totem, what you will. He may be merely a grateful being, eager to repay a kindness casually done. He may be all three of these in one. But, whatever his motive is and however he has been acquired by the hero, he is in his functions simply a friend in need, and as such, of course, he is likely to appear on any occasion when the hero wants assistance. Wherever there is trouble or difficulty or danger, there is the helpful animal. Thus his presence in any particular tale by no means determines the type to which that tale is referable, or the central idea that governed its conception.

Helpful animals, then, as I have just said, may easily work confusion between our two types of folk-tale. For one of the chief services which they afford is to guide or convey the hero, and in this capacity they are just as usable in one type as in the other. Hence we cannot always be certain whether a given beast in a given story is the *fée's* summoner (type I) or whether he is (type II) the hero's guide, philosopher, and friend, helping him to the Other World for the nonce on a voluntary errand.

This is a long excursus *de partibus animalium*, but I think it not altogether otiose. There is some danger that we may allow the Fairy Mistress to slip into the throne recently left vacant by the tiresome Sun God of the comparative mythologists; and we must not let her achieve this bad eminence by the aid of helpful animals. In short, the presence of such a beast in any folk-tale or romantic poem does not even create a presumption that the heroine is a *fée*, unless we can make sure that the creature acts as her messenger or agent.[1] This once determined, we may safely entrust ourselves to the animal's guidance.

Three things, then, may be more or less alike in the incidents of our first and our second type — the difficulty of reaching the Other World, the tasks and dangers that confront the hero when he gets there, and the rôle of the

---

[1] On helpful animals see Hartland, *Legend of Perseus*, III, 191–197 (a most useful table).

helpful animals.   Hence it is not surprising that the two types are often confused or even amalgamated in popular fiction.   From their amalgamation arises a third type of folk-tale, and we may call it *The Enchanted Princess*.

The process of its formation is easy to follow.   In type II (*The Giant's Daughter*), as we have already seen, there is a tendency to substitute for the wife or mistress or daughter of the giant, a mortal maiden whom the monster holds captive.   Such a change is due in part to refinement of feeling.   In part, however it comes from religious scruple.   For the hero to marry a creature, however beautiful and virtuous, who was beyond the pale of humanity, was felt to be equivalent to a demonic alliance.[1]   In the first type (*The Fairy Mistress*) the necessity for some modification of the heroine's nature was still more imperative.   Whatever might be thought of a giant's daughter, there could be no doubt that the *fées* who enticed men to their unearthly realm were devils, union with whom was mortal sin.[2]   Enchantment afforded an easy way out of the difficulty, and *fées* became enchanted mortals, whom it was praiseworthy to set free and lawful to wed.   This substitution made it easy for the types to coalesce, especially since, in the second type, the giant or ogre was often regarded as a magician who detained his fair captive as much by spells as by physical force.   When the *fée* of the first type had become an enchanted princess, other changes in her story were inevitable; and these were effected by borrowing features from the second type, or by interpreting features already present in the first type in the light of similar traits belonging to the other.   Thus was developed Type III, which we will now examine and describe.

[1] The change from demon's daughter to enchanted princess may be observed in the *Pançatrantra* itself (cf. Brockhaus, I, 110-113, with II, 175).

[2] The case of the Ritter von Staufenberg is a superb example.

III. *The Enchanted Princess.* — The land where the *fée* lives has ceased to be the Other World. It is simply the hereditary possession of a fair mortal. Wicked spells have made it invisible (except at particular times and under special circumstances) or inaccessible (except to the fortunate hero who can baffle the magic). The same enchantment has made the lady's castle hard to enter and has filled it with hideous defenders, — lions and dragons and serpents. The lady herself is immured in the highest tower or the innermost room, and may be buried in magic sleep or transformed into some horrible monster

The enchanter who has wrought all this evil may or may not be present in person. If present, he sometimes acts simply as one more opponent whom the hero must overcome; but sometimes he is the suitor of the lady, whom he will set free if she will be his wife.[1] The tests or tasks which the ruler of the Other World imposes upon the aspirant for his daughter's hand in type II, and which in type I the *fée* may require as proofs of her chosen lover's worthiness, become in type III magic obstacles contrived by the enchanter. The helpful animal of type II may be regarded in type III as owing his beast's form to the malice of the magician. In that case, he is commonly a brother or other relative of the princess, and the conditions of the spell allow him to roam about in search of a champion who will attempt to undo the mischief. Thus he inherits the office of the guiding beast of type I. And as the hart or boar or *biche blanche* of type I may be an attendant nymph (or even the *fée* herself) in a temporary disguise, so the enchanted animal of type III resumes his human shape when the spells are

[1] In this latter case, the story melts so completely into one variety of the type II (that in which a captive woman has been substituted for the wife or daughter of the giant) that it is hard to tell from which side to begin its analysis.

broken.[1]   The *dénouement* of the story involves the disenchantment both of the lady and her realm, and the acceptance of the hero as the husband of the one and the king or feudatory of the other.

Before we leave this third type, a word must be said of the condition to which the land or the city of the enchanted princess has been reduced by the spells of her persecutor. Very often it lies desolate; no inhabitants are visible; the houses stand empty and are falling into ruin.   On the dissolution of the spell, however, everything returns to its normal state.   The streets are filled with citizens, the palaces once more resound with the voice of feasting.   In this trait of the *gaste citée* or the " waste land," so familiar in Arthurian romance, it is not difficult to recognize a survival of one of the best known laws of the Other World; for the feature exists quite independently of the type of *märchen* which we are discussing, and is easily intelligible whenever we encounter it.   Knights errant are always entering vacant palaces and finding a feast spread for them.   They continually see splendid castles where nothing of the kind was known before, enter, and after romantic adventures wake up to find themselves in the open field or under a tree in the forest.[2]   This means simply that the *fées* or spirits of the supernatural realm are not ordinarily visible to mortals, but that at times they become so.[3]   The general tendency to convert all these beings into devils or magicians explains the shape in which we frequently encounter such stories in mediæval and later literature.   Philosophy and Christianity

---

[1] For examples of the disenchantment of the helpful animal, see p. 200.

[2] In this form of story we have in part a survival of the belief in lustful demons like Lilith, or the Lamia in Philostratus.   Their prestigious enchantments are partly for the satisfaction of their desires, and the hero is discarded when the *fée* (enchantress) is weary of him.

[3] Cf. Newell, *Journal of American Folk-Lore*, XIII, 232.

account for the phenomena as diabolical illusions. The title of John Wier's book is the solution of the whole matter: *De Praestigiis Daemonum*. May not Satan himself appear as an angel of light ? [1]

This substitution of enchantment is due to rationalizing. It brings the supernatural personages down to the level of humanity and makes them thoroughly reasonable and natural creatures. For the enchanter is a primeval figure and magic is an art that has been practised from the earliest known times down to the present day. A magician is nothing but a man who commands powers and forces inaccessible to the general run of his fellow-creatures. He was hardly stranger to the minds of our remoter ancestors than the expert electrician or chemist is to us. The process, then, is of the same kind as that by which gods became heroes, or by which animal-spouses became, not real animals (for that was abhorrent to reason and sensibility), but men transformed for the time into brute shape and transformable into mortal guise if the proper means could be discovered. As time goes on, however, the very idea of enchantment may itself come to seem unreasonable, and therefore an attempt is sometimes made by the story-teller to represent the strange events as due to natural causes or to tell them as facts, with no mention of the superhuman. This kind of rationalizing is extremely common in Arthurian romance, and it frequently results in contradiction or sheer incomprehensibility. A magician is permitted by the laws of his art to make the conditions of disenchantment as bizarre as

---

[1] The degradation to which the poetical and innocent fancy of a wife from the Other World may submit is well illustrated in the account of an unfortuate Italian priest, manifestly insane, in the *Strix* of the younger Pico della Mirandola. Witch trials are crowded with similar horrors. Here again we note the survival of the very ancient belief in lustful demons.

he likes. The more nearly they approach the unachievable, the better for the wizard, who of course desires his régime to be permanent. And the counter-magic or unspelling devices that baffle the villain of the piece may be just as preposterous (if there is truth in magic anyhow) as the original spells, and still be quite reasonable. Thus in *Walewein* a king's son is changed into a fox by his step-mother. He must retain this shape until he shall be in the company of King Wonder, King Wonder's son, the princess Assentijn, and Walewein, all at the same moment — and this, the queen thinks, will never come to pass. Yet it does, and the fox returns to his human form; for no enchantment can be quite indissoluble — there must always be a way out. Here there is also a counter-spell, imposed upon the wicked stepmother by the prince's aunt: she must become a toad and squat under the doorsill until he is released from the charm.[1] Such stories are perfectly consistent and easy to understand so long as they keep the magical machinery; but if the adventures alone are kept by the narrator, and the magic causes are ignored or rationalized, the whole thing becomes a farrago of inconsequent absurdities.[2] The incoherence or lack of adequate motive which critics censure in the Arthurian romances, is not seldom due to the fact that the rationalizing process has been applied (perhaps only partially, when the confusion is the greater) to stories which in their original form were coherent if the data as to enchantment and the like (which no ancient would have dreamed of disputing) were once admitted as true.[3]

[1] *Walewein*, vv. 5696 ff., 5736 ff., 10942 ff. (ed. Jonckbloet, I, 189 ff., 360–361).

[2] Cf. the Challenge in *Perlesvaus* (pp. 52 ff., above).

[3] I do not mean to extend this principle to every late and merely imitative piece; for some of these are mechanical works of fiction, cobbled together out of old materials and *données* with no regard to sense or structure.

A good example of progressive rationalization may be seen by comparing Wauchier's continuation of *Perceval li Gallois* with the *Modena* (or *Didot*) *Perceval* in the adventure of the Perilous Ford. Here we have a contamination of two motifs — the Fairy Mistress and the Disenchantment. The former is doubtless the original and proper motif in this episode, but disenchantment is expressly mentioned in the Modena version as the result of the hero's feat, and the effects of the unspelling are described. In Wauchier, on the other hand, the adventure is rationalized and all traces of the supernatural have vanished.[1]

The fact that we can detect so much rationalizing in the French Arthurian material, and that too in very early texts, — in Chrétien, for example, — shows that these texts, even if they do come early in extant French literature, come late in the development of the particular story which each tells. They stand, in a sense, at the end rather than at the beginning of a long course of development. And even the Celtic materials which the French authors followed had already been more or less subjected to the same process before they came into French hands. Middle Irish documents often exhibit similar misapprehensions or perversions.[2] From whatever quarter the Celtic material reached French writers, much of it had undergone extensive modification before they received it.

Fortunately we are able to bring to bear upon such problems the testimony of a huge mass of folk-tales, which the devotion of collectors for the past hundred years has accumulated from every nation under heaven. These are

---

[1] *Modena Perceval*, in Miss Weston's *Legend of Sir Perceval*, II, 50–55; *Perceval li Gallois*, vv. 24182 ff. (Potvin, IV, 134 ff.). See Miss Weston's remarks, *Legend of Sir Perceval*, II, 204 ff.

[2] An example that is very striking on account of its great age may be seen in the story quoted on p. 276.

now and then belittled by scholars, stigmatized as "modern," and denied the right to be heard. In fact, if circumspectly dealt with, they are witnesses of first-rate importance, for they have often preserved, in their naïveté, the ideas and incidents which courtly or otherwise sophisticated writers disguise or distort or suppress.

With this in view, I have attempted to define with some exactness the three types of folk-tales which we must bear in mind if we are to analyze the plot of *La Mule sanz Frain,* — *The Fairy Mistress, The Giant's Daughter,* and *The Enchanted Princess.*

The first two of these types are doubtless older and more "primitive" than the third. But here we must walk circumspectly and not be deceived by mere words. As soon as a type of folk-tale gets firmly established, the complexity of its pre-history ceases to be significant. Our third type, *The Enchanted Princess,* despite its heterogeneous origin, had become, long before the time at which *La Mule sanz Frain* was written, a simple, independent unit — a "type-märchen" — capable of reproducing its kind indefinitely, without regard to the sources from which it sprang. In our study of *La Mule,* therefore, it must be admitted to equal standing with *The Fairy Mistress* and *The Giant's Daughter.*

La Mule sanz Frain has suffered from both excessive rationalization and from misunderstanding. It has also lost some of its incidents. Paien, it is easy to see, is following in the main a popular tale which he disorders very much in his attempt to eliminate the frankly supernatural or to fit the whole to the requirements of chivalric romance. In some particulars he probably had no clear conception of the real nature of the personages and the phenomena.[1]

[1] For convenience, I have ascribed this rationalizing procedure to Paien. More probably the condition in which we find the story is the result of a

In the first place, the lady of the castle is nowhere spoken of as a *fée* or as an enchanted princess, nor is it said that the state of things in her " waste city " is caused by spells, nor is there any statement that Gawain's adventures in the castle are the work of magic. Perhaps Paien thought that magic might be taken for granted.[1] Anyhow, a very slight examination of the plot shows that it is closely related to the third of the types just defined — *The Enchanted Princess*. Indeed, it is a particularly instructive example of the formation of this type, for the first and second types (*The Fairy Mistress* and *The Giant's Daughter*) are imperfectly amalgamated so that the poem is full of contradictions.

A single feature of *La Mule* is enough to associate it with type I (*The Fairy Mistress*) in unmistakable fashion. The waste castle lies beyond a rapid stream, spanned only by a narrow rod of iron [2] which bends under the passenger as he crosses it on the (magical) mule provided for his conveyance. The river is very horrible: —

> Gauvains chemine tote voie
> Tant que il vint a l'eve noire
> Qui estoit plus bruianz que Loire;
> De li tant voil dire sanz plus,
> C'onques si laide ne vit nus,
> Si orrible ne si cruel.
> Ne sai que vos en deisse el
> Et si vos di, sanz nule fable,

gradual working over by various tellers. Since Paien, however, is the only redactor on whom we can lay our hands, we may conventionally regard him as the representative of all. The argument is not affected; it is merely simplified.

[1] Heinrich von dem Türlîn, in borrowing the plot of *La Mule*, deemed it wise to explain that enchantment had been at work, and even took pains to bring in the figure of a magician, with the sober statement that he was " ein pfaffe wol gelêrt " (see p. 51).

[2] It is only a *dor* (three inches) in width (v. 404).

Que ce est li fluns au deable
Par sanblant et par avison,
Ni voit-l'en se deables non [1] (vv. 390–400).

One might doubtless argue that *La Mule* is tricked out
with scraps from Chrétien. Thus the river and the bridge
correspond to the river and the sword-bridge in the *Charrette*;
the herds of beasts that do homage to the mule, to those
which the questers pass in *Ivain*; the fountain which is
reached soon after passing through the forest of wild beasts,
to that in *Ivain* or in the *Charrette*;[2] the fact that the mule in
darting through the gate of the turning castle loses part of
her tail (vv. 468–470), to the cutting in two of Gawain's
horse by the portcullis in *Ivain*; the *vilain* who appears to
have the lions and serpents under control, with the monstrous herdsman in the same poem. But such a derivation
from Chrétien would be erroneous. In the first place, these
traits are not the personal property of Chrétien.[3] In the
second place, one of the best parallels (the docking of the

[1] These lines suggest Christian and Moslem legends in which those who
cannot cross to Paradise by a bridge fall into hell. The Christian idea (as
found in *The Purgatory of St. Patrick* and elsewhere) was certainly present
to the mind of Paien, as his language shows. The valley of fire-breathing
serpents, where it is very cold from the north wind (vv. 169 ff.), may also
have been tricked out in Christian legendary embellishments. It suggests
the alternations of cold and heat which increase the torments of the damned.
It should be observed, however, that the introduction of details from Christian legend in no way invalidates the claim of the story to belong to the
category of Visits to the (heathen) Other World. Even if the narrow bridge
be taken from Chrétien, that would not change the main situation. Cf.
Fritzsche, *Romanische Forschungen*, II, 266–267, 275–276; Baist, *Zeitschrift
für Romanische Philologie*, XIV, 159–160; Miss Hibbard, *Romanic Review*,
IV, 166 ff.

[2] This spring in *La Mule* shows no magical properties; yet it is emphasized
in a way somewhat out of proportion to its apparent unimportance, as if it
once meant more than it now does (vv. 217 ff., 385–386, 1094).

[3] For Celtic parallels of capital importance see A. C. L. Brown, *Publications of the Modern Language Association*, XX, 693 ff.

mule's tail) is much more primitive than the corresponding incident in *Ivain* and cannot possibly be taken from it. The whirling castle belongs to the same general category as perpetually slamming doors and clashing cliffs (*symplegades*). It is proper and primitive for an animal or bird to dart or fly through and lose its tail. Chrétien has remade the incident.[1]

Even if all these features, however, were mere copies from Chrétien, the case would not be altered, for enough would still be left to keep the tale (in part) in the other-world category. The lady of the castle is a *fée*,[2] clearly enough, who wishes to summon her chosen mate; the damsel who goes to court and purports to be the lady's sister, is the messenger of the *fée*; the mule which carries Gawain safely through the forest of beasts and the valley of serpents and across the narrow bridge, is the guiding animal familiar in such stories, — like the boar or the white hart or the *biche blanche*. The turning castle has also its significance with respect to the Other World.

So far we have examined only certain traits or incidents which mark *La Mule* as a version of *The Fairy Mistress*. But the case has quite another aspect when we look at the condition of the castle (including a town) where the lady resides. Here we find all the characteristics of our third type, *The Enchanted Princess*.

---

[1] For whirling castles see Sypherd, *Studies in Chaucer's Hous of Fame*, Chaucer Society, pp. 144 ff., 173 ff. Note that in *Fled Bricrend* Curoi the enchanter is expressly said to set his house in motion every night by his magic arts (§ 80), whereas in the Old French *Pilgrimage of Charlemagne* the equally magical revolving palace of the Emperor Hugo is scientifically, even if humorously, accounted for on the principle of the weathervane: it stands still unless the wind blows (vv. 334 ff.). For symplegades in general see Lowie, *Journal of American Folk-Lore*, XXI, 106 ff.; A. C. L. Brown, [*Harvard*] *Studies and Notes*, VIII, 81 ff.

[2] See Brown, as above, pp. 80 ff.

"A jolly place," said he, "in times of old,
But something ails it now: the spot is curst."

It is a "waste city," though Paien has suppressed the customary trait of ruinous houses. Not a soul is to be seen in
the streets except, after awhile, a mysterious dwarf, and
later a black and shaggy *vilain*, who comes out of a crypt,
axe in hand. Yet after Gawain has achieved the adventures
required of him, the streets are suddenly filled with great
companies of people singing and dancing. He learns that
they have been hiding in holes and corners for fear of the
beasts. God has delivered them through Gawain,

> Et de toz biens enluminéz
> La gent qui en tenebre estoient.[1]

In short, we have a plain case of a waste city, and Gawain
has released it from enchantment.

Are there any traces of the enchanter? Certainly. Two
personages have shared his rôle between them — the *vilain*
who proposes the *jeu parti* to Gawain and who brings forth
the lions and serpents for him to contend with, and the
knight with whom Gawain has a combat. It is the latter
who has decapitated all previous questers and has set up
their heads on the battlements, after a fashion common in
disenchantment stories and in tales of the type of *The
Giant's Daughter*.[2] The heads on stakes are unheard-of
adornments for the abode of a fairy mistress, except in cases
where this has borrowed scenery from other tales. The
whirling castle itself, by the way, which we have treated as
a sign of the Other World, may just as well belong to the
enchantment part of the story. But the case is complete

---

[1] Vv. 1032–1033: a bit of Scripture (*Isaiah*, ix, 2; *Matthew*, iv, 16).

[2] See many examples in Child, *Ballads*, I, 417, note; II, 507; III, 507;
IV, 459; V, 216; Schofield, [*Harvard*] *Studies and Notes*, IV, 175 ff.

without it. Still, example being better than argument, one may cite *Li Beaus*, which contains both a fairy mistress and a bespelled princess. The complete contrast between the state of things in the Isle of Gold [1] and that in the waste city of Sinadoun (Snowdon) [2] is an object lesson in descriptive folk-lore.

Gawain, we may conjecture, had to win thrice in order to unspell the waste city — he had to fight with lions, with serpents, and with the enchanter himself. When he swept off the magician's head, it returned to his shoulders. Instructed perhaps by the helpful animal, the hero knew what to do the next time: he either destroyed the head or chilled the spinal marrow with the axe-blade. Then the head stayed off and the enchanter-giant was dead. [3]

Next should come, if Paien were sticking to the type of *The Enchanted Princess*, an interview with the lady, her expressions of gratitude, and a happy marriage. But here the author suddenly returns to type I. The lady summons Gawain to her presence and greets him in the following contradictory terms: —

> " Gauvain, bien soiez vos venu!
> Si m'est il par vos avenu
> Mout granz anuiz et granz domages,
> Que totes mes bestes sauvages
> Avez mortes en ceste voie.
> Si vos covient il tote voie
> Avec moi orendroit mengier;
> Onques voir mellor chevalier
> Ne plus preu de vos ne conui " (vv. 921–929).

She declares that the death of the lions and the serpents is a loss to her; yet she welcomes Gawain cordially and offers

---

[1] Vv. 1859 ff., ed. Hippeau, pp. 66 ff.
[2] Vv. 2829 ff., pp. 100 ff.
[3] See pp. 49–50, 148.

him her hand and all her possessions. The death of the beasts, as the poem runs, is a benefit, not a damage, for it is necessary to her liberation and the release of her city from the ban. But now she is no longer an enchanted princess, but an all-powerful *fée* who has simply been proving her chosen warrior. The *vilain* and the knight appear to have been acting under her orders. In short, we are at liberty to imagine, if we choose, that all Gawain's adventures in the town have been illusions, like the tricks of the *fée* on Li Biaus in the Isle of Gold.[1] We may profitably compare the strangely disordered but still intelligible episode of Lancelot and the forthputting damsel in Chrétien's *Charrette*.[2]

Nevertheless, when the lady offers Gawain her hand, she becomes once more, in a spasm of rationalization, an enchanted princess — a fair mortal who owns thirty-nine castles and is eager to entrust them all to a husband strong enough to defend them. The confusion between our first type (*The Fairy Mistress*) and our third (*The Enchanted Princess*) is complete, and it is idle to interpret Paien's poem as belonging exclusively to either of them.

A still further embroilment is caused by the introduction of the Bridle. The damsel who started Gawain on the whole adventure had come riding up to Arthur's hall on a mule that lacked this piece of furniture. She had complained bitterly of its having been taken away from her, and had promised her hand to any knight who should recover it. When Gawain has supped with the lady of the castle, he asks her to give him the bridle. She offers him instead her hand and her territories in gratitude, she says, for the service he has done to her sister — that is, to the damsel with the mule. Gawain declines both, — " Many thanks, gracious lady! But let me have the bridle, please, for it is time for me to be

---

[1] See p. 264.   [2] See pp. 263 ff.

going." She accedes at once. The bridle is hanging on a silver peg in her chamber.

The situation is utterly incomprehensible. If the lady is really the mistress of the beasts and the contriver of the whole affair, it must be her own fault that the bridle is so hard to get, and there is no sense in her loving Gawain for doing a favor to her sister in the winning of an article that she herself must desire to retain. Nor is the tangle unravelled by what follows. Gawain rides back to court on the mule and is joyfully received by the damsel. We take it for granted that he delivers the bridle, though Paien neglects to say so. King and queen and knights beseech her to remain with them, but she protests that it is not within her power; she must go at once. She cannot even accept an escort. And so she mounts her mule and rides away alone.

> Congié prent et si s'en depart;
> Si se remist en l'anbleüre.
> De la damoisele a la mure,
> Qui s'en est tote seule alée,
> Est ci l'aventure finée.

The end is pretty, but, from the point of view of a *märchen*, quite unsatisfying. Folk-tales do not leave the point of the story in the dark. Their hearers object to puzzles. " What did the damsel want of the bridle " ? " Why had it been left in the city ? " " Where did she go with it when it had been returned to her ? " " Back to the city ? " Such are the questions which a *märchen* has to answer. " Did the ears of Donatello really resemble those of the Faun of Praxiteles ? " As the poem reads, they find no reply.

We have regarded the mule as filling the part of *fée's* messenger or enticing beast. Let us look for a moment at the other side of the story, — at the type that we have called *The Enchanted Princess*. In this type, as we have noted, the helpful animal is often a human being, a relative of the princess, perhaps her brother, and he owes his beast's shape to the spells of the same magician who has brought both her and her city under the ban. The assistance that he gives the hero has for its object in part his own release from the magic that has transformed him.[1] Such an animal is likely to be a horse and to convey the hero to the enchanted city, where alone the unspelling adventures can be carried through.

The mule, then, is a man or woman under spells. This Paien, perpetually vacillating between the two types, has either forgotten or suppressed. But somehow Paien has kept the bridle, though nobody in his poem makes any use of it or seems to have any ideas about it; for a bridle is supererogatory on a creature that needs no guidance or control. Its function, however, is obvious, for it is a talis-man that may be seen in active operation in the folk-tale of *The Magician and his Pupil*, of which versions innumerable have been printed.[2] *It is by virtue of the bridle that the mule can resume his human shape.* Its loss condemns the be-spelled man (or woman) to retain the form of an animal until it is recovered.

With these points in mind, one can have no difficulty in reconstructing Paien's plot in the form of a *märchen* of the type that we call *The Enchanted Princess*. Let us try: —

---

[1] See pp. 200 ff., 237.

[2] See Bolte and Polívka, *Anmerkungen zu den Kinder- u. Hausmärchen der Brüder Grimm*, II, 60 ff. (No. 68); William of Malmesbury, *Gesta Regum Anglorum*, ii, 171 (ed. Stubbs, Rolls Series, I, 201); J. F. Campbell, *The Celtic Dragon Myth*, pp. 105, 107; Mac Innes, *Folk and Hero Tales*, p. 173; *Scottish Celtic Review*, I, 73–74, 77; Mc Kay, *Ancient Legends of the Scottish Gael*, pp. 20–25; Mackinlay, *Folklore of Scottish Lochs and Springs*, pp. 174 ff.; Hutchinson, *Historical Essay concerning Witchcraft*, 2d ed., 1720, pp. 266–267; Teit, *Traditions of the Thompson River Indians*, p. 88; Loth, *Les Mabinogion*, 2d ed., II, 63, note.

An enchanter has laid spells upon a princess and her city. The lady is immured in the donjon keep and the city is reduced to solitude and ruin, — there are wild beasts in its desolate houses and dragons in its pleasant palaces. The lady's brother is changed into a horse, and the bridle which alone can undo the charm that keeps him in that shape is locked up in the tower with the imprisoned lady. The horse associates himself with a hero and acts as guide and helpful animal. The enchanter is slain and the city is restored to its pristine splendor. The lady is released and marries the hero. But first either she or the hero applies the talismanic bridle — now happily in good hands — and the prince her brother resumes his human likeness.

This sketch of a plot is offered for what it is worth. Every reader of *märchen* will at least acknowledge that it does no violence to folk-lore. As for Paien's little romance, our sketch accounts for quite as much of it as can ever be reduced to consistency. For he has so jumbled together his materials, whatever they were, that there is no adjusting them. Still, if we are willing to pass incessantly to and fro from *fée* to enchanted princess and from enchanted princess to *fée*, we can read his poem with pleasure. For my part, I find it charming, and would not change a word of it.

Enough has been said to show that the main plot of the *Mule*, from whatever point of view we look at it, has no significance for the history of the Challenge. That episode must be studied by itself, as we have studied it, and not in the accidental context in which it occurs in *La Mule sanz Frain*.

Heinrich von dem Türlîn, early in the thirteenth century, inserted almost the whole of Paien's little romance of *La Mule sanz Frain* into the vast compilation which he entitled *Diu Crône*.[1] In weaving it into his loose fabric he allows himself certain changes which, though of no significance for the history of the Challenge, are not without interest for the student of fiction. Heinrich sees well enough that Paien's

[1] Vv. 12627 ff., ed. Scholl, pp. 155 ff.

treatment of the subject is inconsistent, contradictory, and obscure, and he takes some pains to clear up the story. His efforts, however, are characterized rather by zeal than by felicity.

In his new construction, Heinrich makes free use of an episode known as *The Rival Sisters*, which occurs in the following quite intelligible form in Chrétien's *Ivain*:[1] — A lord dies, leaving his realm to his two daughters to hold in common. The elder ousts the younger. Both appeal to the Round Table for aid, and each is eager for the championship of Gawain. He is secured by the elder; the younger gets Iwain. After an indecisive combat between them, Arthur divides the heritage between the sisters.

This is a very simple episode (something like Eteocles and Polynices) and neither has nor requires (indeed, it does not properly admit) an enchanted castle and all sorts of proofs of valor. It is quite possible that Paien knew the episode, either from Chrétien or from some other source, for he makes the damsel of the mule and the lady of the castle sisters, and he represents the former as deprived of a bridle which turns up in the possession of the latter. But Paien, if he was acquainted with *The Rival Sisters*, used it very sparingly, and his poem can by no means be regarded as a version of that story.[2]

Heinrich, however, is thoroughgoing according to his lights. Here is his tale: —

A certain king at his death has left his kingdom to his two daughters, Amurfina and Sgoidamur, to hold in common, and has bequeathed to them a bridle, informing them that, so long as they keep it they will keep their realm. Amurfina, the elder, has got possession of this talisman and has ousted her sister from the inheritance. Sgoidamur

[1] Vv. 4703 ff.

[2] Orlowski in his edition of *La Mule* (*La Demoiselle à la Mule*, Paris, 1911) attempts to derive Chrétien, Paien, and Heinrich from a common source,

has set out for Arthur's court to lodge a complaint. Amurfina enlists the services of Gawain, whom her messenger finds at a castle. At Amurfina's residence Gawain has an adventure which appears to be derived, with variations, from the *Chevalier à l'Épée.* He is toying with the lady when a sword, which hangs over the bed, shoots from its sheath and encircles his waist like a girdle, pressing him so hard that he looks for nothing but death; but it releases him when he swears everlasting fidelity to Amurfina (vv. 8509–8610). She then becomes his *amie.* A magic potion deprives him of his memory and makes him think that he has been living there as Amurfina's husband for thirty years! He even forgets his own name. After a time, however, he comes to himself and takes his leave, in order to pursue the adventure on which he had been bound when his attention was diverted by Amurfina's summons. He promises to return as soon as possible (vv. 9080–9084).

After various happenings, Gawain reaches Arthur's court (vv. 12,391–12,426). Soon after, Sgoidamur arrives, in quest of a champion who shall win the bridle for her, and the episode derived from *La Mule sanz Frain* begins (v. 12,627). After an unsuccessful attempt on Kay's part (as in the French poem), Gawain undertakes the enterprise and carries it through in complete oblivion of the fact that he is acting against the interests of Amurfina. When he learns the truth, he takes both Amurfina and the bridle to Arthur's court, where he marries Sgoidamur to a knight and is formally wedded to his own *amie.*

Heinrich, we observe, has found Paien's account of the bridle incomplete and has invented a function for it. The father of the young ladies left it to them as a talisman that ensured them possession of the kingdom. This is quite absurd in itself — which might be pardoned in a romance — but it is doubly unsatisfactory because it brings the bridle into no proper relation with the mule.

The person who challenges Gawain to the beheading game is, in the *Crône*, the uncle of Amurfina and Sgoidamur, — one Gansguoter. When Gawain has made his way into

and holds that Chrétien has departed from it most widely of the three (p. 63). His arguments are not worth a moment's consideration and have, indeed, met with no favor from his reviewers (see R. T. Hill, *Romanic Review*, IV, 392 ff.; Roques, *Romania*, XL, 144 ff.).

the Whirling Castle by the aid of the mule, he sees a fine-looking man, splendidly attired. Immediately, however, this man is changed into a frightful shape, which he wears during the beheading game, and, apparently, during the whole of Gawain's stay at the castle. This is Gansguoter, who is said to be " ein pfaffe wol gelêrt " (v. 13,025). He seems to be the contriver of all the enchantment.

A number of differences between *La Mule sanz Frain* and the *Crône* may be specified. Gansguoter has an axe (" ein breit helmbarten," v. 13,052) but no block. He strikes two harmless blows, both of which miss: —

> Die helmbarten vuorte
> Gansguoter unde tet zwên slege,
> Daz er vervælte alle wege
> Und ime den lîp versêrte niht (vv. 13,164 ff.).

He merely wished to test Gawain's valor. The knight with whom Gawain afterwards fights loses his life. Gawain unlaces his helm and decapitates him, and Gansguoter sticks the head on the single vacant stake (vv. 13,384 ff.). These, and other variations, are certainly the work of Heinrich and have no significance for our problems.

But the German romancer does good service in one respect. The Bern MS., our sole authority for the text of *La Mule sanz Frain*, expresses the terms of the *jeu parti* as follows: —

> " Te partis orendroit .i. jeu,
> Et por ce que je voi mon leu,
> Si pren tot a ta volenté."
> Et .G., li a creanté,
> Qu'il en prendra loquel que soit.
> " Di, fet .G., que orendroit,
> Si m'ait Dex, l'un en prendré,
> Ne de mot ne te mentiré,
> Que je te tieng a mon bon oste."
> " Anuit, fait il, la teste m'oste

> A ceste jusamre trenchant,
> Si la m'oste par tel convant
> Que la toe te trencherai
> Lou matin, quant je revenrai:
> Or pren, fet il, sanz contredit."
> " Mout sauré, fait .G., petit,
> Se je ne sai louquel je preigne;
> Je prendré, conment qu'il aviegne.
> Anuit la toe trencherai,
> Et lou matin te renderai
> La moie, se viax que la rende."
> " Mal dahez ait qui miax demande,
> Fet li vilains, or en vien donc." [1]

There is undoubtedly a lacuna after v. 578. The *vilain*
should subjoin the alternative, — " Or I will cut off your
head to-night and you may cut off mine to-morrow." Otherwise the *jeu parti* lacks one of its terms, and Gawain's reply
is inept. Fortunately Heinrich von dem Türlîn had the use
of a text of *La Mule* which had no lacuna here, and his verses
enable us to fill the gap in the sense.[2] In the *Crône* the
challenger is perfectly explicit: —

> " Vriunt Gâwein, nim
> Under zwein spiln ein spil,
> Diu ich dir beidiu teilen wil,
> Und daz ich daz ander habe:
> Slach mir iezunt mîn houbet abe
> Mit dirre barten, die ich trage,
> Und lâz mich morgen bî dem tage
> Dir abe slahen daz dîn,
> Oder lâz mich hînt slahen ê.[3]

Gawain replies: —

> " Swie ez ergê,
> Sît sîn niht mac wesen rât
> Und ez alsô dar umbe stât,
> Sô wil ich hiute der êrste sîn
> Und wil dich morne daz min
> Abe slahen lâzen."[4]

[1] Vv. 565–587.
[2] Paris, *Histoire Littéraire*, XXX, 75.
[3] Vv. 13104 ff.
[4] Vv. 13113 ff.

Thus we are able to correct the text of *La Mule* in the important feature of the *jeu parti*.

The figure of the *vilain* in *La Mule sanz Frain* tempts to comparison with the personage who keeps the beasts in Chrétien's *Ivain*.[1] There are points of resemblance in the description. Chrétien's *vilain* is a sufficiently friendly personage who directs adventurers to the magic fountain and tells them what they have to do, at the same time warning them of the risk they are running. It is proper enough to conjecture, if one wishes, that some such well-disposed *vilain* was a part of the machinery of the enchanted castle in Paien's source. We may note that Paien's churl has charge of the lions and the serpents and lets them loose for Gawain to fight withal, and that Chrétien's churl is the herdsman of similar cattle. In Chrétien's *Perceval*, too, a *vilain* attached to the service of the enchanted castle of the Perilous Bed, lets loose the lion with which Gawain has to fight in his task of raising the enchantment under which the castle and its inhabitants labor.[2] Perhaps, then, Paien found in his source a *vilain* who was *not* friendly but acted merely as the keeper of the animals and let them out to combat with such knights as essayed the adventure. All this does not affect the course of our argument. If Paien had a *vilain* in his source, then he identified him with the churl of the Challenge story when he inserted the latter into his plot. Such details can never be settled, and need not detain us.

[1] Vv. 286 ff. See A. C. L. Brown, *Iwain*, [*Harvard*] *Studies and Notes in Philology and Literature*, VIII, 70 ff., and *Romanic Review*, III, 165.

[2] Vv. 9225 ff.

VII. THE CARL OF CARLISLE

THE central incident in the Old Norse *Saga of Illugi* affords a striking parallel to *The Carl of Carlisle*.[1]

The Danish prince Sigurðr, son of King Hringr, accompanied by his friend Illugi, has been on a viking expedition against the Orkneys and Scotland. In the autumn he sails for home, but his ship is driven north by a great storm. At last they take shelter in an inlet in Finnmark. They have no fire, and Illugi rows across the fjord to seek some. He enters a great cave, which is inhabited by a frightful troll-wife Grídr, whose ugliness is described in detail. She says that Illugi shall get no fire unless he says three true things,[2] adding, " If thou dost that quickly, thou shalt lie with my daughter." Illugi consents, without seeing the daughter, who, however, appears immediately and is so fair that he falls in love with her on the spot. The three true speeches are made and accepted, and Illugi goes to bed with the girl, whose mother gives him the same permission that Gawain received from the Carl.[3] When he attempts to act in accordance with this permission, however, Grídr seizes him by the hair and, brandishing a sharp knife, threatens him with instant death. Illugi lies quiet, and is not at all alarmed. His heart, he says, has never felt fear, and a man can die but once. A second and a third time she subjects Illugi to the same test, with a like result. Thereupon she hails him as the bravest of mankind and declares that he shall have her daughter in very truth. She thanks him also as her benefactor, averring that he has released her from powerful spells, in obedience to which she has already killed sixteen brisk young men, all of whom quailed before her terrible knife. She thereupon tells Illugi her history.

Her real name, it now appears, is Signý, and she is daughter to Ali, king of Alfheimar. Her stepmother Grímildr had laid spells

---

[1] *Illuga Saga Grídarfóstra*, chaps. 3–6, Rafn, *Fornaldar Sögur*, III, 651–660.

[2] Cap. 4, III, 653 ("þrjú sannyrði). See Babrius, ed. Lachmann, No. 53. Many parallels are cited by Reinhold Köhler in Gering's *Íslenzk Æventyri*, II, 180 ff. Compare the requirement of discovering the right answer to the question " what woman most desire " in the *Wife of Bath's Tale* and related stories.

[3] See p. 88, above.

upon her, that she should become a troll-wife and live in a cave.
Signý's daughter Hildr was to accompany her, " and every man that
sees Hildr, shall fall in love with her, and thou shalt murder everyone
that thou seest in her bed." Signý's seven stepsisters (terrible witchwives) are to attack Signý every night and wound her sore.   She is
never to be free from these enchantments till she meets with a man
whom her knife does not terrify — and such a man, adds Grímildr,
cannot be found.   When the tale is finished, seven witchwives (*skessur*)
come into the cave and maltreat Signý, but Illugi slays them all and
burns them to ashes.   " Gríðr said then: ' Now hast thou, Illugi,
freed us both from these monsters, who have tormented me for eleven
winters." " A rather long time that! " replies Illugi.   Illugi gets
fire, and, after a month, the ship returns to Denmark, Hildr accompanying Illugi as his wife.   Signý arrives in Denmark somewhat later,
and is married to Sigurðr, whose father has died in the meantime.   The
marriage was happy, and the pair had many children; but Hildr and
Illugi had none.

The same story occurs in the Danish ballad *Hr. Hylleland
henter sin Jomfru.*" [1]

King Løver's daughter is taken away by a troll.   He promises her
to whomsoever of his men can bring her back.   Only young Hyldeland dare undertake the quest.   He sails to Norway, where he finds a
sea-woman and bids her fetch the maid.   He must go to the mountain
and fetch her himself, is the reply.   Entering the mountain, he sees
the maid, who is very fair.   But the troll-wife requires three truths,
as in the saga.   On their utterance, she allows the pair to sleep together,
adding, however, that she will have Hyldeland's life before sunrise.
Early in the morning, she stands by the bedside, whetting her knife.
Hyldeland has recourse to runic charms, and the troll-wife bids them
sleep in peace.   Hyldeland is allowed to take his bride home with him,
and also receives rich presents from the troll.   Nothing is said of the
disenchantment of the troll-wife.

The Norwegian ballad of *Kappen Illhugin* [2] is more like
the *Illuga Saga*, as the identity of names would lead
us to expect.   There is the request for fire and the battle
with the troll-wife's sisters seven [not stepsisters].   The

---

[1] Grundtvig, *Danmarks Gamle Folkeviser*, No. 44, II, 94 ff., IV, 820 ff.
[2] Landstad, *Norske Folkeviser*, No. 2, pp. 22 ff.

troll-wife herself is killed. Other parallels are noted by Grundtvig.[1]

It is difficult not to agree with Grundtvig that the saga-incident is an extended and beautified version of the simpler story preserved in the ballads. The disenchantment of the troll-wife and the double marriage certainly look like later additions.

Apparently, then, we have in the *Illuga Saga* the story of the rescue of a maid from a troll-wife worked up in such a way as to be attached to personages of rank. The disenchantment of the troll-wife, and the fact that the damsel is her daughter, may be later modifications. Yet, on the other hand, it is possible that we must regard the whole rather as an account of the winning of the fair daughter of a troll — as belonging to the same class of stories as the type of *märchen* in which the hero subdues or kills a supernatural being and takes his daughter to wife.[2]

An Icelandic tale taken down in 1863 or 1864 [3] has remarkable points of agreement with *The Carl of Carlisle* and the *Illuga Saga*.

The hero, a young peasant named Tritill, pays court to princess Ingibjörg. Her father in anger threatens him with death in three years unless he can tell him what he (the king) thinks.[4] Tritill betakes himself to a giant, one Kolur, for counsel. On his way he is warned that nobody has ever visited Kolur and escaped with his life. Various persons, however, give him advice as to what to say to the giant. He is to ask him three questions. He hides under the bed in Kolur's cave, but the giant, on his return, smells human flesh, and bids him come

[1] *Danmarks Gamle Folkeviser*, II, 95, 663; III, 823. Grundtvig does not mention the *Carl of Carlisle* or the *Chevalier à l'Épée*.

[2] See p. 232.

[3] Rittershaus, *Die neuisländischen Volksmärchen*, No. 1, pp. 1–4.

[4] This is a familiar requirement in tales and ballads on the theme of *King John and the Bishop*: see Child, *Ballads*, No. 45 (I, 403 ff.; II, 506–507; IV, 459; V, 216, 291); Torrey, *Journal of the American Oriental Society*, XX, 209.

forth. Tritill creeps out and the giant threatens him with instant
death. The lad replies that he came hither for that very purpose,
but begs the privilege of asking three questions first. Kolur says he
will answer the questions next morning and gives Tritill his choice of
sleeping places — the floor or the giant's own bed. He chooses the
bed and sleeps sound. In the morning the giant leads him out and
declares that he will kill him at once. Tritill is calm. He allows himself to be laid on the ground and tells Kolur to cut off his head without
delay. The giant laughs: he has never seen so bold a fellow; as a
reward, he shall live.

Tritill then asks the giant to tell him what the king thinks. " He
thinks you may perhaps be his son-in-law," is the reply. Then
Kolur answers the other questions and gives his guest a horn and a
spear. He charges him to invite him to the wedding. Tritill wins the
princess, and does not forget to invite Kolur. In return for his good
counsel, the giant asks to be allowed to pass the night with Ingibjörg,
promising not to touch her, and offering to allow Tritill to watch
with a light and a sword. In the course of the night Tritill sees a
giant's skin on the floor and a prince in the bed. He burns the skin.
The prince thanks Tritill and Ingibjörg for releasing him from spells.
A part of the enchantment had consisted in his being forced to kill
every visitor who showed fear of death.

An important variant of the foregoing is the Icelandic
Blákápa, in which the heroine is condemned by a curse to
take the form of a giantess and to kill her maidservants one
after another until she finds one not susceptible to fear.[1]

An adventure in the Welsh *Peredur* [2] bears a certain
resemblance to the *Carl*.

Peredur enters a valley by means of a narrow pass. The pass is
guarded by a chained lion. Below him is a chasm full of the bones of
men and animals. Finding the lion asleep, Peredur is able to throw
him into the pit and thus to make his way into the valley. Here he
finds a beautiful castle. Before it, in a meadow, sits a grayhaired
man, the tallest man that Peredur has ever seen, watching two young
men, his sons, who are throwing knives. Peredur salutes the gray
lord of the castle, who curses the porter (the lion) for letting him pass.

[1] Rittershaus, No. 2, pp. 7–9.
[2] Loth, *Les Mabinogion*, II, 87–80; 2d ed., II, 83–87.

All of them now enter the castle. In the hall are tables, with abundance of meat and drink. From the bower come an elderly woman and a damsel, — the tallest women that Peredur has ever beheld. The gray man takes the head of the table, his wife by his side; Peredur and the maiden sit together, and the two young men serve. The maiden grows mournful as she gazes at Peredur. She tells him that she has fallen in love with him and that she is sad to think he is doomed to speedy destruction; to-morrow the giants who are her father's subjects will kill him. Next morning the mother and daughter beg the gray man to take a pledge of secrecy of Peredur and spare his life, but he refuses. Peredur kills many of the giants and one of the sons of his cruel host. The lord of the castle sends his daughter to ask mercy of Peredur, who grants it on condition that he and his subjects (the giants) go to Arthur, do homage, and say that it is Peredur who sent them. They must also accept baptism. In return, Peredur promises to request Arthur to grant this valley to the gray man and his heirs forever. The gray man accepts the terms, remarking that Peredur is the only Christian who has ever escaped with his life. Peredur spends the night at the castle, and goes his way the next morning. The gray man fulfils his part of the engagement, and after making submission to Arthur returns to the valley as the king's vassal.

The gigantic man, the lion, and the pit full of bones remind one strongly of *The Carl of Carlisle*. It is not said that the gray man is under spells, but there is a manifest parallelism between his receiving Christianity and the Carl's disenchantment. Of course we are to infer that the gray man, like the Carl, gives up his evil custom of causing the death of all comers. Like the Carl, he becomes Arthur's vassal, and as the Carl receives Carlisle, his hereditary domain, as a fief at the king's hands, so the gray man receives his own domain, the Round Valley, on similar terms. Peredur does not, like Gawain, take his host's daughter as his wife or *amie*, but she is in love with him, and the omission of the natural consequence is accounted for by the fact that Peredur's heart is already engaged. Indeed, Peredur protests his fidelity to his own lady at the very point in the story at which we might expect him to receive the love of the gray man's daughter.[1]

The whole episode shows plain traces of adaptation. Where it came from, it is impossible to say. It may be a Welsh tale, influenced in some of its details by the Arthurian story into which it fitted. It may (less probably) be a Celtized French romance. In either case, its parallelism to *The Carl of Carlisle* confirms the view at which we have arrived regarding the essential character of that poem. If the *Peredur* episode is really a derivative from some French romance, it may even go back to the French source of the *Carl* itself, though the absence of the Temptation makes that hypothesis improbable.[2] At all events, the enrolment of the gray man among Arthur's vassals is welcome testimony to the correctness of the similar incident in the English poem.

Stories of an imperious or truculent host whose daughter falls in love with a visitor are not uncommon, and in such cases the quester regularly has to fight with the host or to perform stupendous tasks. Here belong the episode of Wolfdietrich and the knife-throwing heathen and the juvenile adventure of Lancelot with Galagandreis.[3] The general type is well enough represented by Jason and Medea and has already been considered under the title of *The Giant's Daughter*.[4] The girl's honor may be magically guarded, as by the sword in the *Chevalier à l'Épée*.[5] The same purpose is served by the sleeping potion in *Wolfdietrich* and by the tricks of the *fée* in *Li Biaus*, which have many parallels in popular fiction.[6]

---

[1] Loth, p. 79 (86).

[2] One might hold that the substitution of conversion to Christianity for disenchantment occasioned the omission of the Temptation and the beheading. This would be hard to confute, but it is equally hard to prove, and the question must be left in abeyance.

[3] Pp. 218 ff.   [4] Pp. 232 ff.   [5] P. 91.

[6] For the use of charms or sleeping potions in a situation more or less

Such tales as these do not belong to the special category that concerns us particularly here — that in which the host tempts his guest by means of a fair and seductive wife, with her cognizance and without any love on her part toward the stranger. In other words, they are not versions of the story that we have called the Temptation. But they frequently approximate it closely, and it is very likely that the Temptation (in our sense) is a development from the type of *The Giant's Daughter*. At all events, the omission of the wife from any version of the Temptation (as in the *Chevalier*) [1] brings the two kinds of plot very close together. The episode of the Imperious Host in *Humbaut*,[2] might almost as well be referred to one as to the other.

As an example of the complexities and uncertainties of such discussions, we may examine a curious episode in Chrétien's *Charrette*.[3]

Lancelot meets a fair damsel who offers him hospitality on outspoken terms:

> " Mes osteus,
> Sire, vos est apareilliez
> Se del prandre estes conseilliez;
> Mes par itel herbergeroiz
> Que avuec moi vos coucheroiz " (vv. 950–954).

He accepts the hospitality but wishes to be excused from the terms. She is firm, however, and he complies since needs must. Supper is ready when they enter the hall, but no attendants are visible. Indeed, there is no one but the damsel herself in the whole enclosure, which is surrounded by a high wall and a deep " water." After supper the lady asks Lancelot to go out and amuse himself until he thinks she has gone to bed, reminding him of his promise. When he returns,

similar, see Child's observations on the ballad of *The Broomfield Hill*, No. 43 (I, 390 ff., 508; II, 506; III, 506; IV, 459; V, 290).

[1] P. 92.
[2] Pp. 99 ff.
[3] Vv. 941 ff. (ed. Foerster, *Der Karrenritter*, pp. 35 ff.). Cf. Paris, *Romania*, XII, 468; Rhŷs, *Arthurian Legend*, pp. 102, 140.

she is not to be seen, but Lancelot says he will seek her in order to keep his word. As he enters a chamber, he hears a loud cry from another room. Going thither, he discovers a knight attempting to force the damsel, who is calling for help. The door is open, but it is guarded by two knights with drawn swords and four men-at-arms with axes. Forcing his way in, he "aert parmi les tanples" the knight who is attacking the damsel, and, leaping between the bed and the wall, faces the others, who have followed him from the door. The lady then sends away the knights and men-at-arms. They retire obediently, and she then remarks to Lancelot —

> " Sire, bien m'avez desresniee
> Ancontre tote ma mesniee.
> Or an venez, je vos an main " (vv. 1201–1203).

Then Lancelot fulfils his promise, but he is so offish that she rises, bids him good-night, and retires to her own chamber. Next morning she conducts him some distance on his way.

Here we have one of the many instances in which Chrétien has failed to understand his original (whatever it was) or in which, though retaining the incidents, he has suppressed their significance. Nothing can be clearer than that the damsel is a *fée*, like the *fée* of the Île d'Or in *Li Biaus Desconeus,* and that the knights and men-at-arms are acting in accordance with her directions in order to test Lancelot. We are at liberty to take them as illusions, if we like.[1] As the *fée* of the Île d'Or plays tricks on her lover, though eager to receive him,[2] so this *fée* plays tricks on Lancelot. It would, of course, be the proper conclusion of this adventure for Lancelot to become the lover of the *fée*, but his passion for the Queen, and his devotion to his quest, prevent that, and the catastrophe is changed (whether by Chrétien or some predecessor) to fit the circumstances.

---

[1] Foerster (note on v. 1194, p. 372) sees that the whole adventure, so far as the rescue of the damsel is concerned, is " ein elendes Blendwerk, ein abgekartetes Spiel," but he draws no inference. His note on v. 1371 (p. 373) gives the impression that the nature of the situation escapes him.

[2] Vv. 4460 ff., ed. Hippeau, pp. 159 ff.

An amazing parallel (hitherto, I believe, unrecorded) to the tricks of the *fée* of the Île d'Or, may be found in the *Eachtra mhic na Miochomhairle* ("Adventures of the Son of Bad Counsel") by Brian Dhu O'Reilly (?), who was living in or about 1725. Part of this tale is given by Kennedy in his *Legendary Fictions of the Irish Celts*, pp. 133 ff. (cf. pp. 233 ff.) Magic tricks of this nature are not seldom resorted to, in popular fiction, by a woman in defence of her honor, and it would take an Œdipus to untwist the tangles and arrange the clues in order. Fortunately, nothing of the kind is my duty at present.[1]

If we had Lancelot's adventure in its original form, we should probably find that the intent of the trick was to prevent the knight from winning the lady unless he had valor enough to take long odds in a fight. Very likely there was no " forcing " in this original.

There is a curious place in Malory's Seventh Book that bears this out.

When Gareth had succeeded in relieving Dame Lyones, the lady of the Castle Perilous, and had been accepted as her betrothed husband, she agreed to come to his bed, which was to be made in the hall. But her sister, the damsel Lynet, perceiving what was afoot, and thinking the lady " was a lytel ouer hasty that she myghte not abyde the tyme of her maryage," used "her subtyl craftes" (enchantments, of course) to hinder. There appeared at the bedside " an armed knyght with many lyghtes aboute hym, and this knyghte had a longe Gysarme in his hand and maade grym countenaunce to smyte hym." Gareth leaped out of bed and sprang towards him. The knight wounded him, but Gareth struck him down, and, unlacing the helmet, cut off his head. Dame Lynet "toke vp the hede in the syghte of

---

[1] Cf. Rua, *Novelle del 'Mambriano' del Cieco da Ferrara*, pp. 85 ff; R. Köhler, *Kleinere Schriften*, I, 163; Prato, *Zeitschrift für Volkskunde*, I, 113–114; Rittershaus, *Die neuisländischen Volksmärchen*, pp. 421–422; Macdougall, *Folk and Hero Tales*, pp. 164 ff.; Straparola, night 2, tale 3; Menghin, *Aus dem deutschen Südtirol*, p. 50; *Folk-Lore*, V. 155; Webster, *Basque Legends*, 2d ed., pp. 128–129.

hem alle, and enoynted it with an oyntement there as it was smyten of, and in the same wyse she dyd to the other parte there as the hede stak. And thenne she sette it to gyders, and it stak as fast as euer it did. And the knyghte arose lyghtely vp, and the damoysel Lynet put hym in her chambre." Gareth had a similar experience some nights later. This time he cut the head into a hundred pieces and threw them into the moat; but Lynet's ointment was still efficacious. The result contemplated by Lynet (antenuptial continence) appears to have been achieved.[1]

This episode, by the way, is not a version of the Challenge (or Beheading Game). It has nothing in common with that story except the axe and the replacing of the head. The strange knight is simply one of those supernatural beings whose heads come on again when severed. The use of ointment is a bit of rationalization, as in the Dutch ballad of Halewijn.[2]

The Temptation is in some form or other a very ancient story. We may even detect its main outlines in the myth of Ixion and Hera. Ixion has incurred the wrath of the gods and is a fugitive. Zeus takes pity on him and receives him as a guest. But he falls in love with Hera, who informs her husband. Zeus, to test Ixion,[3] causes a cloud to take the shape of the goddess, with results that are familiar to everybody.[4] This is not our story, but it is much more like it than some mediæval documents are to the conjectural reconstructions of us theorists. It may pass, at all events, as complete proof that the idea of a host's testing his guest by means of a wife, and with her cognizance, is not necessarily a freak of mediæval fancy.

[1] Malory's *Morte Darthur*, book vii, chaps. 22–23 (ed. Sommer, I, 247 ff.).

[2] P. 157.

[3] " Test " is the very word: δοκιμάζων αὐτόν (Lucian, *Dialogi Deorum*, 6); βουλόμενος δοκιμάσαι (scholium on Euripides, *Phoenissae*, 1192).

[4] See the passages collected and discussed in Roscher's *Ausführliches Lexicon*, II, i, 766 ff.

This idea, without which our special story of the Temptation has no existence, is by no means simple in origin. We have seen that it has connections with the theme of the Fairy Mistress and the theme of the Giant's Daughter, and so, undoubtedly with the hideous but venerable superstition of lustful demons of the Lilith order. But these relations by no means exhaust its complex pedigree. The idea goes back also to a custom that still survives among savages and may be traced in the ancient history of some civilized nations. To lend a female slave or one's daughter or even one's wife to a guest is a trait of barbarous hospitality too familiar to require extensive illustration.[1] The custom obtained in ancient Ireland and ancient Wales.[2]

This derivation supplies us with one element of the Temptation story — that which gets frankest expression in Pucci's poem. The host is carrying hospitality to its utmost conceivable limit in an act which may well provoke the guest to a polite ceremoniousness of protest. We have here a fine instance of the mediæval fondness for superlatives, for depicting a quality *per se* in its most extravagant development — the same tendency that gave us patient Griselda, discourteous Kay, uncompromising Cordelia. It would be a mistake to regard these types, however, as invented *ad hoc*. Such invention, though sporadically possible, is unusual in mediæval fiction. The ethical type is usually developed out of a primitive custom (as here) or a bit of fairy-lore (like Griselda) or mythology (like Cordelia) which

[1] Westermarck, *History of Marriage*, pp. 73 ff.; Spencer and Gillen, *Native Tribes of Central Australia*, pp. 93, 101 ff.; W. E. Roth, *Ethnological Studies among the North-West-Central Queensland Aborigines*, Brisbane, 1897, p. 182; Marco Polo, ii, 47 (Yule, III, 48); Liebrecht, *Orient and Occident*, II, 543–544.

[2] See, for example, Stokes, *Revue Celtique*, XI, 43; *Fled Bricrend*, § 63; *Kulhwch and Olwen*, Loth, *Les Mabinogion*, 2d ed., I, 252; d'Arbois de Jubainville, *Cours*, V, 7–8; VI, 320; *Ossianic Society*, II, 178–179.

originally had little or no *tendenz*. Anything can be allegorized or worked up into an *exemplum*. Touchstone moralized the sundial and Jaques the weeping deer into a thousand similes.

But disenchantment is an essential point in the Temptation, as exemplified by the *Carl of Carlisle*. Here we may see connections of some sort with the well-known idea of disenchantment by personal contact, especially by kissing or by admitting the bespelled person to one's bed.[1] This is a very old and widespread belief. Nevertheless, in many stories, it may easily be recognized as a substitution for another conception, perhaps more primitive.[2] The woman who is released from spells by the kiss or by marriage is often merely a surrogate for an immortal. Union with a man reduces her to the condition of humanity, at least for the time being. This is the essential point in the swan-maiden story, which is found throughout the earth. As time goes on and Christianity stigmatizes all such supernatural creatures as demonic, the situation is saved by regarding them not as nymphs, but as mortals under spells, and the old means of bringing them into the ranks of mankind is regarded as a means of release and restoration. Thus nymphs become enchanted princesses, and gods become bespelled knights.[3] As stories grow more complicated, the conditions of restoration increase in complexity, until at last mere union with a mortal may become only one of a number of conditions necessary to reverse the spell. Thus a final beheading (which slays the enchanted body) may be

[1] See Child, *Ballads*, I, 288 ff., 297 ff.; II, 502; IV, 454; V, 213, 289; Schofield, *Studies on the Libeaus Desconus*, pp. 199–208; Maynadier, *The Wife of Bath's Tale*, pp. 19 ff., 191. Cf. p. 205, above.

[2] It is possible, however, that both notions are equally old. The point is impossible to determine.

[3] See p. 236.

necessary to enable the bespelled person to come to life in his proper form. The fact that these two conditions (contact and decapitation) are so often associated (as in the class of *märchen* known as *The Frog Prince*) is significant here, for the Temptation and the beheading are similarly associated in *The Carl of Carlisle*, and this tends to prove that the test with the wife in that romance gets its efficacy as an unspelling operation (in part, at least) from the principle of disenchantment by personal contact. In this way our Temptation enters into relations of an interesting nature with *The Wife of Bath's Tale* and other members of that group, in some of which the loathly lady is disenchanted not by marriage merely, but by the *complete submission of her husband to her will*. Compare the unspelling of the Carl by the test with the wife and other means which, taken together, constitute a similar submission to his will on the part of Gawain.

It is to be observed that the brother of the loathly lady in the ballad of the *Marriage of Sir Gawain* is a terrible fellow in a " carlish " shape armed with a club,[1] but that he owes his monstrous figure, as she owes her ugliness, to enchantment.[2] The ballad does not say that the brother gives up his ferocity or is released from spells when Arthur learns the answer to the question " what women most desire " and Gawain accepts the loathly lady; but the dame's marriage with Gawain and her husband's complaisance suffice to disenchant *her*, and one would expect her brother to be freed likewise. In the closely related romance of *The Wedding of Sir Gawain*,[3] there is at all events a reconciliation between King Arthur and Dame Ragnell's brother and Arthur

---

[1] Child, No. 31, I, 288–296.
[2] Stanza 48.
[3] Madden, *Syr Gawayne*, pp. 298 ff.

promises to take him into favor.[1] In the romance, however,
only the Dame is said to have been a victim of " nygram-
ancy." [2] As to the brother, he is described as " a quaynt
grome, armyd well and sure; a knyght full strong and of
greatt myght." [3] His quarrel with Arthur is that the king
has wrongfully bestowed his land upon Gawain.[4] In both
the romance and the ballad he is angry with his sister for
betraying the secret " what women most desire." [5] Such
anger does not seem reasonable if he is under enchantment;
but there appears to be a contradiction anyway, since —
whether he is under enchantment or not — he ought to be
willing to have his sister freed from spells, and the betrayal
of the secret was necessary to that end. It is hard to avoid
the inference that, if we had the story complete and un-
sophisticated, we should find that brother and sister were
unspelled, and that the brother joined Arthur's company of
knights as the Carl of Carlisle does.[6]

It may or may not be significant, in connection with the
reconciliation between Arthur and the carlish brother in
The Wedding of Gawain, that Sir Gromer Somer Joure
(which is the brother's extraordinary name) appears under
a similar appellation as a Knight of the Round Table in
Malory: — " syr Grummore gummursum a good knyghte
of Scotland" is mentioned in vii, 27 (Sommer, p. 256) and
again as "Grummore grummorssum " and " syre Gromere
Gromorson " in vii, 29 (p. 258). " Syre Gromore somyr

---

[1] VV. 812–817.

[2] V. 692.

[2] Vv. 50–52.

[4] Vv. 55–60. Compare the complaint of Sir Galleroun of Galloway in
The Awntyrs of Arthur, st. 33, vv. 404–409 (Madden, *Syr Gawayne*, p. 115);
st. 33 (Robson, *Three Early English Metrical Romances*, p. 16).

[5] Romance, vv. 474–485; ballad, sts. 29–30.

[6] On the whole matter, see Maynadier, *The Wife of Bath's Tale*, 1901.

Ioure " in xx, 2 (p. 799) must be the same person. Malory
throws no light on his history. The knight who sets Arthur
the task of discovering " what women love best " in the
Wedding of Sir Gawain is called " Gromersomer Jourer " in
v. 62, " syr Gromer somer Joure " in v. 766, " syr Gromersomer " in v. 64. Elsewhere in the same text he is called
simply " syr Gromer " (vv. 445, 453, 456, 492) or " Gromer
syre " (v.473). All the *-er*'s are represented by the familiar
sign of contraction, and " Jourer " is clearly an error for
" Joure " (the sign being accidentally added in v. 62). Of all
these forms " Gromere Gromorson " looks most intelligible.
It is tantalizing like Icelandic (" Gormr Gormsson "), but we
should not expect the nominative *-r* to be kept in English.
" Joure " is an unsolved riddle. The Rawlinson MS. to
which we owe *The Wedding of Gawain* is perhaps late
enough to have been influenced by the printed text of
Malory,[1] though the poem itself is much older than the
manuscript. In the ballad of *The Marriage of Gawain*
(Child, No. 31), neither Gromer nor his sister Ragnell
receives a name. The name of the transformed Turk in
The Turk and Gawain is Sir Gromer.[2]

We may just notice, in parting, that the group of stories
to which *The Wife of Bath's Tale* belongs is undoubtedly
Irish, but that in Chaucer, as well as in the romance and the
ballad, the plot has been brought into the cycle of King
Arthur.

Two texts and one fragment of Étienne's *exemplum* of
The Three Knights and the Three Inns[3] are appended, from
manuscripts in the British Museum. I follow copy.

---

[1] MS. C. 86, fols. 128 v° ff. (Bodleian Library). Madden (p. lxiv) assigns
this portion of the manuscript to a period " towards the close of Henry the
Seventh's reign."

[2] P. 120.   [3] See p. 97.

I

Additional MS. 16589, fol. 88, col. 2 (late 13th century).

DE TRIBUS MILITIBUS

Item dicitur quod tres milites conduxerant ad invicem quod querunt fortunam que dicitur aventure et cum ingrederentur Civitatem quandam dictum est eis quod non essent ibi nisi tria hospicia. in primo equi bene procurentur ut equites fame moriuntur. In secundo e contra fiebat. In tercio tam equi quam equites bene procurantur sed uix accideret quin ibi procurentur.[1] Tres igitur milites tria hospicia acceperunt et invenerunt sicut eis dictum fuerat. Tercius vero miles qui in tercio hospitaverat sine verberibus illesis[2] exivit, et cum tamen quereret quare non fuerat percussus dictum est eis[3] quia domino illius domus ita obediens fuisset quod propter tantam obedientiam ei pepercisset. Civitas est mundus in quo tres sunt hospites. Quidam sunt qui nimiam curam gerunt de equo procurando et militem fame perire permittunt. Equus est corpus. Miles est anima. vnde Iob obliviscatus ejus misericordia dei qui sterilem carnem suam pavit et anime sue non bene fecit. Item alii qui corpus suum nimis indiscrete artant et curac[i]o[nem] temporalium non gerunt. Tercii sunt qui utrique discrete discernunt et cum in omnibus suo creatori obediunt, hii sine magno flagello a mundo ibunt in vitam eternam.[4]

II

Additional MS. 24641, fol. 210 (first half of 14th century).

Tres erant milites querentes adventuram, qui convenerunt et mutuo propositum sibi apparuerunt, qui cum ingrederentur quandam civitatem; dictum est eis non esse ibi nisi tria hospicia. In uno equus bene procurabatur, et dominus fame moriebatur. In alio e contro.[5] In tercio vero equus et dominus bene, sed vix erat quod dominus in exitu non bene verberaretur. Tres igitur tria hospicia acceperunt, et sicut eis [6] fuerat invenerunt, excepto hoc quod tercius quod non fuit verberatus. et cum alii causam quererent, dixit quod domino domus in omnibus fuerat obediens. Civitas hec est mundus: tres hospites; tria hominum genera significant: quidam enim sunt qui nimis curant de equo procurando, neglecto domino. Equus corpus, miles spiritus, Job. 24. Obliviscitur ejus misericordia dei qui sterilem

___

[1] Read *verberarentur*.   [2] Read *illesus*.   [3] Read *ei*.

[4] See Herbert, *Catalogue of Romances*, III, 468.

[5] Read *contra*.   [6] Supply *dictum*.

pavit et vidue non benefecit. Alii sunt qui indiscrete corpus atterunt et spiritus tantum curam gerunt. Tant charge hom le char qe le brise. Tercii sunt qui utrique discrete intendunt et per omnia obediunt. et tales absque flagello transeunt.[1]

III

Sloane MS. 3102, fol. 7 v° (15th century).

Deinde notandum quod illi qui sunt ducti timore humano magis eligunt malum anime quam corporis similes sunt etc. . . .

Item similes sunt militi de quo dicitur quod intrans civitatem cum audisset quod erat ibi duo hospicia unum in quo equus male tractabatur sed dominus bene, aliud in quo dominus male sed equus bene, eligit secundum timens magis equo quam sibi.[2]

[1] Herbert, III, 536.   [2] Herbert, III, 93.

VIII. THE TURK AND GAWAIN

THE *Turk and Gawain* is an adaptation to Arthurian romance of that kind of folk-tale in which the hero, on a visit to a giant or similarly oppressive being, is forced to undertake tasks that seem impossible, but triumphs by the aid of one or more supernaturally gifted comrades.[1] To the same general class belong very numerous *märchen* in which the hero is assisted by an animal. Such helpful beasts we have already studied,[2] and they need not here occupy us. It will suffice to note that the animal is often a bespelled man, whom the hero frees from the ban by decapitation[3] or otherwise, and that a tale of this class has actually been worked up into a long romance of Gawain — the Middle Dutch *Walewein* of about 1250,[4] founded unquestionably on a French poem. Nor is it necessary to discuss the well-defined cycle in which the hero enjoys the coöperation of " skilful companions " — the swift runner, the dead shot, the man with telescopic vision, and so on.[5] We may confine our attention chiefly to the more limited category in which the hero has an ugly or deformed or uncouth attendant, recently taken into his service, who performs the tasks for him, and who is freed from spells and resumes his natural shape when the adventure is achieved. Some of these tales include the unspelling decapitation of the servant, and the resemblance to *The Turk and Gawain* is often very striking.

---

[1] P. 121. [2] Pp. 233 ff. [3] Pp. 200 ff.

[4] Edited by Jonckbloet, Leyden, 1846. The *Walewein* has been studied by Ker, *Folk-Lore*, V, 121 ff., and is summarized by Paris, *Histoire Littéraire*, XXX, 82–84 (under the title of *Gauvain et l'Échiquier*).

[5] See Benfey's classic essay, *Das Märchen von den " Menschen mit wunderbaren Eigenschaften*," in *Ausland*, 1858, pp. 969 ff., reprinted in his *Kleinere Schriften*, II, iii, 94 ff. Other papers are cited in [*Harvard*] *Studies and Notes*, VIII, 226, note 3.

A first-rate example makes an episode in the Gaelic *King of Albainn*.[1] There is throwing of the venomous apple, and the defeated contestant is roasted. Compare the brazen tennis-ball [2] in *The Turk and Gawain*, and the boiling of the giant in his own cauldron. The nominal hero (the young king) does nothing. Everything is performed by his servant, who first appears as a big ugly lad, but who before the journey is undertaken becomes a fine-looking fellow. Nutt's remark [3] that the servant has been " doomed to loathsome transformation " until " a hero could be induced to take up and carry out the quest " is sound. The change to a handsome young man is misplaced. It should come after the accomplishment of the tasks, not at the outset. There is a first-rate example of the duel with the venomous apple in the Irish story of Finn and Lorcán mac Luirc. Lorcán is a fearful-looking warrior of immense strength, but not deformed.[4]

The King of Albainn is a " modern " tale, " but as in so many other cases its fidelity to ancient tradition is avouched by a venerable parallel. Cormac's *Glossary* [5] contains a

---

[1] MacInnes, *Folk and Hero Tales*, pp. 91–93.

[2] See p. 120.   [3] MacInnes, p. 454.   [4] See p. 222, above.

[5] S. v. *prúll*, Stokes, *Three Irish Glossaries*, pp. 36–38; Cormac's *Glossary*, O'Donovan's translation, ed. by Stokes, pp. 135–137. O'Curry, *Manners and Customs*, II, 89, first called attention to the passage, and Nutt (note to MacInnes, pp. 467–468), has compared it with the *King of Albainn* and has discussed its true character. See also Nutt, *Revue Celtique*, XII, 194–195, where is the remark that the Welsh *Peredur* shows the same theme (obscured in the French), the black ugly girl being transformed into a handsome youth when the tasks in which she assists have been performed by Peredur (Loth, *Les Mabinogion*, 2d ed., II, 103–104, 116–119). Cf. Nutt's *Legend of the Holy Grail*, pp. 138–139, 205–206; Maynadier, *The Wife of Bath's Tale*, pp. 65 ff. The utility of the Welsh, Irish, and Scottish examples of the transformation of the helpful attendant for our present purposes is, it should be observed, in no wise dependent on Nutt's theories as to the position of *Peredur* in the history of the Grail legend, nor, indeed, on any particular theory of the " matter of Britain."

fragment of the *Tromdam Guaire* which probably belongs to the oldest portion of the text [1] and is therefore of the tenth century, at the very latest, doubtless considerably earlier. Senchán with his retinue of poets and students visits the Isle of Man — the scene of the Turk's exploits. A frightfully ugly youth asks permission to accompany them and climbs into the boat. He is described in great detail: " Rounder than a blackbird's egg were his two eyes; . . . black as death his face; . . . yellower than gold the points of his teeth; greener than holly their butt; . . . his belly like a sack; . . . his neck like a crane's neck " — in short, he is a worthy mate for the loathly lady of Celtic story. On their arrival, they find an old woman on the strand. Learning that the leader of the party is " Senchán, Poet of Ireland," she asks an answer to a problem, and it is unwarily promised. She then speaks two verses of poetry and calls for the other half of the quatrain. All the poets are nonplussed. The ugly lad springs forward and supplies the missing lines. The same test is repeated. Senchán recognizes her as a lost poetess, for whom there has been much searching. " Then she is taken by Senchán, and noble raiment is put upon her," and she accompanies the bards to Ireland. " When they came to Ireland they saw the aforesaid youth before them; and he was a young hero kingly, radiant; a long eye in his head: his hair golden yellow: fairer than the men of the world was he, both in form and dress. Then he goes sunwise round Senchán and his people, *et nusquam apparuit ex illo tempore.*" The glossator adds that he was without doubt the " spirit of the poem," an oracle which suggests certain formulas of modern literary criticism. [2]

---

[1] Zimmer, Kuhn's *Zeitschrift*, XXVIII, 438.

[2] Rhŷs, *Hibbert Lectures*, pp. 567–568, has an ingenious but unconvincing theory to reconcile the lad's ugliness with the *spiritus poematis.*

Old as it is, this tale is far from being in its original form. It is nothing but a *märchen*, artificially worked up into a literary anecdote. The glossator who has recorded it did not understand its real significance, and interpreted it in a highly artificial way. At bottom, it is no mere technical contest in capping verses, but a clear case of a hideous hag who requires the answer to a riddle [1] and of an ugly bespelled attendant who enables the quester to escape destruction at her hands and accomplishes his own disenchantment thereby. In the later text of the saga [2] the incident is modified into a Christian legend: [3] the hideous youth is a leper who turns out to be St. Caillin in disguise.[4]

In a mixed-up Gaelic story called *Osgar*, a little shaggy man assists the Fenians at a giant's house and kills the giant. Shortly after he meets them in the form of a fine young man (the son of the King of Greece) and tells them he has been under spells for eight years.[5] The Knight of the Full Axe gets Finn safe through many adventures. He has previously been disenchanted (through Finn's means) from the form of a blackbird. He is " a little man not more

---

[1] The hag herself is also bespelled, and the whole story thus comes very near to the *Marriage of Sir Gawain* in its ballad form (Child, No. 31). In the *Marriage*, there is the question "what women most desire," which King Arthur must answer or accept death at the hands of a monstrous carl, and the solution is furnished by a hideous hag. It appears that both hag and carl are enchanted, and the upshot of the ballad is the hag's release. In the story of Senchán, it is the hag who propounds the problem and the ugly lad who solves it. For riddle-contests see Child's index, s. v. (*Ballads*, V, 493); Laistner, *Ratsel der Sphinx*, I, 17 ff.

[2] Ed. Connellan, Ossianic Society, V, 115-121.

[3] Zimmer, Kuhn's *Zeitschrift*, XXVIII, 438.

[4] We may compare the kissing of St. Caillin in the guise of a leper with the repulsive leper legend in the Irish *Life of St. Féchin of Fore* edited by Stokes, chaps. 37-38 (*Revue Celtique*, XII, 342 ff.), and the Latin life in Plummer, cap. 13 (*Vitae Sanctorum Hiberniae*, II, 80-81).

[5] Campbell, *Popular Tales of the West Highlands*, III, 299-300.

than three feet high."[1]   Similarly Finn has tasks performed
by him by the Big Lad in *The Lad of the Skin Coverings*.[2]
There is, however, no disenchantment.   In another tale the
Fenians are assisted by the friendly champion Ceadach,
who does all the work.[3]   A forester assists Dyeermud in still
another Irish story, and is finally disenchanted by decapitation.[4]

In a surprising Irish story, *The King of Ireland's Son*,[5]
" a short green man," who has the ability to increase his
size enormously at will, helps the hero in fulfilling the tasks
that win his bride — indeed, fulfils a number of them himself; the rest are performed by the well-known Skilful
Companions (the marksman, the blower, etc.).[6]   The green
man reveals himself as a " thankful dead " helper.[7]   His sole
reward is to have the first kiss.   The wife " was full of
serpents " (this is a very archaic feature) and the king's son
would have been killed by them when he went to sleep, but
the short green man picked them out of her.   We have
essentially the same thing in Larminie's *Beauty of the World*.
Here the grateful dead man takes the shape of a red-haired
youngster; there are no skilful companions; and, instead of
serpents, three " lumps of fire " (which are three devils)
come out of the lady's mouth.[8]   Kennedy has what is
practically the same story, but in some ways not so well

[1] Curtin, *Myths and Folk-Lore of Ireland*, pp. 235 ff.

[2] Macdougall, *Folk and Hero-Tales*, pp. 35 ff.

[3] Curtin, *Hero-Tales*, pp. 477–482; so Kaytuch, in Larminie, *West Irish Folk-Tales*, pp. 77 ff.   Cf. also J. F. Campbell, II, 414 ff.; Curtin, *Myths*, pp. 124 ff., 258 ff., 262 ff.

[4] Curtin, *Hero-Tales*, pp. 510–511.

[5] Hyde, *Beside the Fire*, pp. 18 ff.

[6] See p. 274, note 5.

[7] On the Thankful Dead Man, see Max Hippe, Herrig's *Archiv*, LXXXI, 141–183; Gerould, *The Grateful Dead*, London, 1908.

[8] *West Irish Folk-Tales*, pp. 155 ff.

preserved; it is said that the princess was enchanted, but there is no mention of serpents or of " lumps of fire." [1] A red-haired man, barefoot and wobegone, acts as servant and performs the tasks in a Highland story. He too is one of the thankful dead.[2] The tale is an oddly varied version of *The Lady that Loved a Monster*.[3]

In *Bioultach*,[4] the hero is helped by a ragged green man, who throws the giant and otherwise proves invaluable; also by a hag, who makes him promise to grant her any request she may make if he returns in safety. The adventures being successfully performed, Bioultach goes back to the hag's house, accompanied by the ragged green man, who disappears as Bioultach enters. Bioultach takes a seat, and a beautiful woman appears to welcome him. He is in despair, for he feels sure the hag's boon will be marriage, and he had rather die than wed her after seeing this woman. But the fair damsel reveals herself as the hag transformed. Soon enter eleven other beautiful women, and presently a handsome gentleman. The latter is Keeal-an-Iaran, son of the King of Underwaves; the transformed hag is his sister, and so are the eleven others, formerly seen by Bioultach in their haggish guise. All have been " under bonds to the Bocaw More." The resemblance of this story to the *Wife of Bath's Tale* is patent.

In *The Bare-Stripping Hangman*,[5] Cormac and Alastir, sons of the king of Ireland, are on their travels. When they are about to visit the King of Riddles to sue for the hand

---

[1] *Legendary Fictions of the Irish Celts*, pp. 32 ff. On the connection between the " thankful dead " and " thankful beasts," see Laistner, *Rätsel der Sphinx*, I, 26 ff.

[2] *Celtic Magazine*, XIII, 20 ff.

[3] Cf. [*Harvard*] *Studies and Notes*, VIII, 188, note, 250, note.

[4] Larminie, *West Irish Folk-Tales*, pp. 35 ff.

[5] Macdougall, *Folk and Hero-Tales*, p. 80.

of the princess for Cormac, Alastir says: " Thou shalt travel
as the King of Ireland, and I will travel as the Servant.   If
thou art told to do anything thou shalt say it is the Servant
who does that in the country out of which thou hast come."[1]
Alastir conquers in the riddling contest, and Cormac gets
the king's daughter to wife.   This is very similar to the
situation in the fine English ballad of *King Estmere*.[2]
Alastir, like Adler, Estmere's brother, has wonderful powers.
He is not ugly.

It is unnecessary to carry the subject farther.   Tales of
this type are by no means confined to Celtic territory, but
they have been very much at home there for more than a
thousand years.   Phenomenal ugliness made a powerful
appeal, as the evidence demonstrates, to the Celtic love for
the grotesque and the exaggerated.   On the whole, we have
every reason to accept *The Turk and Gawain* as an Irish
folk-tale which made its way into English *via* Celtic Scotland and became attached to the Arthurian saga, more
especially to the saga of Gawain.   I can see no ground for
insisting upon a French source for the little romance.   It is
much more likely to come from a popular ballad.   The story
now known as Caradoc and the Serpent,[3] which came into
the Arthurian cycle at least seven centuries ago, was told
to Campbell of Islay in Gaelic by a travelling tinker[4] and

---

[1] This part of the tale is like part of Campbell's *Ridere of Riddles* (*Popular Tales of the West Highlands*, II, 29–30); cf. Groome, *Gypsy Folk-Tales*,
p. 12.   Cases in which a servant or casual assistant answers riddles in place
of his or her master are studied by Laistner, *Rätsel der Sphinx*, I, 17 ff.; cf.
his whole chapter on *Puss in Boots*, I, 26 ff.

[2] Child, *Ballads*, No. 60, II, 49 ff.   Formerly in the Percy MS., but torn
out.   For our knowledge of the ballad we are therefore dependent on the
text furnished by Percy in his *Reliques*, edition of 1794, compared with that
printed in the edition of 1765.   Both texts were adapted by Percy (see Child,
loc. cit.).   For riddles see p. 277, above.

[3] Cf. pp. 228–230.   [4] *Tales of the West Highlands*, I, xcv–xcvi.

was circulating orally in Scotland as a ballad (in Scots English) late enough to be captured and printed by Peter Buchan.[1]

In conclusion, we may note that the Old French romance of *Humbaut,* in that portion which has a real plot,[2] affords an excellent instance of the attachment to Gawain of the story of the " quest with a helpful companion." Humbaut has visited the domain of the King of the Isles [3] before, is well and favorably known there, and proves indispensable to Gawain at every turn. He is not an ugly servant, however, but a knight without reproach.

[1] *Ancient Ballads and Songs of the North of Scotland,* 1828, I, 46 ff. (*The Queen of Scotland*); Child, No. 301, V, 176–177 (Sargent and Kittredge, pp. 626–627). On Buchan's good faith see William Walker, *Peter Buchan and Other Papers,* Aberdeen, 1915. Scholars are indebted to Miss Harper for bringing the tale and the ballad into comparison with the *Livre de Caradoc* (*Modern Language Notes,* 1898, XIII, 209 ff.; cf. Paris, *Romania,* XXVIII, 214 ff.; Lot, *Romania,* XXVIII, 568 ff.).

[2] Vv. 1–1775, about one-half of the extant fragment. Cf. pp. 61 ff., 199 ff.

[3] This is the Other World by many infallible signs.

IX. THE GREEN KNIGHT OF THE PERCY MANUSCRIPT

FOR the reader's convenience I have here brought together most of the passages in the short *Green Knight* (P) of the Percy Manuscript that show verbal resemblance to the long romance (G).[1] A certain number of other comparisons and remarks are interspersed. Few of the parallels are at all impressive, but on the whole there is quite as much of this kind of thing as was to be expected in such condensing (about 2500 lines to about 500), with complete transformation in metre, vocabulary, and poetic style. The list strengthens the argument for derivation of the shorter English romance from the longer rather than from the French.[2]

1. In both there is a short historical introduction (*G* 1–26, *P* 1–18); but in *G* it concerns chiefly the pre-Arthurian period, in *P* it explains the founding of the Round Table. The "brethren of the Round Table" are mentioned in *G* 39. Perhaps this suggested to *P* the desirability of accounting for the institution, since he was addressing an unlearned audience.

2. With rych reuel oryȝt, and rechles merthes;
   Ther tournayed tulkes bi-tymeȝ ful mony,
   Iusted ful Iolile thise gentyle kniȝtes,
   Sythen kayred to the court, caroles to make,
   For ther the fest watȝ ilyche ful fiften dayes,
   With alle the mete and the mirthe that men couthe a-vyse;
   Such glaumande gle glorious to here,
   Dere dyn vpon day, daunsynge on nyȝtes (*G* 40–47).

   Some chuse them to Iustinge,
   Some to dance, Reuell, and sing;
      Of mirth thé wold not rest (*P* 241–243).

---

[1] See pp. 131, 135. The line-numbers follow Morris for *G* and Furnivall for *P*.

[2] Pp. 130 ff.

3. Now wyl I of hor seruise say yow no more (G 130).
   Now of King Arthur noe more I mell (P 37).

4. In both the visit of the Green Knight takes place
during the Christmas festivities (G 37, P 19). Arthur is
holding court at Camelot in G 37, at Carlisle in P 85. The
special localization at Castle Flatting " in the Forest of
Delamore " in P 86–87 is due to the author of the short
version or to some reviser.

5. Both lay stress on the multitude that assembled and
on the abundance and excellence of the viands (G 38–59,
121–129; P 20–36).

6. This kyng lay at Camylot vpon kryst-masse
   With mony luflych lorde (G 37–38).
   Itt fell againe the christmase
   Many came to that Lords place (P 19–20).

7. The grayn al of grene stele and of golde hewen (G 211).
   A green weapon in P 81.

8.   " Wher is," he sayd,
   " The gouernour of this gyng ? gladly I wolde
   Se that segg in syȝt " (G 224–226).
   Hee said, " I am a venterous Knight,
   And of your King wold haue sight " (P 94–95).

9. Arthour con onsware,
   And sayd, " syr cortays knyȝt,
   If thou craue batayl here,
   Here fayleȝ thou not to fyȝt " (G 275–278).
      Certein thus can he say:
   " As I am true knight and King,
   Thou shalt haue thy askinge!
      I will not say thy nay,
   Whether thou wilt on foote fighting,
   Or on steed backe iusting " (P 123–128).

10. Now hyȝe, and let se tite
    Dar any her-inne oȝt say (G 299–300).
    Let me see who will answer this,
    A knight that is doughtye of deed (P 143–144).

11. Gawain begs the king to allow him to accept the challenge, reminding him of his relationship (*G* 339–361, *P* 164–169).

> Bot for as much as ȝe ar myn em̅, I am only to prayse (*G* 356).
> Remember I am your sisters sonne (*P* 149).

12. " Kepe the cosyn," quoth the kyng, " that thou on kyrf sette "
(*G* 372).
" Sett the buffett well " (*P* 174).

13. That thou schal seche me thi-self, where-so thou hopes
I may be funde vpon folde, and foch the such wages (*G* 395–396).
Let him come to me and seicth his paye [1] (*P* 146).

14. Gauan gripped to his ax (*G* 421).
Sir Gawaine to the axe he braid (*P* 188).

15. That the scharp of the schalk schyndered the bones,
And schrank thurȝ the schyire grece and scade it in twynne (*G* 424–425).
He stroke the necke bone in twaine (*P* 190).

16. The fayre hede fro the halce hit [fell] to the erthe (*G* 427).
The head from the body fell (*P* 192).

17. The blod brayd fro the body (*G* 429).
The blood burst out (*P* 191).

18. The hede in his honde he haldeȝ vp euen (*G* 444).
Bare his head in his hand (*P* 201).

19. Halled out at the hal-dor (*G* 458).
Forth att the hall dore he rode right (*P* 202).

20. Knyȝtes ful cortays and comlych ladies,
Al for luf of that lede in longynge thay were (*G* 539–540).
Knights and Ladyes waxed wann (*P* 260).

21. The extraordinarily elaborated description of the arming of Gawain and Gringolet in (*G* 567 ff.) is certainly the work of the English poet, who delighted in such things. The French is not likely to have had more than a line or two on the subject. The Percy version, however, short as it is, gives several verses to this matter (265–278), and these

---

[1] Miswritten " praye."

are apparently reminiscent of *G*.   The absurd stirrups of
Indian silk (*P* 275) may or may not be a misunderstanding
of *G* 589.   Cf. also *G* 609, 617, with *P* 271–273; *G* 603–604
with *P* 278.

22. So mony meruayl bi mount ther the mon fyndeȝ,
    Hit were to tore for to telle of the tenthe dole.
    Sumwhyle wyth wormeȝ he werreȝ, and with wolues als,
    Sumwhyle wyth wodwos, that woned in the knarreȝ,
    Bothe wyth bulleȝ and bereȝ, and boreȝ other-quyle (*G* 718–722).
    Many furleys there saw hee
    Of wolues and wild beasts sikerlye (*P* 283–284).

23. Ther fayre fyre vpon flet fersly brenned (*G* 832).
    Fier in chambers burning bright (*P* 310).

  24. The lord of the castle makes clever observations and
enquiries which reveal that his guest is Gawain (*G* 901–906).
Cf. *P* 331–339.

25. Then frayned the freke ful fayre at him-seluen,
    Quat derne dede had hym dryuen, at that dere tyme,
    So kenly fro the kyngeȝ kourt to kayre al his one (*G* 1046–1048).
    One thing, Sir, I wold you pray:
    What you make soe farr this way (*P* 328–329).

26. For I schal teche yow to tha[t] terme bi the tymeȝ ende,
    The grene chapayle vpon grounde. . . .

    .   .   .   .

    Mon schal yow sette in waye,
    Hit is not two myle henne (*G* 1069–1078).
  He saith, " As to the greene chappell,
    Titherward I can you telle.
    Itt is but furlongs 3 " (*P* 343–345).

27. ȝe schal lenge in your lofte, and lyȝe in your ese

    .   .   .   .   .   .

    And I schal erly ryse,
    On huntyng wyl I wende (*G* 1096–1102).

    You shall abyde and take your rest,
    And I will into yonder fforrest
      Vnder the greenwood tree (*P* 352–354).

28. It is quite clear that three hunts have been reduced to one in the Percy text, whether by the author of the short version or by some scribe or oral reporter nobody can determine. The first hunt in *G* takes up more than fifty verses (1126–1177, 1319–1322), not to mention the celebrated account of the " breaking " of the deer (1323–1361).[1] In *P* the hunting is despatched in six lines: —

> The greene Knight went on hunting (*P* 361).
>
> .   .   .   .   .   .
>
> The Knight in the fforrest slew many a hind,
> Other venison he cold none find
>   But wild bores on the plaine,
> Plentye of does and wild swine,
> Foxes and other ravine,
>   As I hard true men tell (*P* 406–411).

These few verses, however, seem to preserve fragments of a passage in *G* which was in all probability lacking in the French source. According to *G*, Bernlak let the harts and bucks go, forbidding his men to touch the male deer, since it was " fermysoun tyme " or close season, but —

> The hindeȝ were halden in, with hay and war,
> The does dryuen with gret dyn to the depe sladeȝ (*G* 1158–1159).
>
> And ay the lorde of the londe is lent on his gamneȝ,
> To hunt in holteȝ and hethe at hyndeȝ barayne,
> Such a sowme he ther slowe bi that the sunne heldet
> Of dos and of other dere, to deme were wonder (*G* 1319–1322).

A wild boar is the quarry in the second hunt in *G* (1561 ff.) and a fox in the third (1698 ff.). I see no likelihood that the hunting was described in detail in the French *Gawain*, and the passage in the short *Green Knight* looks much more like a resolute condensation of those in the long English romance than like a reminiscence or reproduction of anything that stood in the French source. If the two English poems are

---

[1] Cf. Bruce, *Englische Studien*, XXXII, 23–36.

read side by side at this point, I feel sure that any unpreju-
diced judge will find evidence in the comparison for the
view that the short *Green Knight* comes from its English
predecessor.

29.   " And I haf worthyly this woneȝ wyth-inne,
       I-wysse with as god wylle hit wortheȝ to ȝoures."
       He hasppeȝ his fayre hals his armeȝ wyth-iune,
       And kysses hym as comlyly as he couthe awyse:
       " Tas yow there my cheuicaunce, I cheued no more,
       I wowche hit saf fynly, thaȝ feler hit were" (*G* 1386–1391).

       Sir Gawaine sware by St. Leonard,
       " Such as God sends, you shall haue part."
          In his armes he hent the Knight,
       And there he kissed him times 3,
       Saith, " Heere is such as God sends mee,
          By Mary most of Might " (*P* 421–426).

   30. In *G* the lady says to Gawain:

       " And now ȝe are here, I-wysse, and we bot oure one;
       My lorde and his ledeȝ ar on lenthe faren,
       Other burneȝ in her bedde, and my burdeȝ als.

              .   .   .   .

       ȝe ar welcum to my cors " (*G* 1230–1237).

In *P* the old lady does the talking, but the following passage
may well be derived from that just quoted from *G*: —

       " Take her boldly in thine armes,
       There is noe man shall doe thee harme; "
          Now been they both heere (*P* 376–378).[1]

   31. Speaking of the green lace, the lady says in *G*:

       " For quat gome so is gorde with this grene lace,
       While he hit hade hemely halched aboute,
       Ther is no hathel vnder heuen to-hewe hym that myȝt " (*G* 1851–
       1853).

---

[1] The last line is corrupt. Perhaps we should read it as a part of the old
lady's speech: " Now been ye both y-feere."

So in *P*: —

> " For heere I haue a lace of silke,
> It is as white as any milke,
>   And of a great value."
> Shee saith, " I dare safelye sweare,
> There shall noe man doe you deere
>   When you haue it vpon you " (*P* 397–403).

32. The Green Chapel is a hallow mound in *G*, " over-grown with grass " (2180–2181), " with erbeȝ ouer-growen " (2190). It is not described in *P*, but is said to be " couered with euyes " (450).

33. The whetting of the axe is described in *G* in a fine passage (2199–2204, cf. 2219–2220), which is probably due to the English poet. Compare *P* :

> He hard him wehett a fauchion bright,
> That the hills rang about (*P* 452–453).

In *G* the sound of the whetting " clatered in the clyff, as hit cleue schulde " (2201).

34. The Green Knight appears in his former likeness: —

> And the gome in the grene gered as fyrst,
> Bothe the lyre and the leggeȝ, lokkeȝ and berde (*G* 2227–2228).
> The greene knight rode another way;
> He transposed him in another array,
>   Before as it was greene (*P* 442–444).

35. " Gawayn," quoth that grene gome, " God the mot loke!
> I-wysse thou art welcom, wyȝe, to my place " (*G* 2239–2240).
> The Knight spake with strong cheere,
> Said, " Yee be welcome, S[ir] Gawaine heere " (*P* 454–455).

36. The word *shunt* is used of Gawain's dodging or shrinking in both poems. "Quoth Gawain, 'I schunt oneȝ'" (*G* 2280); "He saith, 'Thou schontest'" (*P* 460).

37. In striking Gawain, the Green Knight —

> Bot snyrt hym on that on syde, that seuered the hyde;
> The scharp schrank to the flesche thurȝ the schyre grece (*G* 2312–
> He stroke, and litle perced the skin,   [2313).
> Vnneth the flesch within (*P* 457–458).

38. Gawain's actions and words after receiving the blow are very similar in the two versions. In *G* he " braydeʒ out a bryʒt sworde " (2319); in *P* " soone he drew out his sword " (463).

39. " I haf a stroke in this sted with-oute stryf hent.

> . . . .
>
> Bot on stroke here me falleʒ " (*G* 2323, 2327).
> " I had but one stroke att thee,
> And thou hast had another att mee " (*P* 466–467).

40. In *G* Bernlak, with reference to the concealment of the lace, says to Gawain " Lewte yow wonted " (2366); in *P*, " Thou wast not leele " (478). The strange accusation that the Green Knight brings against Gawain of having lost his " three points " (*P* 476) looks temptingly like a muddling up of Bernlak's remark in G 2356: " At the thrid thou fayled thore." But no stress need be laid on this.

BIBLIOGRAPHICAL NOTE

For convenience the most important documents are here enumerated, with a summary account of each.

I. FLED BRICREND

Fled Bricrend (or *Bricriu's Feast*) is contained in the manuscript known as the *Lebor na hUidre* (or *Book of the Dun [Cow]*), pp. 99–112, where it is incomplete at the end on account of the mutilation of the manuscript. Fragmentary texts occur also in other codices. The text of the *Lebor*, with a collation of Egerton MS. 93 (British Museum), was edited by Windisch in 1880,[1] and the whole saga by Henderson in 1899.[2]

Maelmuire mac Ceileachair, who was killed by freebooters in 1106,[3] has long passed for the scribe who not only collected the materials for the *Lebor na hUidre* but wrote the whole manuscript. Mr. Best, however, has recently shown[4] that this famous codex is the work of at least three scribes, whom he designates as A, M, and H. M, who transcribed the major portion, was undoubtedly Maelmuire, and to his pen is referable most of the *Fled Bricrend*, including the page (112) that contains *The Champion's Bargain*. After p. 112 several leaves are lost (five, according to Best), so that Maelmuire's text is incomplete. The portion that is pre-

---

[1] *Irische Texte*, [I], 235 ff.

[2] London, Irish Texts Society, Vol. II. On the manuscripts see Henderson, pp. xxiv ff.

[3] Four Masters, *ad ann.* See Zimmer, Kuhn's *Zeitschrift*, XXVIII, 671 ff.

[4] *Notes on the Script of Labor na hUidre*, *Ériu*, VI, 161 ff. (1912).

served corresponds to §§ 91–94 of Henderson's edition. These sections are also preserved in Egerton MS. 93 and in a Leyden MS.[1] For the conclusion of *The Champion's Bargain*, and consequently of the *Fled Bricrend* (§§ 99–102 in Henderson), we must depend solely on Edinburgh Gaelic MS. XL, which contains no part of the *Fled Bricrend* except *The Champion's Bargain* (in a hand, as it seems, of the sixteenth century), but fortunately has this in its entirety. There is no doubt in anybody's mind that the Edinburgh text is safely usable to fill the lacuna in in the *Lebor na hUidre*. §§ 95–98 are also in the Leyden MS.

The Edinburgh copy of *The Champion's Bargain* was summarized by Kuno Meyer in 1887 (*Celtic Magazine*, XII, 215 ff.) and edited by him with a translation in 1893 (*Revue Celtique*, XIV, 450 ff.),[2] and the whole of the *Fled Bricrend* is Englished in Henderson's edition. There is a German version of the *Fled Bricrend* by Thurneysen in his *Sagen aus dem alten Irland* (Berlin, 1901), pp. 27 ff., in which an attempt is very skilfully made " die zu Grunde liegende Erzählung wieder herauszuschälen." In the translation of *The Champion's Bargain* on pp. 10–14 I have made free use of the work of these three scholars, comparing the Irish throughout and keeping as close to the original as possible. My friend and colleague, Professor Robinson, has had the kindness to criticise my attempt, and I owe much to his scholarship and care. *The Champion's Bargain* has some claims to be regarded as a separate and distinct tale, and has a title of its own (*Cennach ind Ruanada inso*) in the *Lebor na hUidre* as well as in the Edinburgh MS.

---

[1] *Is. Vossii Cod. Lat. Quart.*, No. 8 (see Stern, *Revue Celtique*, XIII, 27 ff.; *Zeitschrift für celtische Philologie*, IV, 143 ff.). The last page of the Leyden MS., containing the conclusion of the adventure, is so faded as to be illegible. Thus we lack §§ 99–102.

[2] Cf. Meyer, *Revue Celtique*, VI, 113, 191.

The Uath version of the Challenge (§§ 75–78 in Henderson) is preserved in the *Lebor na hUidre* only (p. 110). It was long ago shown by Zimmer [1] to belong to a version of the *Fled Bricrend* quite distinct from that which ended with *The Champion's Bargain*, and he ascribed the presence of these doublets in the text of the *Fled Bricrend* in the *Lebor na hUidre* to the industry of a compiler. See also Thurneysen's important study, *Die Überlieferung der Fled Bricenn* in the *Zeitschrift für Celtische Philologie*, 1902, IV, 193 ff. In 1912 Best pointed out in his fundamental *Notes on the Script of Lebor na hUidre* (*Ériu*, VI, 161 ff.) that the leaf of the manuscript that contains the Uath sections is in a hand (H) quite different from that of Maelmuire (M) and is actually an insertion in Maelmuire's text, made bodily after he had finished his work and probably after his death. Still, the date of H cannot be much later than 1106, and the version of the *Fled Bricrend* that he took pains to amalgamate (rather poorly) with Maelmuire's was an old one. The translation (pp. 17–18, above) follows Henderson in the main, but with comparison with the Irish in an endeavor to render the original closely. Here again I have had the benefit of Professor Robinson's criticism.

In 1888 Gaston Paris, on the basis of a communication from d'Arbois de Jubainville, compared the Challenge in *Gawain and the Green Knight* with the Uath episode.[2] In 1891 d'Arbois called particular attention to this episode, inquiring if it might not be connected with the legend of St. Denis.[3] In 1892 he published a French translation of the *Fled Bricrend* from the *Lebor na hUidre*, but of course it lacks the concluding sections.[4] In the same year Nutt

---

[1] Kuhn's *Zeitschrift*, 1887, XXVIII, 623 ff.; cf. Henderson, pp. xxxii ff.

[2] *Histoire Littéraire de la France*, XXX, 77, note.

[3] *Revue Celtique*, XII, 166–167; cf. *Cours*, V, 147.

[4] *Cours de la Littérature Celtique*, V, 81 ff. (cf. 535).

adverted to the resemblance between our romance and the
Fled Bricrend in an article [1] on the Irish documents that
concern *The Marriage of Gawain* and its analogues.[2] Henderson refers to the subject in his edition of the Irish saga
(pp. 199 ff.). The resemblances between the romance and
the two Irish versions of the Challenge are considered by
Miss Weston, in her *Legend of Sir Gawain*, chap. ix (pp.
85 ff.), where she also treats the other forms of the Challenge. The *Fled Bricrend* is discussed by A. C. L. Brown
in his *Iwain*, 1903 ([*Harvard*] *Studies and Notes*, VIII, 51–
56), from the point of view of the Other-World Journey. On
Curoi mac Daire, who plays the part of the axeman in
The Champion's Bargain, see Thurneysen, *Die Sage von
CuRoi, Zeitschrift für celtische Philologie*, IX, 189 ff., 336;
cf. *Ériu*, II, 1 ff., 18 ff.

II. GAWAIN AND THE GREEN KNIGHT

Gawain and the Green Knight is found in a single manuscript (Cotton MS. Nero A. x., fols. 91–124 v°, in the
British Museum), described by Sir Frederic Madden, *Syr
Gawayne*, 1839, pp. xlvii ff., 299–301. The manuscript consists of three parts (originally distinct manuscripts), of
which the second alone concerns us. This is assigned to
the reign of Richard II by Madden (p. 301), to the " end
of the fourteenth century," by Ward (*Catalogue of Romances*, I, 387) [3]; it contains four poems (without titles),
all written in the same hand: *The Pearl, Cleanness, Patience,*
and our romance.

[1] *Academy*, No. 1043, April 30, 1892, p. 425. Nutt cites the summary of
the *Lebor* text given by Zimmer in Kuhn's *Zeitschrift*, XXVIII, 623 ff.

[2] See Maynadier, *The Wife of Bath's Tale*, 1901, pp. 25 ff., 195–196.

[3] Cf. Gibson, *The Library of Henry Savile of Banke* (Bibliographical
Society, *Transactions*, IX, 135; Gollancz, *Patience*, 1913, pp. [ix–x]).

Gawain and the Green Knight was first edited by Madden, *Syr Gawayne*, 1839, pp. 1–92 (Bannatyne Club); then by Richard Morris for the Early English Text Society, 1864 (reprinted 1869, 1893, and with a revision of the text by Gollancz, 1897). The poem is studied by Gaston Paris in the *Histoire Littéraire de la France*, XXX, 71–78. There is a convenient bibliography by Gollancz, *Cambridge History of English Literature* I, 472–473, drawn up to accompany his chapter on this and the other poems usually ascribed to the same author (I, 320 ff.). See also Schofield, *English Literature from the Norman Conquest to Chaucer*, London, 1906, pp. 215–217. There are translations by Miss Jessie L. Weston (London, 1898; New York, 1905), and the Rev. E. J. B. Kirtlan, (London, [1912]), and one from the pen of K. G. T. Webster will soon be published (Neilson and Webster, *The Chief British Poets of the Fourteenth and Fifteenth Centuries*).

Several of the most important documents for the study of the romance are cited by Madden (pp. 305 ff., 345). He refers to the Caradoc story in the prose *Perceval*, to *La Mule sanz Frain*, to *Perlesvaus*, to *The Carl of Carlisle*, and to *Le Chevalier à l'Épée*. He regards the Challenge in the English poem as derived from the Caradoc story. The *Chevalier* he supposes to be the original of the *Carl*. The idea that the English poet drew from the *Livre de Caradoc* (in the verse *Perceval*) was carefully worked out by Miss Thomas, *Sir Gawayne and the Green Knight*, Zürich, 1883, pp. 34 ff.[1] This was before the Irish versions of the Challenge had been brought into the discussion.

In 1897 Miss Weston discussed *Gawain and the Green Knight* in connection with her theories about Gawain and

[1] Reviewed by Paris, *Romania*, XII, 376–380.

his fairy wife or mistress.[1] She compared the various documents, but came to no very definite results as to their historical relations to each other. She was convinced, however, that the beheading game was " one of the special deeds of valour by which [Gawain] won the hand of his ' other-world ' bride " (p. 102). This view, with some modification, has been revived in a recent paper by J. R. Hulbert, *Modern Philology*, XIII, 433 ff. A few sentences give his theory with admirable precision: " A *fée* loved Gawain, and sent an emissary to lure him to her. He traveled for a long time until he came to a hospitable castle where he was entertained until the appointed day by a shape-shifter, the same who had enticed him from court; then he was conveyed to the entrance to the Other World. There he had to submit to the beheading test; when he succeeded in that he was admitted to the Other World and led to the fairy. Probably he stayed with her some time, and then after having been given a magic talisman — the green lace — he was allowed to return to his own land. Now at some time, a story-teller conceived the idea of making this story a poetic explanation of the founding of an order, probably because the green lace reminded him of the badge of that order. Wishing to associate with the order the idea of loyalty, he altered the nature of the material slightly by having Gawain resist the love of the lady, and he transferred the incident of Gawain and the lady to the hospitable castle, so as to bring the beheading test after it and make the test an evidence of Gawain's loyalty " (p. 459). It will be noted that Hulbert's views differ *toto caelo* from mine, and that the method of his paper and that of my essay in Part One are dissimilar. A second article from Hulbert is announced.

---

[1] *The Legend of Sir Gawain*, pp. 85–102.

A connection between the romance and " the romantic origin of the Order of the Garter " was maintained by Gollancz in his edition of the *Pearl* (1891). There is an eccentric paper on the subject by I. Jackson in *Anglia*, XXXVII, 393 ff. (*Sir Gawain and the Green Knight. Considered as a " Garter " Poem*).

III. The Green Knight

The Green Knight, a romance in six-line stanzas, extending to 516 verses, is in the Percy MS., pp. 203–210. It has been thrice edited: by Sir Frederic Madden, *Syr Gawayne*, 1839, pp. 224–242; by Child, *English and Scottish Ballads*, I, 35–57 (1857); and by Hales and Furnivall, *Bishop Percy's Folio Manuscript*, II, 56–77 (1868). It is reprinted (from the text of Hales and Furnivall) in *The Percy Folio of Old English Ballads and Romances*, London, at the De la More Press, 1906, II, 120–137. Percy mentioned the romance in 1765 (*Reliques*, III, xix). A copy made for him is among the Percy Papers in the Harvard College Library. He intended at one time to hand this poem over to his nephew, the younger Thomas Percy, for inclusion in a volume supplementary to the *Reliques*.[1]   Madden,[2] Hales,[3] and Gaston Paris [4] agree in regarding the piece as a late and much altered condensation of *Gawain and the Green Knight*. Hulbert dissents (*Modern Philology*, XIII, 461).

IV. The Turk and Gawain

The Turk and Gawain (*The Turke and Gowin*) is found only in the Percy MS., pp. 38–46. It was mentioned by

---

[1] Percy to Pinkerton, March 12, 1785, Nichols, *Illustrations of the Literary History of the Eighteenth Century*, VIII, 108.

[2] *Syr Gawayne*, p. 352.   [3] *Bishop Percy's Folio Manuscript*, II, 56.

[4] *Histoire Littéraire de la France*, XXX, 78.

Percy in 1765 (*Reliques*, III, xix), and has been edited by Madden, *Syr Gawayne*, pp. 243–255, and by Hales and Furnivall, *Bishop Percy's Folio Manuscript*, I, 88–102. Paris refers the poem to the sixteenth century,[1] but it may well go back to 1400 or shortly after. Hales remarks that the exchange of buffets proposed at the beginning of the piece " is apparently forgotten as the story proceeds "; but this is an error. There can be no doubt that the return buffet came in where it should, after v. 267 on p. 44 of the MS., but is lost because half that page is torn out. In fact, leaves 1–26 of the manuscript are mutilated, so that each of the first 52 pages is half-gone.[2] It is the lower half of each leaf that is torn away. The beginning of *The Turk and Gawain* is preserved, and so is the conclusion, since the poem begins at the top of p. 38 and ends before the rent on p. 46. Thus there are eight gaps in the narrative, each of about six stanzas (or 36 verses).

V. Le Livre de Caradoc

Le Livre de Caradoc is inserted in the first continuation of the *Perceval* of Chrétien de Troyes (the " Pseudo-Wauchier "). It occupies approximately vv. 12,451–15,792 of Potvin's text (*Perceval li Gallois*, III, 117–221). Undoubtedly it forms a poem by itself, having nothing to do with the romance in which it is inserted.[3] Potvin follows the Mons MS., but gives many variants from the Montpellier MS., which differs considerably. There are, in fact, two main versions of the *Livre de Caradoc* and some varieties, but all of them contain the Challenge (or Beheading Game),

[1] *Histoire Littéraire*, XXX, 68, note.
[2] See Hales and Furnivall, I, 14, 16, 138. The pages are oddly numbered, the first being 5 (5–12, 15–58).
[3] See Paris, *Romania*, XXVIII, 214–215, 231, note 1.

which takes up vv. 12,592–12,885 of Potvin's text (III, 125–133). See the discussions of the *Livre* by Hugo Waitz (*Die Fortsetzungen von Chrestiens' Perceval le Gallois nach den Pariser Handschriften*, Strassburg, 1890, pp. 47 ff.) and Miss Weston (*The Legend of Sir Perceval*, I, 309 ff.). The *Book of Caradoc* (*Karados Buoch*) forms a portion of the *Parzival* of Claus Wisse and Philipp Colin (1331–1336), vv. 1971 ff., ed. Schorbach, cols. 45 ff. The translation of the adventure of the Challenge (vv. 2131–2467, cols. 49–56) gives us no help in our study. For the *Livre* in the prose *Perceval*, see pp. 31–32, above.

On the *Livre*, as a whole or in part, see Madden, *Syr Gawayne* pp. 305–306; Heinzel, *Ueber die französischen Gralromane*, Vienna *Denkschriften*, 1892, p. 32; Miss Thomas, *Sir Gawayne and the Green Knight*, pp. 34 ff.; Warnatsch, *Der Mantel*, pp. 62 ff.; Child, *The English and Scottish Popular Ballads*, I, 257 ff.; Miss Weston, *The Legend of Sir Perceval*, I, 309 ff.; Miss Harper, *Modern Language Notes*, XIII, 209 ff.; Paris, *Romania*, XXVIII, 214 ff.; Lot, *Romania*, XXVIII, 568 ff.; Rhŷs, *Celtic Folklore*, II, 689–690; Nitze, *The Old French Grail Romance Perlesvaus*, p. 68; Kittredge, [*Harvard*] *Studies and Notes*, VIII, 208, note 1; Friedwagner, *La Vengeance Raguidel*, pp. clxxix ff.

VI. LA MULE SANZ FRAIN

La Mule sanz Frain (or *La Demoiselle à la Mure*) is in the same Bern MS. that contains *Le Chevalier à l'Épée*. The author names himself in v. 14: " dist Paiens de Maiseres." The poem has been edited by Méon, *Nouveau Recueil de Fabliaux et Contes*, 1823, I, 1–37; by R. T. Hill, *La Mule sanz Frain*, Baltimore, 1911 (Yale dissertation); and by Boleslas Orlowski, *La Demoiselle à la Mule*, Paris, 1911.

For discussions, see A. Duval, *Histoire Littéraire de la France*, XIX, 722–729; G. Paris, the same, XXX, 68–69; A. C. L. Brown, *Iwain*, [*Harvard*] *Studies and Notes*, 1903, VIII, 80 ff.; the same, *The Knight of the Lion*, *Publications of the Modern Language Association*, 1905, XX, 692 ff.; Hill's review of Borlowski, *Romanic Review*, IV, 392–395; Roques's review of Hill and Borlowski, *Romania*, XL, 144–147. Both Hill and Roques reject the strange theories of Orlowski as to the relations among Chrétien, Paien, and Heinrich von dem Türlîn. Hill very properly remarks that " the conclusion reached by Orlowski is made contrary to his own evidence." See pp. 252 ff., above.

Diu Crône, a Middle High German romance of the Round Table, by Heinrich von dem Türlîn, is edited from two manuscripts by G. H. F. Scholl, Stuttgart, 1852 (*Bibliothek des Litterarischen Vereins in Stuttgart*, XXVII). It extends to a little more than thirty thousand verses and is supposed to date from about 1220 or ealier. Heinrich inserts *La Mule sanz Frain* with variations of his own (vv. 12627 ff., pp. 155 ff.); see pp. 251 ff., above. He also has the adventure of the Perilous Bed (vv. 8504–8616) apparently imitated from *Le Chevalier à l'Épée* (see p. 303, below), and again in another form in vv. 20598 ff. On his method and sources, see particularly Warnatsch, *Der Mantel* (Breslau, 1883), pp. 118 ff.

VII. PERLESVAUS

PERLESVAUS, an Old French romance in prose, is edited by Potvin only (*Perceval li Gallois*, I, Mons. 1866), but printed texts occur in incunabula. It must have been finished before 1212, probably about 1200. There is a Welsh translation among the Hengwrt MSS., which was published, with an English rendering, by the Rev. Robert Williams in

1876 (*Selections from the Hengwrt MSS.*, Vol. I, *Y Seint Greal*, pp. 171–433, 547–720). Potvin's text has been translated into English by Sebastian Evans (*The High History of the Holy Graal*, London, 1898). For further particulars see Nitze, *The Old French Grail Romance Perlesvaus, a Study of its Principal Sources*, Baltimore, 1902 (Johns Hopkins dissertation). He treats the Challenge (or Beheading Game) briefly on pp. 66–68.

The episode of the Challenge is to be found in Potvin, I, 102–104, 231–234, and the coming danger is mentioned in the interval (I, 196–197); cf. Evans, I, 164–167; II, 23–24, 78–83. For the Welsh see Roberts, chaps. 139 (pp. 259–260, 605–606), 189 (pp. 327, 649–650), 199–201 (pp. 347–350, 663–665).

There is no certain evidence that the author of *Perlesvaus* was acquainted with that continuation of Chrétien's *Perceval* (the so-called Psuedo-Wauchier) that contains the *Livre de Caradoc*. Nitze thinks he shows such a knowledge in certain episodes, but on insufficient grounds (*The Old French Grail Romance Perlesvaus*, 1902, pp. 66–73). But, even if Nitze's arguments are accepted, they do not carry with them the consequence that the author of *Perlesvaus* knew the *Livre de Caradoc*, which is certainly intrusive in the Psuedo-Wauchier; and Nitze himself has no thought of deriving the Challenge in *Perlesvaus* from the *Livre* (pp. 66–67).

VIII. Humbaut

Humbaut (or Hunbaut) is an unfinished French romance found only in the Chantilly MS. of Arthurian pieces (the same that contains *Rigomer* and *Li Biaus Desconeus*), which was written in the second half of the thirteenth century. The romance is very briefly summarized and discussed by

Gaston Paris (*Histoire Littéraire*, XXX, 69–71, 75–76), who calls attention to its resemblance in one episode to *The Carl of Carlisle* and *Le Chevalier à l'Épée*, and in another to *Gawain and the Green Knight*. It is edited (under the title of *Hunbaut*) by J. Stürzinger and H. Breuer as Vol. XXXV of the publications of the Gesellschaft für Romanische Literatur (Dresden, 1914). The romance may be safely referred to the first quarter of the thirteenth century. It contains both the Challenge and an episode resembling the Temptation (see pp. 61 ff., 99 ff., above).

IX. The Carl of Carlisle

THERE are two texts of *The Carl of Carlisle*: (A) *Syre Gawene and the Carle of Carelyle*, Porkington MS. No. 10, fols. 12–27, edited by Madden, *Syr Gawayne*, pp. 188–206; (B) *Carle off Carlile*, Percy MS., pp. 448–455, noticed by Percy, *Reliques*, 1765, III, xx; edited by Madden, pp. 256–274; by Child, *English and Scottish Ballads*, I, 58–79 (1857); and by Hales and Furnivall, *Bishop Percy's Folio Manuscript*, III, 275–294. There are two copies of B (made for Percy and one containing some notes in his hand) among the Percy Papers in the Harvard College Library. A is in tailrhyme stanzas of six verses and runs to 660 lines; B is in irregular short couplets and runs to 500 lines. The Porkington MS. is put by Madden at the close of the reign of Henry VI (d. 1471);[1] the Percy MS. was written about 1650. A and B are two texts of the same poem. A, however, is not from B,[2] for the conclusion is better preserved in B than in A. Probably B is to be regarded as a poor copy of a poem in

---

[1] *Syr Gawayne*, p. 344.

[2] Madden thought that A was "the original from which the modernised copy in the Percy MS. was taken" (pp. 344–345).

couplets, and A is a working over of this same poem into the
tail-rhyme form. In the main (except for the conclusion) A
affords a better text than B. The *Carl of Carlisle* is certainly derived from the French, but not (as Madden
thought) [1] from *Le Chevalier à l'Épée*. The *Carl* and the
Chevalier go back independently to a common French
source, which is lost, and the *Carl* preserves the story much
better than the *Chevalier*.

That *The Carl of Carlisle* preserves a much more correct
version of the story than the *Chevalier à l'Épée* is the opinion
of Paris, emphatically stated in *Histoire Littéraire*, XXX,
68. Paris also comments on the beheading for disenchantment at the end of the Percy MS. version of the *Carl* (which
he calls a ballad): — " Il est remarquable qu'on y trouve un
dénouement qui doit être primitif et qui ne figure pas dans
le poème [i.e., the Porkington MS. version]. Comme ce
dénouement a un caractère très fantastique, on peut croire
qu'un copiste l'a trouvé absurde et l'a supprimé; la fin du
poème anglais, dans la manuscrit unique qui l'a conservé,
présente quelque chose de gauche qui rende une mutilation
assez vraisemblable." [2]

X. Le Chevalier à l'Épée

Le Chevalier à l'Épée (*Espée*) is contained in an MS. of the
fourteenth century in the Bern Municipal Library (*Bib-
liotheca Bongarsiana*, No. 354). The poem belongs to the
first quarter of the thirteenth. It has been published by
Méon, *Nouveau Recueil de Fabliaux et Contes*, 1823, I, 127 ff.;
by Legrand d'Aussy, *Fabliaux ou Contes*, 3d ed., 1829, I,
Appendix, pp. 3 ff.; by Jonckbloet, *Roman van Walewein*,
Part II, 1848, pp. 35–74; and by E. C. Armstrong, *Le*

---

[1] P. 345.   [2] Cf. also *Romania*, XXIX, 597, and note 1.

Chevalier à l'Épée, Baltimore, 1900 (Johns Hopkins University dissertation). Armstrong's edition contains much valuable material besides the text; cf. the review by Paris, *Romania*, XXIX, 593 ff. The poem is also examined by A. Duval, *Histoire Littéraire*, XIX, 704 ff.; by Paris, the same, XXX, 67–68; and by Friedwagner, *La Vengeance Raguidel*, 1909, pp. clxxxv ff. Madden regarded it as the source of the *Carl of Carlisle* in the Porkington MS.[1]

It consists of two stories: (1) the Temptation (vv. 1–859), in which Gawain wins an *amie*, and (2) an anecdote contrasting the fidelity of dogs with the faithlessness of women, in which she deserts him (vv. 860–1206). The Perilous Bed, which occurs in the first part (vv. 534 ff.), is found twice in Chrétien — in his *Perceval*[2] and his *Chevalier de la Charrette*.[3] Since the author of *Le Chevalier à l'Épée* mentions Chrétien with approval in his prefatory lines,[4] he doubtless borrowed the contrivance from him.[5] Comparison shows that he was indebted rather to the *Charrette* than to the *Perceval*,[6] but the use to which he puts the machine (to guard chastity) is his own invention.[7] In the *Perceval* the weapons that assail Gawain when he sits on the " lit de la merveille" are darts and arrows; in the *Charrette*, it is a lance with a burning pennon that grazes Lancelot. The substitution of a sword by the author of *Le Chevalier à l'Épée* I have explained by conjecturing that in his original

---

[1] *Syr Gawayne*, p. 345.

[2] Vv. 9054–9222 (Potvin, II, 302–306; III, 1–2).

[3] Vv. 463–538, ed. Foerster, pp. 19–21.

[4] Vv. 17–22.

[5] For other versions, see Armstrong, pp. 59–62.

[6] Armstrong, pp. 60–62.

[7] For the imitation of the *Chevalier* in this point by Heinrich von dem Türlin (*Crône*, vv. 8504–8616), see p. 253. Paris, *Romania*, XXIX, 597, thinks that Heinrich did not get the incident from the *Chevalier*, and Friedwagner agrees with him (*Vengeance Raguidel*, p. clxxxix).

Gawain laid his own sword between his host's wife and himself (p. 92).

The anecdote of the contrasted fidelity of dogs and women occurs in variant forms in the *Chevalier à l'Épée*,[1] the *Vengeance Raguidel*,[2] the prose *Tristan*,[3] and the Dutch *Lancelot*.[4] It has been studied by Paris, *Histoire Littéraire*, XXX, 60 ff. (cf. *Romania*, XXIX, 598–599), by E. C. Armstrong, *Le Chevalier à l'Épée*, pp. 63–67, and by Friedwagner, *La Vengeance Raguidel*, pp. clxxxv ff. Cf. Kittredge, *Arthur and Gorlagon*, [*Harvard*] *Studies and Notes in Philology and Literature*, VIII, 245–254. G. Doncieux (*Revue des Traditions Populaires*, VIII, 513 ff.) prints a modern French poem, *La Maîtresse Volage et le Chien Fidèle*, which he thinks was composed on the basis of the summary of the *Chevalier à l'Épée* given by Legrand d'Aussy in 1779 in his *Fabliaux ou Contes*, I, 34 ff.

XI. THE CANZONI

The anonymous Italian poem is edited, with a study of its literary relations, by Rajna, *Zeitschrift für romanische Philologie*, I, 381 ff. The present investigation shows that Rajna's combinations will not hold in some particulars. Pucci's poem was printed (from *L'Etruria, Studi di Filologia*, anno secondo, Florence, 1852, pp. 124 ff.) by Carducci, *Rime di M. Cino da Pistoia e d'Altri del Seccolo XIV*, Florence, 1862, pp. 460–463, and from Carducci's edition by Wesselofsky, *Rivista di Filologia Romanza*, II, (1875), 221 ff.[5] Wesselofsky (p. 225) says that it is impossible to decide whether

---

[1] Vv. 861–1191 (the poem ends with v. 1206).

[2] Ed. Hippeau, vv. 4446–4861, pp. 154–168; Friedwagner, vv. 4452 ff.

[3] Löseth, pp. 128–130.

[4] Vv. 13055–13180, ed. Jonckbloet, II, 89–90.

[5] It it also published by Ferri, *La Poesia Popolare in Antonio Pucci*, Bologna, 1909, pp. 217–219.

Pucci's source was the *Chevalier à l'Épée* or some French fabliau more similar to Pucci's own poem. Cf. Paris, *Histoire Littéraire*, XXX, 68, and see especially E. C. Armstrong, *Le Chevalier à l'Épée*, Baltimore, 1900, pp. 67–68. Rajna, Armstrong, and Paris (*Romania*, XXIX, 597) all agree in ascribing both *canzoni* to Pucci, but comparison with the *Carl of Carlisle* and *Le Chevalier à l'Épée* makes it probable that they are from different hands (see pp. 93 ff. above).

XII. THE EXEMPLA

There are two versions of the Latin *Exemplum* of *The Three Knights and the Three Inns*: (A) in a collection of stories in a manuscript written in Italy in the sixteenth century (Harleian MS. 3938, fol. 121, British Museum), printed on pp. 96–97, above; (see Herbert, *Catalogue of Romances*, III, 710); (B) in a treatise by Étienne de Bourbon (who died about 1261) known as *Liber de Septum Donis Spiritus Sancti* or *Tractatus de Diversis Materiis Praedicabilibus*, from which it is printed by Lecoy de la Marche, *Anecdotes Historiques . . . tirés du Recueil Inédit d'Étienne de Bourbon*, p. 17 (see p. 97, above). Other texts of B occur in additional MSS. 16589 (late 13th century), fol. 88, col. 2, and 24641 (first half of 14th century), fol. 210, and there is a part of the story in Sloane MS. 3102 (15th century), fol. 7v°: see Herbert, *Catalogue of Romances*, III, 468, 536, 93. These three pieces are printed on pp. 272–273, above.

XIII. RAUF COILYEAR

The *Taill of Rauf Coilyear* was printed at St. Andrews by Robert Lekpreuik in 1572 (unique copy in the Advocates' Library, Edinburgh). There is no manuscript extant. The poem has been edited by David Laing, *Select Remains of the*

Ancient Popular Poetry of Scotland, Edinburgh, 1822 (reprinted 1884); the same, reëdited by John Small, 1885; by W. Carew Hazlitt, *Early Popular Poetry of Scotland*, I, 212–249; by S. J. Herrtage, *English Charlemagne Romances*, Part VI (Early English Text Society), 1882; by F. J. Amours, *Scottish Alliterative Poems*, pp. 82–114 (Scottish Text Society); (5) by M. Tonndorf, Berlin, 1894; (6) by William Hand Browne, Baltimore, 1903. For similar stories (without the lesson in courtesy), see Child, *Ballads*, III, 55, 74–76, 220 ff.; V, 67–87, 303; W. H. Clawson, *The Gest of Robin Hood* (*University of Toronto Studies*, 1909), pp. 102 ff. A curious parallel to the contention in courtesy (but without the violence of Rauf's lesson) is quoted by Clawson (p. 109, note 2) from Andrew Small's *Interesting Roman Antiquities recently discovered in Fife*, Edinburgh, 1823, pp. 278–279.

INDEX

INDEX

[*Bibl.* refers to the Bibliographical Note, pp. 290 ff.]